PRAISE FOR

## PROTECTING THE GIFT

"DE BECKER HAS DONE IT AGAIN in a field that is
full of pseudo advice on protecting America's most valuable
asset—our children. *Protecting the Gift* leads the way
in this field. It's a must for all parents raising children
in an ever increasingly violent society."

—Robert Ressler, FBI behavioral scientist,
author of *Whoever Fights Monsters*

"De Becker offers insights into the behavior and strategies
of predators to help parents protect their children."

—*The Denver Post*

"PROTECTING THE GIFT IS THE ANTIDOTE FOR EVERY
PARENT'S WORST NIGHTMARE. A rare opportunity to converse
with a master observer of the human condition."

—Dr. John Monahan, professor of psychology and law,
University of Virginia, author of *Predicting Violent Behavior*

"DE BECKER WRITES ELOQUENTLY AND
COMPASSIONATELY ABOUT THE REAL DANGERS FACING
CHILDREN. De Becker delivers his message not only through
emotionally resonant real-life stories . . . but also through
a distillation of the teachings of major criminal justice
and psychological researchers. He has achieved what the
academics have not been able to effectively do—make
the research understandable and useful to the average person."

—Paul Mones, children's rights attorney,
author of *When a Child Kills*

"THIS IS TOP-DRAWER CHILD-REARING STUFF."
—*Booklist*

*Please turn the page for more extraordinary acclaim. . . .*

*Also by Gavin de Becker*

THE GIFT OF FEAR

# PROTECTING THE GIFT

· · · ·

## Keeping Children
and Teenagers Safe

### (AND PARENTS SANE)

## GAVIN DE BECKER

A DELL TRADE PAPERBACK

A DELL TRADE PAPERBACK

Published by
Dell Publishing
a division of
Random House, Inc.
New York, New York

DTP and the colophon are trademarks of Random House, Inc.

ISBN: 978-0-440-50900-4

Library of Congress Catalog card number: 99-22006

Reprinted by arrangement with The Dial Press.

Printed in the United States of America
Published simultaneously in Canada

May 2000

22 21 20 19 18 17 16 15 14

BVG

*For Olivia and George—*
*courageous, compassionate, and capable*
*protectors of family.*

*For Camille and Bill,*
*who showed that great parents never stop*
*protecting their children—no matter what happens*

# AUTHOR'S NOTE

Much of the language in this book is gender-specific to men; I don't always write *he or she, his or hers,* etc. That's because men, at all ages and in all parts of the world, are more violent than women. My language may not always be politically correct, but when it comes to violence, it is statistically correct.

Every story in this book is true. Though a few names and identifying features have been changed to protect privacy, 90 percent are the actual names of the people involved.

# CONTENTS

CHAPTER ONE
THE SEARCH FOR CERTAINTY                    1

CHAPTER TWO
INTUITION—THE SOURCE OF SAFETY              24

CHAPTER THREE
WORRY                                        41

CHAPTER FOUR
SURVIVAL SIGNALS                            60

CHAPTER FIVE
TALK TO STRANGERS                           79

CHAPTER SIX
## THE CHANGING OF THE GUARD                91

CHAPTER SEVEN
## BABY-SITTERS AND NANNIES                 103

CHAPTER EIGHT
## CHILDREN AWAY FROM HOME                  128

CHAPTER NINE
## SEXUAL PREDATORS                         148

CHAPTER TEN
## CHILDREN AT SCHOOL                       175

CHAPTER ELEVEN
## PROTECTING OPHELIA                       191

CHAPTER TWELVE
## TOM SAWYER AND HUCKLEBERRY FINN
## AND SMITH & WESSON                       218

CHAPTER THIRTEEN
## FRIENDS AS ENEMIES                       232

CHAPTER FOURTEEN
## ALL IN THE FAMILY                        247

CHAPTER FIFTEEN
## PROTECTING THE VILLAGE                    269

CHAPTER SIXTEEN
## PROTECTING THE GIFT                       280

ACKNOWLEDGMENTS                              287

APPENDICES                                   291

RECOMMENDED READING                          323

INDEX                                        327

# PROTECTING THE GIFT

# CHAPTER ONE

# THE SEARCH
# FOR CERTAINTY

Friday was the one evening each week that Holly spent entirely with Kate, usually along with other mothers and their daughters met through Kate's school. This particular Friday, the plan was an early meal at a restaurant, followed by a movie. At dinner, the women were protective, as always, but they'd recently initiated a new freedom: letting the girls sit at a nearby table on their own. The tables were close enough for Holly to see that her daughter wasn't eating much—it interfered with talking—but she didn't bug Kate about that in front of her friends; she was eight now, old enough to be embarrassed.

If you took away their twenty-five-year age difference, Holly and her daughter were like twins: both slender with short dark hair and large blue eyes, both liked to talk and to laugh, and both loved movies. This particular Friday, their movie would be *Jurassic Park*. After dinner Holly decided to leave the car at the restaurant and take advantage of the extra-warm night by walking the two blocks to the theater with Kate. None of the other mothers chose to walk, one of them noting, "The sun will be down when we get out, and I don't want us to have to make our way back to the car in the dark." So Kate and Holly enjoyed the walk on their own.

At the theater, they joined the six other mothers and their seven daughters, who were already doing what Steven Spielberg has made worthwhile for millions of people: standing in line. A man ahead of them looked at Holly as if they knew each other. He was about thirty years old, tall and a little pudgy, with very short blond hair. He was wearing loose-fitting sweatpants and a too-small T-shirt with the words AFRAID OF THE DARK across the chest. Holly was sure they'd never met. Just as he appeared about to say something, she decided to turn away. At that moment, he asked her, "Ladies night out?"

"Uh-huh," Holly (sort of) responded. She was thinking about Jeff Goldblum, her favorite actor. To her, the dinosaurs would be only a distraction. The man had another question. Taking in all the mothers and daughters he asked, "What's the idea, safety in numbers?" Holly nodded, but she was thinking, *Bug off.* She wasn't sure why, but she knew she did not like him.

After the line, after the candy debates with the girls ("But we're still hungry!"), after the who'll-sit-next-to-who contest, and after all the mid-movie trips to the bathroom, the world was saved from prehistoric predators and the group was gathered in the lobby, saying goodnight. One of the other mothers offered Holly and Kate a ride to their car, but Holly declined: "It's just a couple of blocks and even after that film, I'm not afraid of the dark." As she heard herself saying those words, she felt apprehension about walking, just a soft whisper that said *Don't*—so she changed her mind and accepted the ride.

At that moment, Kate needed to use the bathroom (again), so the other girls piled into the van and waited. Keeping an eye on the bathroom door and an eye on the anxious-to-leave kids, Holly overruled that soft whisper and concluded that the logical thing to do was walk back to her car. It didn't make sense to keep everybody waiting, and anyway, she thought, *I don't want to be one of those people who's scared to walk a couple of blocks.*

She called out to the mother driving the van: "Hey, we'll just walk."

"You sure?"

"Yep." But the moment the van pulled out of the parking lot, Holly wasn't sure anymore. She was uneasy about that man, that man she didn't like in line. Not much to be concerned about, she told herself, but as she and Kate walked along the quiet street, past closed shops and empty parking lots, Holly felt something unfamiliar to her, but also unmistakable: fear, fear of that man. But she wondered why. Maybe he'd been within earshot when she'd declined the ride and registered that they'd be walking; that might be part of it. He appeared to be attending the movie alone, and that might have been part of it. He was intrusive and looked at her strangely, and that was definitely part of it, but even without knowing all the reasons, Holly listened to her fear. When Kate said something about their neighbor's dog looking like a dinosaur, Holly laughed but was really just taking an opportunity to throw her head back and look down the street. Bad news: That man was following them.

Should she run? Cross the street? Scream? Just as she started to consider these options, fear took over and said, in effect, *Do what I tell you to do, and I'll get you both through this.* Holly put her hand on Kate's arm and sped up slightly. Though she didn't know it, fear was readying her body for action: Blood flow in her arms and legs was increasing, lactic acid was heating up in her muscles, her vision was becoming more focused, her breathing and heartbeat more determined. To prepare her for any possibility, fear gave her a dose of the chemical cortisol. Cortisol would help her blood clot more quickly in the event of injury.

For a hundred yards, Holly tried not to let her daughter know there was a problem, but the child knew. "Mom, why—"

"There's a strange man following us and I want to get to the car in a hurry."

"Let's run!" Kate said adventurously, but Holly held her daughter's arm firmly in response. Fear had put a solid plan in her head: *Do not run because then he'll have to run after you, and he'll be faster than you and Kate. When you reach the car, unlock it with the key instead of the remote control because the remote control would unlock all the doors and you want to unlock only one. Put Kate in the driver's-side door and have her climb over to her seat. Then get in yourself, lock the door, hold down the horn while starting the car, and drive away.*

Most of that happened according to plan, but as she stood waiting for Kate to get across the inside of the car, the man was already at the passenger door. Holly looked directly at him over the roof of her car. Though no words were spoken, they were communicating. The man's communication was basically this. *You are my victim*, and Holly's response was, *No, actually, I'm not.*

Holly heard the latch as the man tried to open Kate's door: once, twice, and then he gave up. He walked calmly around toward the driver's-side door. By then, Holly was in her seat, watching him get closer. Before she could swing her legs into the car, the man was upon her. He was occupied mostly with trying to control her legs, which were kicking powerfully. Holly watched her own impressive resistance with some detachment because she was trying to figure out the origin of a constant loud noise.

Then she realized she was holding down the button for the car horn, just as fear had told her to do. Loud as it was, she still heard a soft whisper in her head: *Ignition key*.

While her legs kicked, she regarded the key, amazed to find herself thinking about sticking it into this man's eyes. She felt no great rush to act because his full attention was on trying to gain control of her uncontrollable legs, and that wasn't going to happen. Holly worried that he might have a gun, but fear interrupted her with an assurance she accepted: *He does not*. His face was right in front of her, and here is what Holly was thinking: *I don't want to stick a key into someone's eye. I don't want to hurt him that badly. On the other hand, he obviously plans to hurt me, and I have to protect Kate. If I stick a key in his eye, he'll stop this, but I really don't want to blind a person. Obviously though, I'm not going to let him hurt Kate.*

All this thinking was moot. That's because as Holly was going over her options, it turns out she already *had* stuck the key into the man's eye, and already had placed it into the ignition. She had already started the car, and the man was already sitting on the ground beside the open door doing what men do when something sharp is stuck in their eye.

The force of the car accelerating caused Holly's door to slam, and immediately, there was silence. That is when she stopped thinking about what to do and slowly realized she'd already done it.

"Mom, your seat belt's not on."

Holly took Kate's hand to reassure her that they were safe. Without any panic, she explained, "That man tried to get in our car without asking for permission, and I didn't let him. Do you understand?"

"I understand, but you forgot to put on your seat belt."

Holly put on her seat belt, amazed to see that her daughter had gotten into the car and followed the usual procedure, trusting that she was safe while her mother handled that man.

What an odd experience, Holly thought—not frightening or terrible, but almost calm. Too awful to imagine sticking a sharp object deep into someone's eye, but not, it turned out, so bad to actually do it. Each time she went over the experience, the word that came into her head was "natural." *You attack me when I'm with my little girl, and you get the natural consequence.* In fact, she thought the man got away kind of lucky because she could have stuck him in both eyes.

That's when she realized she *had* stuck him in both eyes.

When Holly recounted all this to me months after it occurred, we were standing in the hallway of a television studio where I'd just finished a news interview. I had discussed the fact that violence almost always has detectable pre-incident indicators that we recognize intuitively. Intuition sends many messengers to warn us, messengers such as doubt, suspicion, apprehension, and hesitation, but the most urgent—and often the most valuable—is fear. I had said that true fear is a gift because it is a survival signal that sounds in the presence of danger. "Of course, you're an expert on all that," I told Holly.

"Yes, I am," she said with some pride.

"Why do you think your intuition assured you that he didn't have a gun?"

"Well, he was wearing loose sweat pants, which probably didn't have a waistband strong enough to hold a gun—and his T-shirt was tight, so I'd have seen one. Also, if he had a gun, why would he have fought with me? But these are theories on my part because I don't really know for certain."

Holly had obviously given this a lot of thought, and her theories made sense. I asked if she had any regrets about what happened to her assailant.

"No. He got into something very dangerous: attacking a woman with her child. Maybe if I'd been alone, he wouldn't have been injured so badly, I don't know. But if you attack a mother with her child, well, you've got to expect some serious consequences. It's only natural."

That's exactly what it is, and Holly had experienced firsthand what every mother in nature knows on some level: that she is well equipped to protect her offspring from just about anything. This natural ability is deep, brilliant, powerful. Nature's greatest accomplishment, the human brain, is stunningly efficient when its host is at risk, but when one's child is at risk, it moves to a whole new level, one we can justifiably call miraculous.

The brain built for protecting our children was field-tested for millions of years in the wild. I call it the *wild brain*, in contrast with the logic brain so many people revere. The logic brain couldn't do a thing for Holly once the situation became critical. The logic brain is plodding and unoriginal. It is burdened with judgment, slow to accept reality, and spends valuable energy thinking about how things ought to be, used to be, or could be. The logic brain has strict boundaries and laws it wants to obey, but the wild brain obeys nothing, conforms to nothing, answers to nobody, and will do whatever it takes. It is unfettered by emotion, politics, politeness, and as illogical as the wild brain may sometimes seem, it is, in the natural order of things, completely logical. It just doesn't care to convince us of anything by using logic. In fact, it doesn't give a damn what we think.

To tap into this resource, to reinvest in our intuition, to *know* how to avoid danger, to know, for example, whom to keep our children away from, we must listen to internal warnings while they are still whispers. The voice that knows all about how to protect children may not always be the loudest, but it is the wisest.

A generation ago, in Dr. Spock's *Baby and Child Care*, Benjamin Spock told parents that they already possessed most of the important knowledge about their children's health. Similarly, when it comes to predicting violence and protecting children, I submit that you already know most of what you need to know. You have the wisdom of the species, and the expert voice that matters most is yours. Yet, society has trained us to believe that we don't know the answers, that professionals know what's best and that good parents listen to them. As a result, we have come to believe that we will find certainty outside ourselves. We won't, of course, but we can find the illusion of certainty, particularly if that's what we're willing to settle for.

When the principal tells us our concerns are baseless, when the other parents insist there's no problem, when we're assured that the school-bus driver is a good guy, when the baby-sitter seems great to everyone else, our hesitation may be the only thing that stands between us and a fraudulent feeling of certainty. That hesitation stands there for a reason, and we won't always find the reason with logic. Remember, it was Holly's logic brain that convinced her to ignore the whisper, to disregard the apprehension she felt at the theater. It was her wild brain that made up for the error.

Mothers are frequently required to interpret signals they get from the wild brain. This can be complex because the world of risk to our children is not a flat world whose edges are within view, but a round one with horizons we cannot easily see beyond. It is a world of so many possible risks that two miracles occur every day with most every child and most every parent: The kids survive, and the parents retain their sanity.

It may have been a long while since you pondered what you could stick into a wall outlet: *a hairpin? A spoon handle? Might fit.* Musings such as these suddenly matter to the new parent. By the time we're old enough to have children, we've developed quite a list of life's dangers, but new parents can throw that list away and prepare for one so extensive they'll need an index. It must include not only the topic of these pages—violence and predators—but also elements of life as universal as water and gravity. The list must include electricity, yarn, heat, cold, plastic bags, stairs, sprinkler heads, doors, drawers, appliances, pencils, cleaning products, rocking chairs, bottle caps, staples, medicine, and marbles. Every danger you have overcome and mastered in your entire life, every safety concern you long ago abandoned, now returns to your consciousness.

Babies themselves teach parents to be watchful. Tom, a new father, told me that whenever his baby daughter has a choice, she'll follow the most dangerous course: "The best toy imaginable could be in front of her, but if there's also a red hot wire coming out of the wall, that's what she'll grab every time. It's as if she has an instinct to pursue the riskiest thing available. This skill of hers has made us very alert."

As children grow up, a parent's longing for certainty grows even stronger. "I just want to be sure the park is safe; I just want to be sure she won't be waiting in front of the school by herself; I just want to be sure he'll be supervised at the beach; I just want to be sure that boy will drive carefully."

And you can't be sure. There are, however, things you can be certain about. You can be certain every important decision is made with the best information. You can be certain you've educated yourself, certain you've made the best choice possible with the time and resources available. Above all, you can be certain you will listen to yourself, certain you'll give your hesitations a moment's consideration rather than later regret that you didn't. You can be certain you do not deny or discount intuition, the best resource nature gave you.

Yes, of course, anything can happen. You could hear of a great camp for your son and confirm that the camp conducts background checks on its counselors, you could talk to parents whose children have gone there summer after summer, take comfort in the camp's policy that its personnel are never alone with individual boys, be pleased with the results of your inquiry at the state licensing agency, feel good after meeting the priest who's run the place for twenty-five years, pack off your boy for his adventure, and then a tree branch could fall into the barbecue pit, sending an ember down the cowboy shirt of the guy singing folksongs and as he reels, the neck of his guitar could hit your son in the forehead, endowing him with his first stitch (courtesy of the nurse you confirmed the camp employed).

When you get that call, you needn't lament, "Oh God, I should have checked to see if there were any weak branches above the barbecue pit."

The search for certainty starts and ends within yourself—for example, every time you are open to receive information about your daughter's new boyfriend, conclude he's okay, and then don't torture yourself while she's out on a date. Greater certainty is yours for the taking after you visit the parents of your son's friend at their home, feel good about the sleepover, and approve it.

There is also a role for faith in all this. Ultimately, no matter how well you come to know the parents of your son's new friend, you'll need to have faith that the dad won't drink too much before driving the boys home from a movie. But we decide where to invest our faith and we must invest some of it in ourselves. That means being willing to hesitate even when it's inconvenient, unpopular, or downright rude. Can you imagine canceling the sleepover at the very last moment because of a feeling that something's not right? I hope you can.

If you think the dad might drive drunk, there's probably a reason you think it, and it's worth exploring for a moment. If you think there might be a collection of unsecured guns at their home, your hesitation makes sense. You see, it's one thing to never get a warning about some risk to our children; it's quite another to get a signal and then ignore it. You can be certain you will listen to yourself, because that's up to you. You may conclude on further consideration that your hesitation wasn't called for—but you can give at least a brief consideration to every signal from your wild brain.

That brain is already hardwired with amazing forethought about protecting your children. Take closing the car door, for example. The whole process is broken down to its elements: the exact spot where you place your hand, the leverage you might need to slow or stop the door after it's moving, the amount of energy you use, the amount you hold back. For years, you have pushed a car door and walked away, been several steps off by the time it latched, but now you are right there the whole while, ensuring that no part of your child comes between the door and the car. Everything is different when you have children.

.     .     .

Among all the possible risks to our children, from the freak accident to the predictable accident, from the chemical under the sink to the chemical sold on the street corner, nothing is more frightening to us than the danger posed by people, the danger that is by design, the danger that is conscious.

The danger that is conscious may reside within the fourteen-year-old neighborhood boy who makes us uncomfortable, or the baby-sitter we do not trust, or the mall security guard who stares at our daughter, or the deliveryman who stops by during his lunch hour to give our son an unsolicited gift. Though many people act as if it's invisible, the danger that is conscious is usually in plain view, disguised perhaps, but in plain view nonetheless. Some of the behaviors that precede this kind of danger are designed to distract, confuse, or reassure us, but those behaviors are themselves signals. There is a universal code of violence, and like every parent, you already know that code.

Imagine you've just been blessed with a newborn baby girl. She is the latest model of human being, the proud result of ages of R & D that makes the most fantastic computer seem like an abacus. She has more brain cells than you and me combined, more in fact, than there are grains of sand on your favorite beach. She can learn, teach, design, build. She has within her the cleverness and dexterity to catch an ant or a whale. She can fly—literally. She can travel to another planet, and many of her contemporaries will.

Can you believe, even for a moment, that this astonishing being was designed without a defense system? Nature's investment in this child is far too great for such an oversight. Parents are the defense system designed to spot danger at the earliest possible moment, and qualified to avoid it, evade it, escape it, or destroy it. Nature almost always arranges more than one person for this job, and with good reason: In spite of the power coiled up inside every human being, we each begin as the most vulnerable of creatures. A human infant left to its own resources is left with just one resource: the ability to make noise. That noise, however, lacks clear meaning to those who might hear it. A baby cannot describe its peril, cannot move out of harm's way, cannot hide, cannot mount a viable defense against any predator, even the smallest. But a baby doesn't have to do any of these things because for reasons so deep in our cells that we don't need any scientist to explain them, healthy parents will do anything to protect a child.

When a baby is born, the mother in particular enters into a new, larger relationship with the world. She has become connected to all people. She is part of keeping us on earth—not the "us" comprised of individuals, but the species itself. By protecting this one baby, this gift, a mother accepts life's clearest responsibility.

As the years go on, whose responsibility that is becomes less clear. Does it still belong to the parents, or is it now the day-care center, or the parents of your child's friend, or the school, or the mall, or the police, or the university, or the government? And when does your daughter herself take over?

Is it the first time she is allowed to be alone in the house or the first time she walks herself to school? Or is it that afternoon when she first backs the car down the driveway (and over the sidewalk) into the street?

We are built to consider these questions very carefully because we know how vulnerable children are. In fact, throughout history, half of all children failed to reach adulthood. Half. The odds are far better for children in America today, but the truth remains that childhood is safe only when adults make it so.

Of course, it is also usually adults who make it unsafe, though you are not likely one of those. I say this because you are right now reading a book about protecting children from violence. That means you are willing to look at some hard realities, the first of which is that man does things to man (and to girl and boy) that no other animal would even consider doing.

You may have gotten this far in life without having to acknowledge that violence is a part of humanity, but to protect a child, you will have to take that fact deep into yourself.

Violence, though rarely humane, is always human. It is around your children and it is in them—and it is in you. When I discuss this point in speeches, there is usually an audience member who doubts the universality of violence. It might be a timid woman who raises her hand and says, "I could never be violent; I could never hurt another person." But if I just wait, she will add a telling caveat: "Unless, of course, someone tried to harm my child." In that event, this timid woman not only *might* hurt a person, she would want to. She who said she could never be violent would now hit, punch, scratch, bite, rip, shoot, stab—so the violence is in her, ready to emerge like an assassin if need be. Nature is ruthless, and rather than seek to deny mankind's cruelties, we can accept and draw upon the resources within us—even the ones we wish weren't necessary.

You may have gotten this far in life without the confidence that you can protect yourself, but to protect a child, you'll need that confidence. If you do not accept that you are a creature of nature, fully endowed with powerful defenses, how can you nurture the defenses in your child? If you cannot make a safe place for yourself in the world, can you make one for your child? If you cannot conquer your own unwarranted fears, can you soothe those of your child?

So, safety for children is a matter of safety for parents first. Much as an adult airline passenger is advised to put on her own oxygen mask before putting one on a child, a mother must be safe in order to protect a child. Sacrificing her safety or peace of mind does not add to her child's safety or peace of mind. It isn't either/or—it's both.

If you are a woman with a young child, you'll learn in these pages that it is you and not your child who is most often the predatory prize, you who are more likely to attract violence, and you who must know what it looks like. Do you know the strategies that a predator might use to gain your trust? Do you know the ways your defense system can warn you? If you got this far without learning, now you must.

You can become unwilling to relinquish your control to a predator and you can—after all these years—stop caring about politeness. As parent and child advocate Anna McDonnell says, "To have a child is to have the chance to revisit your own childhood and self, and sometimes to make changes that have been needed for a long while."

Trained for decades to interact with men in ways that serve the patriarchy, the new mother must answer to no man if doing so might place her or her child at risk. The new mother must let go of the idea that violence is a mystery understood only by men.

Safety starts with knowing that your intuition about people is a brilliant guardian. Listening to intuition really means listening to yourself. Like everyone, you've had scores of experiences when you listened and were later grateful, and scores of experiences when you chose not to listen and were later regretful. I can't say it any more clearly than this: To protect your child, you must believe in yourself.

Reluctant enough to learn about protecting themselves, many people are even more afraid to consider the details of how someone might harm their children ("I don't want to *think* about something like that"). I suggest they consider an easier, softer question: Of all the approaches you might take to enhance the safety of your child, do you suppose that ignorance about violence is an effective one?

How about denial? Does it enhance safety? A great irony is that the very people most likely to deny the whole issue of risk to their children, the very ones most eager to invest blind confidence in the neighbor, the school, and the mall—they are the ones who worry most. That raises another question I would ask them: Of all the strategies you might bring to protecting children, do you suppose that worry is an effective one? I can tell you it is not.

I've been helping people manage fear and risk for almost a quarter-century and one of the ironies of worry is that it enhances risk. That's because as you worry about some imagined danger, you are distracted from what is actually happening. Perception and not worry is what serves safety. Perception focuses your attention; worry blurs it. And most ironically, the things we worry about are often chosen specifically because they are more palatable than likelier possibilities. Here's an example: It is easier for the worrier to wring his hands about the possible risk posed by an unknown molester who might wander into the neighborhood than to accept the intuition that someone who was invited into the house is sexually abusing a child. Before you banish that thought, understand that nearly 90 percent of sexual abuse is committed by someone the children know, not by strangers.

Hard as it is to accept the idea that some well-liked neighbor or friend of the family might be sexually abusing a child, imagine the idea that it's someone in your own family. The denier doesn't have to consider this because it's so easy to replace that unwelcome thought with a warmer one like "Not in *this* family." Yet, one in three girls and one in six boys will have sexual contact with an adult, so *somebody* must be responsible. You can be certain that wherever it is happening, a denier is sitting in a box seat watching the performance that precedes the crime, watching a predator snake his way into a position of advantage, watching an adult persuade a child to trust him. During the beginning of sexual abuse, deniers are unconscious co-conspirators. And after sexual abuse, deniers will volunteer for the job of designing theories to explain the onset of a child's sleep disturbances or eating problems or sudden fear of that same adult she liked so much just a week ago.

Speaking of sexual abuse of children, though it is not always committed with force, I treat it as an act of violence throughout this book. That's because for the child victim, it has the same results as violence: demoralization, depression, repression, loss of belief in the ability to protect oneself, fear of people. Not all sexual abuse is committed with sinister intent and not all results in physical injury—but it is all violence nonetheless.

If a discussion requires exploration of these hard realities, the denier will first try to wriggle away: "Talking about those things, you just bring them on yourself"; or "Yes, I know all about that stuff; can we please change to a happier subject?" Under pressure, he or she will acknowledge a given risk, for as a seasoned veteran in a long battle with reality, the denier has learned that appearing to get it, to really get it, is the best defense against unwanted knowledge. And the denier is not stupid—to the contrary, there is brilliance in the creative ways that his or her children can be excluded from the discussion. "You're so right," the denier says, "sexual abuse is an enormous problem, particularly for young teens. Thank God mine aren't there yet."

No, sorry, says reality, the most common age at which sexual abuse begins is three.

"Well, sure, if you have homosexuals around small children, there's a risk."

No, sorry, says reality, nearly 100 percent of sexual abuse is committed by heterosexual males.

"Yeah, but that kind of pervert isn't living in our neighborhood."

Sorry, says reality, but that kind of pervert *is* living in your neighborhood. The U.S. Department of Justice estimates that on average, there is one child molester *per square mile*.

"Well, at least the police know who these people are."

Not likely, says reality, since the average child molester victimizes between thirty and sixty children *before* he is ever arrested. (And anyway, when he is arrested, there's always a denier vouching for him with the familiar mantras: "But he's such a nice man," or "You can't believe everything a child says.")

When all the defenses against reality are taken away, the denier switches to resignation (literally *resigning* from responsibility): "Well, there's nothing you can do about it anyway." This misplaced fatalism actually becomes fatal for some children, and in those cases, the denier sings the ever-popular hit-single: "How Could I Have Known?" The final verse you hear as a denier scuttles away from responsibility is also the most offensive: "Well, kids are resilient. When bad things happen, they bounce back."

Absolutely not, says reality, they don't bounce back. They adjust, they conceal, they repress, and sometimes they accept and move on, but they don't bounce back. In fact, contrary to the apparent belief of some people, children don't bounce at all.

If I seem hard on denial, I have my reasons. One could say that true responsibility, moral responsibility for the bad things people do to children, must lie with the offenders, not the silent witnesses. Fair enough. But understand that the offender is also a denier, a criminal who chooses not to see the roots of violence in himself, chooses not to acknowledge the road he is on even when it's clear where it will carry him, and chooses not to stop himself. Then later, most offenders choose not to see the cruel impact of the behavior they allowed to occur. And they won't be alone in those choices, because for virtually every cruelty done to a child, there is an audience of deniers that stays seated, sees the signals and quickly closes their eyes.

Deniers, more than any other people, have it in their hands to protect our children and change our nation. Why? Because the solution to violence in America is not more laws, more guns, more police, or more prisons. *The solution to violence is acceptance of reality.*

From there, you can hear the messengers of intuition. From there, you can evaluate risk and organize defenses. Reality is the highest ground you can find—and the safest—because from there you can see what's coming.

•    •    •

If you are still reading by this point, you are not a denier. Your acceptance of reality is, all by itself, the greatest asset you bring to protecting children. That's because predicting violence isn't a matter of looking for the obvious; it's about looking *at* the obvious. There is no search involved if you are willing to know, willing to host a difficult thought at least long enough to consider it, willing to treat intuition as the friend it is.

My impatience with denial is fueled by a career of asking people whose children were victimized if they could have seen it coming. Most of them say No, but then add a fact here, another there, until they must acknowledge, "Now that I think of it, I guess there were several signs."

Intuition is knowing without knowing why, knowing even when

you can't see the evidence. Denial is choosing *not* to know something even when the evidence is obvious. It's easy to see which of these two human abilities is more likely to protect children from violence. And that's my purpose in this book. It is not to eradicate violence, for that's not going to happen. Violence is part of the species, even necessary to the species for reasons we can't possibly fathom. But leave that dilemma to anthropologists because the goal here is simply to protect our children. Children in general, sure—but ours first.

Would we sacrifice someone else's children to protect our own? Yes. But leave that dilemma to philosophers, for when we are protecting our children, we are insulated from ideology. We just don't care—and that's the way of our species. If you are a parent, you already know this. Deep inside you are certain you can do what it takes, yet you might worry about missing some detail, acting too late, or failing to recognize danger. These pages, by showing what risk really looks like (as opposed to what you might imagine it looks like) offer ways to be more certain—at least about your own ability. You can come to trust that you will see signals where they exist and not see them where they don't exist. You can be more familiar with risk, and yet less preoccupied by it.

Some parents have become so obsessed with safety that it supersedes much else. One result is that millions of American children learn more about the dangers of strangers than about the wonders new people might bring into their lives.

Risk is part of our experience as human beings, a part that gives life much of its vitality. In her brilliant book, *Parents Who Think Too Much*, author Anne Cassidy discusses our obsession with the safety of children: "The suits of armor we provide them are as dangerous as the world we're protecting them from." She's right, we can be absurdly risk-aversive, like this label that actually appears on a Batman costume: "Parent: Please exercise caution. For play only. Cape does not enable user to fly."

We can be even more absurd about the safety of adults. After a fire on the Mir space station, I saw a TV news exposé proclaiming the space program as unsafe for the astronauts. You mean sitting on top of a missile that's filled with rocket fuel and being blasted out of the atmosphere at 25,000 miles an hour is unsafe? Who'd have thought?

While I won't flinch from reality, this book is not a compendium of every risk a child might face, nor is it a collection of scary stories. My work is far too practical for that. Protecting children from violence is a parental duty that requires expertise in my field, but I know it's just one part of parenting. I'll stay away from all the other parts. I am not writing as a parent or as a judge of people's choices; I'll offer no opinions about whether mothers should work or about single-parent households or alternative-lifestyle families, or about any of the thousand ideological issues and parenting choices that divide us. People have strong feelings about issues that affect their children, of course, but my subject here is not controversial.

I am writing as a consultant, as if you walked into my office each time you were faced with a question about violence, risk, danger, safety, or worry. Sometimes, I'll have a lot to say; other times, I might tell you to quit thinking so much, but I'll remember that you have asked for my opinion on just one topic: safety from violence.

I have studied that topic every day for nearly three decades (longer if you count my own childhood). My consulting firm's seventy associates and I help answer the highest-stakes questions that individuals and nations face. We predict the behavior of mass-killers, stalkers, bombers, angry employees, aspiring assassins, and the more common violent ex-husbands. The clients we advise include presidents (of corporations, universities, and countries), governors, mayors, police departments, movie stars, prosecutors, athletes, and religious leaders. We designed the predictive system used to help protect justices of the U.S. Supreme Court, senior officials of the Central Intelligence Agency, governors of nine states, and all members of Congress.

Whether the most beloved people in the world or the most reviled, whether rich or poor, famous or anonymous, all of our clients come to our office because of a serious safety concern. Most have something else in common, too: They have children they must also keep safe, just like any other parent. They face the same challenges you might: whom to trust, when to let go, what to believe, what to doubt, what to fear, and what not to fear. They are looking for some certainty about life's high-stakes questions, and if you are a parent, you'll have no shortage of those:

• How can I know a baby-sitter won't turn out to be someone who harms my child?
• What can I ask child-care professionals when I interview them?
• What's the best way to prepare my child for walking to school alone?
• How can my child's safety at school be improved?
• How can I spot sexual predators?
• How can I know if my child is being sexually abused?
• What can I do if my child is lost in public?
• How can I teach my child about risk without causing too much fear?
• What must my teenage daughter know in order to be safe?
• What must my teenage son know in order to be safe?

And finally, in the face of all these questions, how can I reduce the worrying?

Holly was able to protect Kate that night because she was with her, but most parents' worries are about the times they can't be with their children. There are more of those times as our children grow, so I'll discuss the safety challenges parents face along the way: from school to sleepovers, from driving to dating. As you read on, you will find yourself questioning the value of the rules children are typically taught: "Go to a policeman if you are lost," "Always respect your elders," "Do what the baby-sitter says," and most popular of all, "Never talk to strangers." These maxims are time-tested, to be sure, but you'll see that they have failed the test.

For a species with a 100 percent mortality rate, we spend our protective resources rather strangely. One would think that children—who have the opportunity to live the longest—would be society's central concern, but often they are not. Punishment for violence against children is less frequent than for the same violence against adults, and compensation for the wrongful death of a child is far less than for the wrongful death of an adult. In America, the safety of children gets less of the government's attention than yours does. This is just another reminder that parents must be experts at protecting their children.

And here's the bigger picture: If we do all we can to protect children and invest them with a deep belief that they are safe, they will be less afraid, and thus less likely to be violent toward others. All creatures are more dangerous when afraid. In the most basic animal sense, if the dominant do not take care of you, you seek to dominate. Domination is sometimes the only way for people to give themselves what society did not: a feeling of safety. For too many young men, that feeling is gained with a gun.

Ultimately, our goal is not merely that children survive, but that they thrive. You are much more than a guard, and I want nothing to do with caution if the price is your child's freedom to grow. I want nothing to do with unwarranted fear. All of these pages, even the ones that address hard topics, are dedicated to getting you through—not into—the subject of violence.

I grew up in that subject—in a violent world. I am not referring to the wars between nations—those were easy for me. I am referring to the wars in my family, the ones that left bullets embedded in the walls and floors of our homes, the wars in which police officers were occasional soldiers and my sisters and I were hostages. I first assumed the role of parent at eight years old, a protector of my younger sister, Melissa. It's clear to me now that predicting and preventing violence was my calling long before it became my profession.

Some years ago, my older sister Chrysti said to me, "Isn't it great to know the worst is behind us?" She was referring to many of our childhood experiences. Our mother was a heroin addict—an intelligent, funny, well-read, and beautiful woman—and a heroin addict nonetheless. While she protected us from some harms, she delivered others, and her addiction brought a collection of people into our lives most parents would recoil from.

I recall a night that I tried to get my mother to stop beating Chrysti; I couldn't, so I sat down on the floor and just watched, reasoning that I'd be there if things got too dangerous. Chrysti and I were used to a lot and our threshold was high, but that night, after two hours of watching the violence escalate, I intervened to calm my mother down. At that moment, Chrysti did something I'd never even thought possible: She ran out the front door. I followed her and we ran like free colts down the center of an empty boulevard.

We stopped at an all-night market and decided to make an anonymous call to the police ("There are two kids loitering around here"). If we didn't give our names to the police, we concluded, they wouldn't be able to take us back home. And it worked just like that. Our ride from the LAPD showed up within a few minutes and took us to jail. They could hardly put a twelve-year-old boy and a fourteen-year-old girl in with hardened criminals (though we might have felt at home), so they put us in our own cell. In the morning, we called our grandfather, who picked us up and took us home. Two kids found bruised and red-eyed and panting at three-thirty in the morning and nobody asked us a thing. It was as if the police saw these dramas every day, and I know now that they do.

I recall another early morning standing in a hallway of the UCLA Hospital emergency room, my mother having taken an overdose of sleeping pills in one of several suicide attempts. A nurse had several questions for me, never asking though, what a barefoot boy was doing there at four A.M., the sole family representative. I now know that emergency-room nurses have seen far younger children playing adult roles in life's dramas, and they've also seen them brought in beaten, shot, raped.

I recall my mother threatening to kill us kids by turning on a gas burner in our apartment while we slept. In response, Chrysti and I modified a screen on our bedroom window so we could get out if we had to. I put a box outside the window and conducted a drill, lifting four-year-old Melissa down to test that I'd be able to get her out quickly. It was my job to be sure the whole family got through those years alive. We didn't. My mother succeeded at her final suicide attempt when she was thirty-nine, and I was sixteen.

Decades went by before I understood why I had invested my life in the prediction and prevention of violence—but now I've got the message.

There aren't many risks discussed in these pages that my sisters and I didn't experience or just barely dodge. Chrysti died recently, but she was happy I was writing a book to help parents protect children. It's good to know that even the hardest of our childhood experiences ended up being valuable, and I commit to share that value with you. I commit that by the end of this book, you'll know more and be uncertain less; see more and deny less, accept more and hesitate less; act more and worry less. How can I be so sure? Because if nature selected you for the job of protecting a child, odds are you're up to it.

# CHAPTER TWO

# INTUITION–THE SOURCE OF SAFETY

*Imagine I throw a spear into the dark. That is my intuition.*
*Then I have to send an expedition into the jungle to find the*
*spear. That is my intellect.*

— INGMAR BERGMAN

China Leonard and her young son, Richard, had just settled into the preop room at St. Joseph's Hospital, where Richard was soon to have minor ear surgery. He usually had a barrage of questions for doctors, but when the anesthesiologist, Dr. Joseph Verbrugge, Jr., came into the room, the boy fell silent. He didn't answer when Dr. Verbrugge asked if he was nervous. "Look at me!" the doctor demanded, but Richard didn't respond.

The boy obviously disliked the abrupt and unpleasant doctor, and China felt the same way, but she also felt something more than that. A strong intuitive impulse crossed her mind: *Cancel the operation,* it boldly said, *cancel the operation.* She quickly suppressed that impulse and began a mental search for why it was unsound. Setting aside her intuition about Dr. Verbrugge in favor of logic and reason, she assured herself that you can't judge someone by his personality. But again, that impulse: *Cancel the operation.* Since China Leonard was not a worrier, it took some effort to silence her inner voice. *Don't be silly*, she thought, *St. Joseph's is one of the best hospitals in the state, it's a teaching hospital; it's owned by the Sisters of Charity, for Christ's sake. You just have to assume this doctor is good.*

With her intuition successfully beaten down, the operation went forward as scheduled, and Richard died during the minor procedure. This tragic story teaches us that the words *I know it* are more valuable than the words *I knew it.*

Later, the investigation revealed that Dr. Verbrugge's colleagues had also been concerned about him. They said he was inattentive to his work, and most seriously, there were at least six occasions when colleagues reported that he appeared to be sleeping during surgeries. For the hospital staff, these were clear signals, but I can't be certain what China and her son detected. I know only that they were perfectly accurate, and I accept that as good enough.

There were medical professionals right at the operating table who heard and then vetoed their intuition. The surgeon noticed that Richard's breathing was labored—and he said so—but nothing effective was done about it. A nurse later said she was concerned with the boy's distress but "chose to believe" that Verbrugge was competent. A doctor who reviewed what happened in that operating room could have been speaking about denial in general when he astutely said: "It's like waking up in your house with a room full of smoke, opening the window to let the smoke out, and then going back to bed."

As you understand how intuition helps protect your children, you'll react to smoke and not wait for fire. You'll care less about protocol and politeness, and you'll be comfortable saying and doing what needs to be said and done. That's no small accomplishment given how often parents think, *What if I speak up and then nothing happens; won't I feel foolish?* Well, if you say something, it's likely nothing will happen, and whatever you might feel will be a cakewalk compared to regret. Can we really look foolish for doing our best to protect our children? In this context, it would seem more embarrassing to keep quiet.

When Holly and her daughter were offered a ride that night after *Jurassic Park*, Holly heard the proverbial "little voice" saying she should accept it. China Leonard got her message through a persistent impulse. Intuition communicates with different people in different ways, sending any of the following messengers:

> Nagging feelings
> Persistent thoughts
> Dark humor
> Anxiety
> Curiosity
> Hunches
> Gut feelings
> Doubt
> Hesitation
> Suspicion
> Apprehension
> Fear

After Holly overruled the subtle signal she received, intuition sent out the ultimate messenger—fear—the one we cannot easily ignore. But people try to silence even that one: *Calm down, calm down, it's probably nothing* some tell themselves, rather than giving a fair hearing to nature's lifesaving signal. Why do they do that? Because they, like all of us, have had experiences where predictions turned out to be inaccurate. Understand, however, that intuition about your children is always right in at least two ways: It is always based on something, and it always has your child's best interest at heart. While some question the accuracy of intuition, nobody can doubt its intent, particularly when it comes to violence. It is there to keep you and your children safe. In fact, the root of the word intuition, *tueri*, means to guard and to protect.

These are subjects I know a lot about, but it's my premise that you too are an expert at predicting violent behavior, just like every creature on earth. (You may also be an expert at denying it, but we're working on that with each chapter you read.) Imagine two wolves meeting on a mountain path: One of them shows his teeth, lays his ears back, growls, digs his back paws into the earth, and then attacks. Do you suppose the victim thinks, *Geez, I had no idea that was coming?* Of course not, because these animals exchanged a series of signals before violence. So do human beings.

Yet people—understandably reluctant to accept that they are in the presence of a person who might harm their children—usually try to explain his behavior some other way. "After all," one mother told me, "if I reacted every time someone gave me the creeps, I wouldn't ever let anyone near me or my children." Actually, that's not so; intuition includes many more people in our lives than it excludes. In fact, we trust people so often that we barely even notice it. The salesperson, the new neighbor, the friend of a friend, the secretary at the tax accountant's office, the guy who towed the car, the couple next to us at the movie theater—we automatically evaluated each of them, felt no hesitation, and that was that.

Since the overwhelming majority of people we encounter will not hurt our children, that is just what our intuition correctly concludes almost all of the time. Accordingly, when we don't trust someone, it's different from our typical experience—and thus noteworthy.

But what about those times we weren't hesitant about someone and should have been? Well, since there are almost always warning signs of violence, most people can later recount what they missed. Often they will say about some particular detail of warning, "I realize this now, but I didn't know it then." Of course, if it is in their heads now, so was it then. What they mean is that only in retrospect have they accepted the significance of a given detail. This has taught me that the intuition process works, though often not as well as its principal competitor, the denial process.

Just as intuition protects us from danger, denial protects us from something too: unwanted information. Denial serves to eliminate the discomfort of accepting realities we'd rather not acknowledge. There are times this protection is valuable for emotional survival, but it is rarely useful for physical survival—and it's downright destructive to the safety of children. Like intuition, denial sends signals you can recognize. When you detect these cues at work in yourself, you can stop and ask one of life's most powerful questions: *What am I choosing not to see here?*

---

# The Signals of Denial

- Rationalization
- Justification
- Minimization
- Excuse-making
- Refusal

---

Psychologist Deborah Mandell recalls a mother's story about taking her three-year-old daughter to visit an elderly neighbor: "She likes going over there because he buys her toys. Plus, he gives her a dollar if she'll kiss him. This worried me at first, but now I think he's just lonely [rationalization]. In any case, my little girl doesn't discourage it so he probably assumes she wants to be kissed [justification]. And they're just kisses, after all [minimization]. He probably doesn't know better [excuse-making]. Anyway, I'm not going to live being suspicious of everyone [refusal]."

We minimize only that which looms large, and the fact that we make an excuse for someone's behavior is, in Dr. Mandell's words, "a sure sign that we perceive something wrong with the behavior." That elderly neighbor made some of the same moves that a pedophile makes. He may be a harmless and dear old fellow—I don't know—but I've seen many parents after the shock of having a child victimized, carried back in their minds to the time when they still had easy choices available, before they acceded to someone's malevolent manipulation.

It isn't only sinister intent some parents deny, it's also negligence: Jane and Sally are friends whose two small daughters sometimes play together. Planning an afternoon play-date for their girls, the mothers decided that Jane's daughter would be driven home by the sitter who worked for Sally. Jane asked, "Your sitter's a good driver, right?" The very fact that the question came into her head meant she had reason to consider the topic—in this case, Jane had once seen the baby-sitter driving too fast with Sally's daughter in the car.

When we ask questions that have only one possible answer, they really aren't questions at all—they are requests for reassurance. In effect, Jane was asking Sally to aid in her denial. On hearing the obvious answer ("Our sitter is a very safe driver"), Jane explained away her concern: "That's good news because I thought I saw her driving too fast one day, but I'm a terrible judge of speed [rationalization]. I know sometimes you've got to rush just to be on time [justification] and since the kids always wear seat belts, they're safe [minimization]. Anyway, we all speed sometimes [excuse-making], so I'm not going to judge her [refusal]."

With denial, the details we need for the best predictions float silently by us like life preservers, and while the man overboard may enjoy the welcome fantasy that he is still in his stateroom, there is soon a price to pay for his daydream.

Many live in that daydream because they believe that human behavior cannot be predicted. We must abandon that myth if we hope to attain any level of confidence in our ability to protect children. We must acknowledge that we successfully predict behavior every day. Driving in big-city traffic, we make amazingly accurate high-stakes predictions about the behavior of literally thousands of people. We unconsciously read tiny untaught signals: the slight tilt of a stranger's head or the momentarily sustained glance of a person a hundred feet away reassures us it is safe to pass in front of his two-ton monster. We expect all the drivers to act just as we would, but we still detect those few who might not—so that we are also predicting their behavior, unpredictable though we may call it.

People predict with some success how a child will react to a warning, how a witness will react to a question, how a jury will react to a witness, how a consumer will react to a slogan, how an audience will react to a scene, how a spouse will react to a comment, how a reader will react to a phrase, and on and on. Predicting violent behavior is easier than any of these, but we fantasize that violence is an aberration done by others unlike us. The human violence we abhor and fear the most, that which we call "random" and "senseless," is neither. It always has purpose and meaning, to the perpetrator, at least. We may not choose to explore or understand that purpose, but it is there, and as long as we label it "senseless," we'll not make sense of it—and we'll think we can't predict it. I submit, however, that you have been attending your academy of predicting violence for most of your life. To pick up your diploma, there is just one truth you must accept: that there is no mystery of human behavior that cannot be solved inside your head or your heart.

•    •    •

The majority of our predictions are so automatic, subconscious, and accurate, we aren't even aware of them. They are handled by intuition, on guard all the time—even when we sleep. That's hard to believe, perhaps, but you've likely had an experience something like this mother's: "I can sleep next to my husband as he watches a loud television show; I can sleep through the phone ringing and my husband answering it—but if our four-year-old son opens the door to his room twenty feet down the hall, I'm up in an instant."

This all goes far beyond mere hearing; intuition is on duty even when we are not, discerning the importance of different sounds while we sleep. That's one reason it's difficult to sleep in a new house: Your intuition has not yet categorized all those little noises. On the first night, the clinking of the ice maker or the rumbling of the water heater might be an intruder. By the third night, your mind knows better and doesn't wake you—until some new unknown sound comes along.

These amazing abilities are even more impressive when used consciously. Because we know more than we think we know, we could make lots of useful predictions in life, but often we appreciate this only after the fact. An example of this is available to anyone who keeps a diary; look back at the pages preceding an event and you'll see the predictive signs. After reviewing her lifelong diary, author Sarah Kortum put it beautifully: "A chill crept up my spine, for inevitably there it was, over and over again: the future, the ending, right there embedded in the beginning, in my own handwriting."

In *Women's Bodies, Women's Wisdom*, Dr. Christiane Northrup calls intuition "the direct perception of truth or fact independent of any reasoning process." She says we are all born with this ability, but that "the more education we get in this culture, the less we trust our natural intuition. Because our society glorifies only logical, rational, left-brain thinking, we are taught to discount other forms of knowing as primitive or ignorant." Dr. Northrup says that the solar plexus, where we usually feel a gut reaction, is in fact a primitive brain. "It's the part of our body that lets us know whether we are safe and whether we are being lied to."

A whole industry of how-to books on child-rearing discourages parents from honoring that primitive brain. In *Parents Who Think Too Much*, Anne Cassidy writes: "Through three pregnancies and our children's early years, books were the answer. They told us when to call the doctor, what stroller to buy, and how to calm a crying baby. Eventually, the information and advice they contained made me analyze almost every decision I made about our kids, ignore my instincts, and continually question myself. I didn't mean for it to happen, but it happened anyway: I had begun to raise my children *by the book*." Cassidy now suggests parents raise kids "by heart," noting that the clarity a parent feels when a child is in trouble "allows instinct to emerge, and suddenly we are not conflicted anymore."

A couple of years ago, a woman named Janet saw me discussing these issues on the *Oprah Winfrey Show* and decided to get my book, *The Gift of Fear*. A few hours later, by coincidence, the book was also suggested to her by her daughter Blair, who was attending college in Arizona. Within weeks, both women had read the book and were about to get a pop quiz on the material.

Blair was living in a small rented house off campus with two other young women, Amanda and Cheryl. They got along well, but there was a persistent problem caused by Cheryl's boyfriend, Nick. Earlier in the year he had attempted suicide and his general instability made them apprehensive. Blair and Amanda did not want Nick visiting, and they had one of the best reasons people can have: He scared them.

When he dropped out of the military and dropped into their house, Blair was alarmed. She refused to join her roommates in denying the obvious: Nick was not looking for a job, he wasn't going anywhere, and the girls were afraid of him.

When Blair discussed the situation with her mother, they both recognized several warning signs of intimate violence: Nick's controlling behavior toward Cheryl (not letting her see friends, deciding what she could wear) and his rabid jealousy (persistently calling Cheryl, demanding to know what she was doing, whom she was with).

Months later Blair wrote to me about how she felt: "I couldn't sleep, I could not feel comfortable in that house, and the whole time a voice in my head was telling me to get out, that something was going to happen. When it came time to be direct with Cheryl, Amanda stunned me by saying she had no problem with Nick. This, after more than a year of telling me she was afraid of him! When it came to standing up for what she believed, she caved. I did not. I was confident that you, your book, and my inner voice knew better than anyone else in that house."

Throughout this period Blair kept her mother apprised of the situation, and Janet decided to contact the parents of the other girls and discuss the situation.

Each parent told Janet that they also disliked Nick. One said she wished he'd leave (but wishing something doesn't make it happen). The theme of these phone calls with the parents was that Janet was overreacting; her daughter could handle it on her own. Admittedly, Janet was torn between being a friend to an adult daughter and mothering someone who had already left the nest, and this made it difficult for her to know what—if anything—to do next. While the other parents had different levels of concern, they solidly agreed on one thing: Nick was not dangerous. The girls apparently didn't feel that way—they had started referring to him as "the psycho."

When Nick learned that he was the subject of discussions between the parents, he stormed into Blair's room and yelled, "This is all your fault. You better be willing to pay the consequences."

A few days later Nick surprised everyone by moving out of the house, but what looked like good news to the other girls looked like trouble to Blair. She felt Nick was not someone who'd just give up. More important, her intuition sent her an emergency signal, and she shared it with her mother: "He's going to kill Cheryl, I just know it."

Janet listened to her daughter (and to herself), and set off without hesitation to get Blair out of that house. Later she told me, "You may stop parenting, but you never stop being a parent." Janet did not rest for a moment after her ten-hour drive to Blair's house. Wordlessly, mother and daughter rushed through their packing. They shared a powerful sense of urgency they couldn't explain, and didn't have to explain to anyone. Soon enough, Blair's stuff was in the car, and so was she, and for the first time in weeks, she felt safe. That's the un-dramatic end of Blair's story—but not the end of Cheryl's.

Within one hour of Blair's moving out, Nick arrived at the house with a gun—and kidnapped Cheryl. He tied her hands and drove first to a remote desert area and then to the small motel where he'd been staying. Nick parked the car there, and as he yelled various threats at Cheryl, some employees of a nearby store looked on and concluded that the couple was just "arguing." A woman shopper with much courage and no denial ran over and yelled to the store employees: "He's got a gun in the car! Call the cops!"

Cheryl's own fears (no longer deniable) were now free to empower her. She struggled with Nick, finally got out of the car, and ran toward the store. The employees locked Cheryl in a storeroom just as Nick arrived. Frustrated at losing her, and filled with rage and self-hate, Nick grabbed a bottle of cleaning fluid from a shelf. Wailing "I want to die, I want to die," he drank it down (a weak attempt at suicide for a man with a gun).

Realizing he couldn't get to Cheryl, Nick fled the store and was ap-prehended by police the following day. He has now been indicted for several offenses, including kidnapping.

It's easy to understand those other parents being unwilling to see hard truths about danger. But even after a kidnapping at gunpoint, they remained experts at denial to the end, choosing to blame Blair for causing Nick's behavior. Thankfully, Blair knows very well that she could not and did not make Nick into a violent man. Would they blame her for his suicide attempt months earlier, his troubles in the military, his abusive and obsessive behavior toward Cheryl? The forces at work inside Nick were there long before he met Blair.

Janet acted as a parent to protect her child in spite of the criticism of others. Because of that, they never had to learn what would have happened if Blair had still been at the house when Nick burst in with a gun.

.   .   .

Melanie is another parent whose intuition had to do battle with several people. She and her thirteen-year-old son, Brian, were taking a trip to a few places around the country. Brian's father had died some months earlier, and this vacation was for healing. The trip went well until Los Angeles, where they ran into a small snag at the hotel, a snag that lasted a year.

At the front desk they were told the rooms wouldn't be ready for at least an hour. Confident in the hotel's reputation, Melanie agreed to leave their bags in the care of the front desk clerk (well, at least in the vicinity of the front desk clerk). Then she and Brian took a casual walk through the department store near the hotel. Back an hour later, the clerk gave them this mixed message: "Your rooms are ready, but if those were your suitcases left over there, they were inadvertently loaded onto our courtesy van and taken to the airport. We're trying to find them." And, oh yeah, "sorry about the confusion."

Melanie asked to speak to a supervisor. "The assistant manager, Mr. Hudson, is already working on the problem," the clerk said, pointing to a man who was speaking to Brian. *That's odd*, Melanie thought, *he's talking to my son instead of to me. Well, at least he's talking.*

As Melanie crossed the lobby to join them, she heard the assistant manager say, "I'm pretty sure I can get you a tennis racket signed by Andre Agassi." Brian had apparently already shared his passion for tennis with this man, and though a signed racket would be a great gift, it wouldn't address their more immediate needs. But Mr. Hudson was prepared to help there too. He arranged for them to have a two-bedroom suite, provided toothbrushes, toothpaste, and two hairbrushes. As a last gesture, even though their bags were found that evening, he arranged to have their air tickets upgraded to first class for the flight back to Chicago. All in all, it wasn't a bad ending for their trip, except that Mr. Hudson's generosity didn't stop there.

One afternoon, several weeks after getting home, Melanie found Brian sitting in the kitchen chatting amiably with someone on the phone. She prided herself on that special skill of many mothers: the ability to tell from only one side of a conversation exactly whom their kids are speaking with. But this conversation didn't track normally. *Was it one of his friends?* Brian seemed too reserved for that. *Was it a stranger?* Too familiar for that. The call covered all the usual topics: sports, computers, the Internet, but it also had some unusual topics: clothes, travel, and a really odd one: local tourism. Finally, the world's leading expert on all-things-Brian admitted to herself that she was stumped. She mouthed, "Who's that?" Brian covered the phone with his hand and said, "Eddie."

"Who's Eddie?"

"You remember, that guy who helped us at the hotel in L.A. I talked to him last week and he said he was coming to town. Well, he's here and wants to know if I can show him the beaches around Lake Michigan."

Melanie recalled how helpful Mr. Hudson (now Eddie) had been, and Brian had certainly liked him. Seeing the guy might be okay, but she wasn't comfortable with the idea of a lake outing.

She told Brian that Eddie could stop by for a visit, but that was all. Eddie arrived at their home the following day with a tennis racket for Brian, not signed, but a beautiful racket nonetheless. He and Brian sat in the living room talking, and Melanie put her head in briefly to say hello.

A few weeks later Eddie visited again. On this trip, he spent some time with Brian and a couple of his friends. After Eddie left, Brian approached his mother with a big request: Eddie had offered to take Brian to a tennis tournament in Atlanta. Melanie told her very disappointed son that they'd have to say No. She did, however, agree to Brian's plea that she at least talk to Eddie about it.

Eddie presented a stronger case for the trip: It would be a once-in-a-lifetime opportunity, Brian loves tennis, and he'd meet lots of other kids his age interested in the game. They would be back in a day and a half—and the entire trip would be free. Just as Melanie was thinking it was all a little too generous, Eddie got more generous: He offered her two round-trip tickets to anywhere in the United States for her own use.

Melanie told Eddie she'd think about it, and she did. She also talked to a few friends; they felt she should accept Eddie's offer. (The friend who most favored the idea was, not surprisingly, the very one who'd get to go on the free trip with Melanie.) Melanie considered the fact that Brian really enjoyed spending time with Eddie. Most of all, she acknowledged that Eddie seemed to be—no, he was—a very nice man.

But something didn't feel right.

In spite of Brian's persistent lobbying and substantial disappointment, Melanie said No to the trip. She also made a far harder decision. One evening after Eddie had taken Brian and two of his friends to a movie, she asked to talk to him alone.

"I am not comfortable about your being in Brian's life, and I've decided that it stops tonight. Thanks for all you've done, and you won't have to explain this decision to my son—I'll do that."

Oddly enough, Eddie didn't appear shocked, didn't ask why, didn't negotiate, didn't, in fact, say much at all. He simply said goodbye and left. Melanie immediately wondered if her intuition had misguided her, but she didn't have to wonder for long. A few weeks after Eddie was out of their lives, he still wasn't out of Brian's mind—and for good reason. Though Brian was reluctant to tell his mother, it turns out that Eddie had regularly discussed sex and pornography with him. One evening when Brian had two friends over, Melanie had gone out for an hour. In that time Eddie had come over with a videotape he showed the boys. It was hard-core pornography.

Melanie eventually got all these disturbing details, but if Brian had been allowed to travel with Eddie, there would doubtless have been many more. She had saved her son from the worst kind of damage, the kind often done by "nice" men.

•    •    •

People are quite conflicted about the value of intuition (not including Holly, China Leonard, Janet, and Melanie). On the one hand, everyone recalls times that they followed some particular course and later said, "I knew I shouldn't have done that." On the other, many believe that people aren't as intuitive as, say, dogs. I have a friend who replaced a building contractor in the middle of a remodel job on the basis of her dog's reaction to the man. "When Ginger growls like that, even if her reason isn't apparent to me, I listen."

"The irony," I offered when she told me this, "is that it's far more likely Ginger was reacting to your signals than that you were reacting to hers. Ginger is an expert at reading you, and *you* are the expert at reading other people. Ginger knows nothing about the ways a contractor might inflate the cost to his own profit, or about the somewhat hesitant recommendation you got from a former client of that builder, or about the slick but evasive answer he gave to your pointed question."

My friend quickly acknowledged that she had relied on Ginger for permission to have an opinion she would otherwise have been forced to call (God forbid) unsubstantiated.

A dog does sense and react to fear in humans because it knows instinctively that a frightened person (or animal) is more likely to be dangerous, but dogs have nothing you and I don't have. The problem, in fact, is that extra something we have that a dog doesn't: It is judgment, and while judgment is often of great value to people, it can get in the way of perception and intuition. With judgment comes the eagerness to cross-examine and convict our own feelings, rather than honor them. Ginger is not distracted by the way things could be, used to be, or should be. She perceives only what is.

Speaking of animals, can you imagine an animal reacting to internal signals the way some people do, with annoyance and disdain instead of attention? Would an animal in the wild that is suddenly overcome with fear spend any of its mental energy thinking, *It's probably nothing?* Yet, too often we chide ourselves for even momentarily giving validity to the feeling that someone is behind us on a seemingly empty street, or that someone's interest in our child might be sinister. Instead of being grateful to have a powerful internal resource, instead of entertaining the possibility that our minds might actually be working for us and not just playing tricks on us, we rush to ridicule the impulse.

A parent could offer no greater cooperation to a predator than to spend time thinking, *But he seems like such a nice man*, yet this is exactly what many people do. For example, a woman is standing with her young daughter waiting for an elevator and when the doors open she sees a man inside who causes her apprehension. Since she is not usually afraid, her feeling may be because of his scruffy appearance or the way he looks at her—it doesn't matter why. The point is, she gets a feeling of fear. How does she respond to nature's strongest survival signal? She suppresses it, telling herself: *I'm not going to live like that, I'm not going to insult this guy by letting the door close in his face.* When the fear doesn't go away, she tells herself not to be so silly, and she gets into the elevator with her daughter.

I would ask which is sillier: waiting a moment for the next elevator, or placing her child and herself into a soundproof steel chamber with a stranger she is afraid of?

No other animal on earth would even consider the question, but we choose not to explore—and even to ignore—survival signals. Every day, people engaged in clever defiance of their wild brain become—in mid-thought—victims of violence and harm. So when we wonder why we are victims so often, the answer is clear: It is because we are so good at it. As you'll see in the next chapter, parents who listen to their wild brain have a lot less to worry about—and a lot less to regret.

# CHAPTER THREE

# WORRY

*As we are liberated from our own fear, our presence automatically liberates others.*

— NELSON MANDELA

Holly thought she had worried about every possibility, but seven months after baby Kate came home from the hospital, life came up with an original. One morning, while Kate was seemingly content playing with her toys, Holly noticed something on the floor—maybe some string—and stepped over it without recognition. Most adults have long ago stopped looking down at small things, for they are of little consequence to us. To seven-month-old Kate, however, the floor was a continent, the string a newly discovered river. She followed it to its glorious destination: the whole ball of string. She was full of baby wonder: *Was this always here, waiting beneath the table?* (No, only since yesterday, when Holly was wrapping a parcel to mail.)

Kate dangled the new plaything around her neck like a piece of jewelry. The other end of string was now invisible, a chameleon somewhere on the light gray carpet. From the hallway Holly saw Kate, now in the center of the floor, engaged in innocuous play. This moment of certain safety (her baby simply sitting on the flat floor) was the opportunity to attend to something Holly had been worrying about all morning: Kate had scooped some soil out of a potted plant and she might put it in her mouth and it might contain dangerous chemicals, and so on. Holly was obsessed about getting every bit of residue vacuumed off the floor.

As she started the vacuum cleaner, she saw Kate's head jerk up, presumably reacting to the noise. Holly rolled the machine once forward, once back—and then froze. There was a scream in her head: *Go to Kate!* That something on the floor, the tiny detail barely seen, that string that wasn't even worth bending over to pick up, was suddenly a critical memory because one end was being consumed by a powerful spinning gear in the vacuum cleaner, and the other end was tightening around Kate.

Even before she knew exactly what was happening, Holly heeded the intuitive signal without hesitation. She yanked the plug from the wall, and the vacuum cleaner went silent. She dragged it toward Kate to slacken the string, and then deftly removed the two tight loops from around her baby's neck. This hazard had come and gone in seconds, but the significance lingered for years, just beneath consciousness, along with so many other averted tragedies. *Even string,* Holly thought, *even string could kill my baby.*

Don't ever wonder why women think about risk more often than men do. It is in the cells—and with good reason. Throughout human history, women have protected the children while men protected the village. As the primary caregiver, a new mother must be more than just a careful person, she must become an explorer who can find hazard no matter how cleverly it disguises itself. Little wonder then that mothers become creative geniuses at imagining frightening scenarios. Little wonder that they sometimes see the shadow of danger where there is no danger. Holly was doing that even before Kate was born— in ways she now considers almost funny.

●    ■    ■

About an hour from giving birth to Kate, Holly could have thought about the things that might go wrong in labor, but she thought instead about more remote risks. Alone for a moment in the maternity ward corridor, she was rehearsing in a sense for her new job of protecting the baby. She was recalling the many scary news reports she'd seen over several weeks at home. The one about babies being switched in the hospital loomed largest in her memory. (Not surprising, given that she'd seen it three times, first on the morning news, then on the five o'clock broadcast, and again at eleven.) She'd also seen a story about babies being abducted from hospitals, which must be common, she concluded. (It isn't.) Holly's gurney was parked in front of the nursery, and as she looked through the window at the four newborns inside, she thought: *They aren't different enough! I don't care what anyone says, they aren't different enough to ensure against accidental switching.*

Between Holly and her husband, she thought, there isn't a single feature so out of proportion, so extreme, so unique that it would make obvious which baby was theirs. In Holly's perfect world, the nurses would glance at her baby and say: "Look at those ears! No question about whose child this is." But Holly's ears and Ryan's ears were nondescript, identical twins to the ears on all the other parents.

When she had first told Ryan about her worries, he responded with one word: *impossible.* Ryan's got a lot of credibility on this one, she thought, recalling that he used the exact same word when she'd told him she was pregnant.

"Who would take our baby?" he had asked, thus prompting Holly to develop her list of suspects: a trainee the hospital hadn't screened properly, an unbalanced nurse angry at never having had her own children, a psychotic woman from the mental ward (it's in the very same building!).

A few days earlier, Holly had called and asked the head maternity nurse about how they protect against switching. "Well, we've never had a baby switched here, Mrs. Mason."

"I'm Holly *Jason*—Jason, not Mason."

"Oh, sorry, we have a Holly Mason on the ward right now. Actually, I think her name is Molly Mason. Sorry."

This was not reassuring.

Holly got to the point: "But how would you know if you'd ever had a baby switched?"

The woman chuckled: "We have so many precautions, and well, let me put it this way: We've never had any complaints."

"But how would parents know to complain if they never knew the baby wasn't theirs?"

"Let me be direct, Mrs. Mason. It just doesn't happen."

"Let me be direct," Holly responded. "My last name is Jason."

"Yes, right. But take my advice and don't give it another thought."

Of course, Holly did give it another thought, and another, and many more, right up until this moment lying on the gurney thinking, *They might not want to admit these things happen, but I saw the news reports—let's just remember that.*

This brought to mind another news report: Doctors with phony medical degrees. Holly immediately thought of a doctor she'd seen on her ward who appeared to be wearing a toupee. "Someone who covers up being bald is covering up other secrets," she concluded. But before Holly could speculate on those secrets, a hospital employee approached her with a few questions for a form. Holly was worried that some error on his part might lead to her getting the wrong medication. The basis for her concern, the proof (if you will) of the man's incompetence: When he walked, he kept his hands down by his sides. He didn't swing his arms. For that odd trait, he became the hands-down winner (literally, hands down) of the *What-Can-Holly-Worry-About-Most Sweepstakes.*

Holly decided she wasn't going to get the spinal anesthetic after all. It might dull her senses (isn't that the whole idea?), and she intended to bear the pain in order to protect her baby. Just then, a terrible contraction revised her plan: "Okay, I'll get the spinal, but I'm going to make Ryan swear to stay with our baby in the nursery. Anything could happen otherwise." Her racing mind screeched to a halt: *Where is Ryan? He probably got stopped for a speeding ticket while rushing here. Can I trust him to drive safely with our baby?*

Holly took a deep, deep breath. *One thing is for sure: I am not going to worry like this for the next eighteen years.*

Maybe not exactly like this.

•    •    •

All the energy a new mother might once have put into protecting herself she now puts into protecting her baby—because it is her*self*, literally a physical part of her. Author (and mother) Elizabeth Stone has said that the decision to have a child is momentous because "it is to decide forever to have your heart go walking around outside your body."

Parents enter into a contract with nature to keep that heart beating, to keep their children alive. That means parents recognize that children could die, yet whenever the thought comes into their heads, they quickly banish it. Journalist Shawn Hubler says, "Preparedness is a funny thing; there's only so much of it a soul can stand. The problem with bracing for the worst is, you have to imagine it first."

Most of Holly's worries that day focused on the nursery; her scenarios assumed that the birth went well. Thus, worrying about remote possibilities allowed her to jump over the only question really relevant as she waited to give birth: Will my baby be all right? A parent's ever-changing worries are usually a mask for the one possibility all parents fear: the death of their child. The specter of that highly unlikely possibility influences our thoughts about adventure and caution, recreation and rest, freedom and autonomy. In short, that ghost puts in his two cents' worth every time we make a decision about our children. But that ghost loses much of his power when we look him in the eye.

Any discussion of death is really about the small details, since the big detail—that we all die—doesn't change. What people are obsessed with is the *schedule* of death. We have an idea of how long a person ought to live and when someone comes in too far below our expectation, we call it a tragedy.

We are equally fascinated by the method of death. We say on hearing a story of someone who died in a fire or who drowned, "What a terrible way to die." If you think about this you'll realize that deaths people describe as terrible have one thing in common: The deceased could see it coming. That forced acknowledgment of death, not the manner of death, is what we're really recoiling from. After all, being burned or crushed or trapped underwater is terrible even if the person survives. Such misfortune could be more accurately described as "a terrible way to live," because dying might be the easiest part of the experience. But we don't want to see it coming. "He died in his sleep" is always said with awe and appreciation, for that's the preferred experience of death. Why? Because it's a *nonexperience* of death.

This desire to be surprised by death, to be unaware of its advance, is ironic since there is such clear benefit to seeing it coming. Seeing it coming is the only way we get a fighting chance to influence the schedule. We'd rather our children never be in grave danger, of course, but if they are, wouldn't it be better to know it? It seems we want it both ways: to be warned of danger and to deny death. To effectively protect our children, we must resolve this conflict.

We protect our children because we love them, of course, but we are also keeping our contract with nature. And we are tempted with a huge incentive: immortality, or at least as close as we get to it. Because we will not see our children die, and because they are a part of us that can keep living for a long while, they are, for all practical purposes, immortal. For a species that fears death as much as we do, this is weighty stuff, and it just may be that *the stakes of our children's safety are higher for us than for them.*

When I've asked parents to list the most serious risks their children face, it's understandable that some say, "I don't want to think about such things," or "I can't imagine." The problem is *if you cannot imagine something, you also cannot predict it, nor protect against it.*

Many people don't have the luxury of deciding to avoid unpleasant thoughts. There are, for example, help-giving professionals who have no choice but to regularly see terrible things. Difficult though they are, the experiences of those people teach them powerful lessons— often instantly. The fireman need pull only one unbelted child out of a gruesome car wreck and he will forever be an advocate of seat belts. The emergency-room surgeon who just once follows the path of a bullet through a child's stomach will finally get rid of that old rifle he last saw in the basement (or was it the garage?).

Since learning about what we dread is the way to overcome it and reduce worry, I want to thoroughly explore the thing parents have told me is their Number One fear: that a child would be kidnapped by a stranger.

It's important to note that this particular outcome is very, very rare. Out of nearly seventy million American children, fewer than a hundred a year are provably kidnapped by strangers. A child is vastly more likely to have a heart attack, and child heart attacks are so rare that most parents (correctly) never even consider the risk. A child is 250 times more likely to be shot with a gun than be kidnapped by a stranger.

I am defining stranger kidnapping here as those cases where a child was gone overnight, was transported a distance of fifty miles or more, was ransomed, was killed, or the perpetrator intended to keep the child permanently. The fear of these things happening is probably not primal, given their rareness, but for Americans, the fear has been encouraged a lot. One outrageous estimate reported in the popular media was that 50,000 kids are kidnapped each year by strangers. An FBI spokesman put this in perspective when he pointed out that the

United States lost 50,000 troops in the Vietnam War. Most everyone knew of a family that lost a son or brother or father there, but, he asked, "How many of us know someone who has had a child abducted by a stranger?" (The year this was said, the FBI investigated fifty-seven cases of kidnapping by strangers; it's been fairly close to that each year since.)

Even though this issue needs a full exploration, there are people who will resist a sober presentation of the facts. Why? Because scores of organizations raise money around this particular fear. Denny Abbott, then national director of the Adam Walsh Child Resource Center, said, "In my twenty-five years in social services, I have never seen an issue as exploited as the problem of missing children." Like most exploitation, there's money involved. Some "nonprofits" pay their executive directors huge salaries. Then there are businesses selling products such as identification kits and "reward insurance." One firm put out an alarming brochure showing a young girl chained to a bed. It turned out the photo was staged and the child was the daughter of the owner. (Thankfully, there are also many well-meaning and effective organizations helping protect children. Several appear in the appendices.)

Every year, there are thousands of kids missing—most are runaways— and thousands of others taken by divorced parents. Some organizations describe these using the phrase "nonfamily abduction," which sounds like kidnapping by strangers. Most often, however, the perpetrator is the boyfriend of the child's mother, or someone else known to the family. There are cases of sexual molestation where a child is lured somewhere for the brief time it takes to commit the offense, and these too are often called kidnappings. All of these are very serious problems, of course, some of which I'll be taking up in later chapters. (For information on what to do if you face one of these situations, the organization I recommend is the National Center for Missing and Exploited Children, 800-THE-LOST.)

Unfortunately, in the jumble of scary statistics it's come to appear that stranger kidnapping is frequent, but in fact, it just isn't one of the things human beings do very often. When you make a deep scratch in the rhetoric and the fear, no matter what rational number you accept, it isn't as high as most people have been led to believe. For example, one year in which there were three such cases in Colorado, most of the people questioned for a *Denver Post* poll felt there had been nearly ten times that many.

You may have seen recent TV news reports about abductions of babies from hospitals. These are, admittedly, frightening stories, but parents would likely worry much less if the stories included this:

> Of the 4.2 million babies born each year in more than 3500 facilities, the total number abducted is fewer than ten.

Still scary I know, but if you studied the details of one hundred baby abductions from hospitals—and you'd have to go back fifteen years to gather that many cases—you'd find that ninety-four of the hundred were quickly recovered unharmed. Ninety-four. No matter how rare such incidents are, when the anchorperson says, "Next up: babies abducted from hospitals!" it places the topic on your agenda, and *voilà*: fear. I guess we can't expect them to say, "Next up: a big inflated waste of your time that'll make you anxious for no good reason."

There's a final irony: While the TV news trumpets cases of abductions from hospitals, from where in the hospital do you suppose babies are taken? The nursery? The pediatric ward? Some. But most abducted babies were taken from the mother's room while in the care of the mother. An exhausted mother with only a few hours' experience at protecting a child might be fooled into giving her baby to someone pretending to be an authorized employee, or she might leave her baby alone in the room. Accordingly, this is one dreaded outcome (like many) that parents can easily prevent.

In addition to alarming TV news reports, there are now products and services that go even farther into the macabre, such as products for gathering DNA samples from your children. One firm boasts that its home kit will preserve a child's DNA for more than eighty years, inspiring us to imagine a long tragedy (longer, ironically, than the lives of all the participants would likely be in any event).

There are firms that store dental records for circumstances only the most masochistic parent would choose to dwell upon. There are even services to affix an ID-coded crown within a child's mouth—stainless steel of course, because it lasts longer than teeth. These schemes do not protect children from harm; to readily identify someone's remains is hardly a safety precaution they'll thank you for. ("True, Caitlin, we never taught you about rape, but if you'd ever turned up in a ditch somewhere, we were sure prepared.")

Such ghoulish services offer vulnerable parents the feeling that they've done something about the unthinkable—so they needn't think of it. I certainly understand that the risks to children can seem overwhelming, a fact made clearer as I met with parents around the country over the last two years. One father worried about a "baby black-market" where infants are taken to Mexico and sold. (Is there a shortage of babies in Mexico? I doubt it.) Whether it was a murderous au pair or a shooting spree at the high school, most parents' fears were programmed by TV news producers. Because of this, I looked beyond the *fears du jour* at the more primal concerns of parents.

Eve, the mother of two girls, told me that when she became a parent, she began to fear her own death for the first time:

> It wasn't for myself at all, but for my children. I cannot fathom leaving them motherless. Sure, some of it is ego, believing that nobody else could raise my children with as much love, understanding, patience and devotion as I do. But mostly it's the

thought that if something happened to me, who would be there for them?

A mother's fear of not being there for her child is probably universal. One mother told me that even though she has always feared flying, she prefers flying with her children rather than without them. "I'm more afraid of leaving them alone than of us all dying together."

When it comes to protecting children from violence, most worries are balanced by a primal feeling of power that comes to new mothers. Again, it is Eve who explains it:

After my daughter was born, the love I felt for her was so intense, so beyond anything I had ever imagined, that I knew I would not allow any harm to come to her. This made me feel, well, dangerous. If someone hurt her, or even tried to, I knew I would take justice into my own hands.

Eve's feeling of power after the birth of her daughter is more than just a feeling—it is a real power. Particularly for women raised to believe they are not able to protect themselves, motherhood gives permission to be dangerous. It connects women to a power they might not ever have felt before: It is the power of violence, a power known to most men. Eve, an otherwise peaceful woman, was expressing her willingness to kill another person if the need arose. I encourage women with children to seize and not retreat from this intimate understanding of violence. Doing so can bring relief from a lifetime's worry about your own vulnerability.

·    ·    ·

While researching parental worry, I found a brilliant, humane, and often funny book written by an unlikely person: the funeral director from Milford, Michigan. In *The Undertaking: Life Studies from the Dismal Trade*, Thomas Lynch explores avoidable death from the perspective of a man who sees it often. Lynch has a lot to say about parental worry, for his own father (also an undertaker) was an expert worrier:

> Whenever I or one of my siblings would ask to go here or there or do this or that, my father's first response was almost always "No!" He had just buried someone doing that very thing.
>
> He had just buried a boy who had toyed with matches, or played baseball without a helmet on, or went fishing without a life preserver, or ate the candy that a stranger gave him. And what the boys did that led to their fatalities matured as my brothers and sisters and I matured, the causes of their deaths becoming subtly interpersonal rather than cataclysmic as we aged. The stories of children struck by lightning were replaced by narratives of unrequited love gone suicidal, teenagers killed by speed and drink or overdosed on drugs, and hordes of the careless but otherwise blameless dead who'd found themselves in the wrong place at the wrong time.
>
> My mother, who had more faith in the power of prayer and her own careful parenting, would often override his prohibitions. "Oh Ed," she would argue over dinner. "Leave them be! They've got to learn some things for themselves." Once she told him "Don't be ridiculous, Ed," when he'd refused me permission to spend the night at a friend's house across the street. "What!" she scolded him. "Did you just bury someone who died of a night spent at Jimmy Shryock's house?"

Thomas Lynch's parents were working their way through a familiar struggle: One parent is reasonably cautious but not fearful, the other unreasonably cautious and always fearful. This is a collision of two distinct protective processes: the management of actual risks as they develop versus the worry about imagined risks. They are rarely the same risks.

When dreaded outcomes are actually imminent, we don't worry about them—we take action. Seeing lava from the local volcano make its way down the street toward our house does not cause worry; it causes running. Also, we don't usually choose imminent events as subjects for our worrying, and thus emerges an ironic truth: Often, the very fact that you are worrying about something means that it isn't likely to happen.

When you worry yourself into a state of artificial fear about your children, you distract yourself from what is actually happening in favor of what you imagine is happening. Since the human imagination is powerful, you can conjure quite a litany of terrors that might befall your children. Anytime you ask yourself the question *Could this happen to my children?* the answer will be Yes—because anything *could* happen, but there are better questions, such as Will this happen? Or, *Is* this happening?

In parenting, as in physics, everything we give energy to takes energy from something else. Thus, needless worry has several costs. For one, there is the cost of the parental conflict itself, a conflict in which the worrier and the nonworrier each has an unfair advantage. Because a child's safety is at the center of these debates, it is difficult to end a discussion of some dreaded possibility without concession to the worrier. On the other hand, the husband who always minimizes his wife's worries gets the luxury of being able to worry less himself—after all, his wife is handling that for him. Hillary Clinton has said, "Like most mothers, I am the designated worrier in our family. When Chelsea arrived, I went from worrying only five days a week to worrying on weekends too."

People worry because it serves them in some way. You've likely known someone who worried so much that people stopped telling that person anything. "Don't worry your mother," or "I'm worried half to death" are phrases that serve worriers by offering protection from too much reality. Excessive worry also helps some people deal with matters they cannot influence. Powerlessness is one of the hardest things for parents to admit and there comes a point with the safety of children where we have to do just that. Worry helps fight off that dreadful feeling that there's nothing we can do, because worrying feels like we are doing something. Thomas Lynch describes it as "the war we wage against those facts of life over which we have no power, none at all." He says, "It makes for heroics and histrionics, but it is no way to raise children."

Children raised by chronic worriers may or may not become victims of violence, but it is absolutely certain they will become victims of worry. In *The Heart of Man*, Dr. Erich Fromm tells of a mother who is always interested in dark prognoses for her child's future, but unimpressed with anything favorable that occurs: "She does not harm the child in any obvious way, yet she may slowly strangle his joy in life." This is an interesting way of putting it given that the literal meaning of the word *worry* is to strangle and choke. People who grew up smothered by unwarranted fears that haunted them into adulthood will see the wisdom in this saying: Everybody dies, but not everybody lives.

True fears and unwarranted fears may at times feel the same, but you can tell them apart. True fear is a gift that signals us in the presence of danger; thus, it will be based upon something you perceive in your environment or your circumstance. Unwarranted fear or worry will always be based upon something in your imagination or your memory.

Worry is the fear we manufacture; it is a choice. Conversely, true fear is involuntary; it will come and get our attention if necessary. But, *if a parent or a child feels fear constantly, there is no signal left for when it's really needed*. Thus, the parent who chooses to worry all the

time or who invests unwarranted fears into children is actually making them less safe. Worry is not a precaution; it is the opposite because it delays and discourages constructive action.

Thousands of airline passengers worry about planes crashing, and
one could say this has been highly effective (considering our exceptional air safety record). But does anybody really believe that worry
will help a flight be safer? For many of the millions of parents away
from their children during the workday, worrying has become a way
of loving from the office—but do they believe that worrying will make
their children any safer? Some do, because they may interpret worri-
some thoughts as intuitive signals sent to remind them of something
important, something they've overlooked, something they haven't yet
considered.

Is worry an intuitive signal? In a roundabout way, it can be. That's
because what we choose to worry about, however bad, is usually
easier to look at than some other less palatable issue. For this reason, a good exercise when worrying is to ask yourself, What am
I choosing *not* to see right now? Worry may well be distracting
you from something important. For example, we worry about the
child molester we saw arrested on the news even though we (and
the police and the newspeople) know who he is, what he looks like,
and where he is—in jail, for God's sake. At the same time, we choose
not to think about the man at the day-care center who gives us the
creeps.

How can you decide which impulses to explore and which to ignore? By learning how you communicate with yourself. When you
honor accurate intuitive signals and evaluate them without denial
(believing that either the favorable or the unfavorable outcome is possible), you will come to trust that you'll be notified if there is something worthy of your attention. Fear will gain credibility because it
won't be applied wastefully. Thus, trusting intuition is the exact opposite of living in fear.

Explore every intuitive signal, but briefly and not repetitively. When faced with some worry or uncertain fear, ask yourself: Am I responding to something in my environment or to something in my imagination? Is this feeling based on something I perceive in my circumstance, or merely something in my memory? Is the fear that my teenage son will have a car accident tonight based on some actual perception that he is unfit to drive tonight, or is it based on that frightening news footage I saw last week?

Aside from encouraging the chronic worriers in your life to avoid watching the local news, there's another home remedy you can suggest to them: Each time you have a worry, define when you expect the dreaded outcome to occur, and mark it down on a calendar. Imagine you are worried that your daughter will be harmed while attending college in the big city. When? In a year, a month, a week, later today? Imagine you choose a week. Write it down, and when that milestone passes without incident, make note of that too. Record these failed predictions for a year, or until you are too embarrassed to keep doing it, whichever comes first.

Another exercise is to ask highly specific questions about a given dreaded outcome, as I did with a mother named Alice who was terribly worried that her daughter would be kidnapped by a stranger. Here's the actual exchange:

Who will do it?
*I don't know; he's a stranger.*
Does he have a history of kidnapping?
*I don't know.*
Where will it happen?
*Maybe on the way to school, I don't know.*
How will he do it?
*He could lure her into a car.*

What kind of car does he drive?
*I don't know, a station wagon.*
When will it happen?
*In the morning.*
How would he get her into the car?
*By offering to take her horseback riding.*
Where will he take her?
*To his apartment.*
He lives in an apartment building?
*Yeah, I guess so.*
Won't neighbors see him bringing her in?
*They all work during the day.*

She was writing quite a novel when she stopped herself and said plainly: "I don't know, I guess I'm just making things up." (No need to guess on that one.) She said, "It doesn't seem very likely, does it?" Few worries survive a cross-examination of highly specific questions which we can ask of ourselves. Anytime we start to invent possibilities or find that the answer to most questions is "I don't know," we're not evaluating real or present risk.

When unable to shake a worry, we can simply acknowledge (and tell others if we choose to) that we are feeling anxiety right now about our son driving on this rainy night. We don't have to justify our feelings with imitations of logic. We don't have to build a case to support our worry or give our anxiety credence by citing all the risks we ever heard of. Trying to persuade someone else to share your worry rarely works anyway, because you can rarely make a very good case. It is enough to just call it worry, find some comfort, and move on.

• • •

Many parents go from worry to worry, never stopping long enough to see that their children are prevailing through life's challenges day in and day out. This is like surviving an air crash and then pausing at the top of the evacuation slide to worry about whether your luggage will make it on time. Sometimes, taking a moment for some gratitude keeps a few worries away.

The best antidote to worry is action. If there is an action that will lessen the likelihood of a dreaded outcome occurring, and if that action doesn't cost too much in terms of effort or freedom, then take it. The worry about whether we remembered to close the baby gate at the top of the stairs can be stopped in an instant by checking. Then it isn't a worry anymore; it's just a brief impulse. Almost all of the worry parents feel about keeping their children safe evolves from the conflict between intuition and inaction.

Your choices when worrying are clear: take action, have faith, pray, seek comfort, or keep worrying. When it comes to violence, you've already chosen to take action by learning. Thomas Lynch's father was too busy worrying about danger to actually learn about it, and that kept him from seeing his children as anything but potential casualties. "For my father," Lynch wrote, "what we did and who we became were incidental to the tenuous fact of our being. That We Were seemed sufficient for the poor worried man."

When Lynch became a parent himself, his father's demons were there: "I remember in those first years as a father and a funeral director, new at making babies and at burying them, I would often wake in the middle of the night, sneak into the rooms where my sons and daughter slept, and bend to their cribsides to hear them breathe. It was enough. I did not need astronauts or presidents or doctors or lawyers. I only wanted them to breathe. Like my father, I had learned to fear."

This could more accurately read "*From* my father, I had learned to fear," for as distinguished psychiatrist Karl Menninger has said, "Fears are educated into us and can, if we wish, be educated out."

As you'll see again and again, the things we've been taught to fear are rarely the things most likely to happen. Still, since so many parents fear stranger kidnapping, I will take a clear-eyed look at one case in the next chapter. We'll understand the experience, put a face on it, learn from it, and then move on.

# CHAPTER FOUR

# SURVIVAL SIGNALS

*People should learn to see and so avoid all danger. Just as a*
*wise man keeps away from mad dogs, so one should not make*
*friends with evil men.*

—BUDDHA

Marilee had had about enough. Sure, Jess had been patient for as
long as one could expect from any nine-year-old, and, yes, the shopping excursion had gone on a long time, but he was pushing it.
Rounds of "Mom, can we go now?" had serenaded Marilee since they
arrived at the department store, and as she looked over the inventory
of shoes, Jess brought out his whole inventory of manipulations: "You
promised," "I'm tired," "I'm hungry."

Marilee reminded her son that as he spoke those words about being hungry, he was literally still chewing on a donut. Her expression
and tone were full of warning when she said, "Jess, stop bugging me.
I'm going as fast as I can and you are only slowing me down."

Marilee heard a sound that made her instantly angry: a slight
chuckle from a man standing nearby. She shot a cold look in his direction, but he responded with a warm smile. Marilee remembers
that he was in his twenties with wavy black hair, dressed casually in

jeans and a green wool sweater. He explained his amusement: "Sorry, it's just that I was having this exact problem with my son a half-hour ago. My wife wasn't as patient as you've been; her solution was to send him a few doors down to the video-game place. Hey, if you want, I'll take your son over there to join my son—they're about the same age—and you can pick him up when you're done shopping."

The man turned to Jess. "What's the name of that place?"

"Electra," Jess answered.

"Right, Electra, where we always go when I've got quarters in my pocket. You know, that place was started by a dad and his son, and now they're equal partners." The man laughed and turned back to Marilee. "Since we're in the same boat, I'll be glad to give you a few minutes off, and we'll meet up at Electra when you're done."

Marilee looked at this easygoing guy like he was crazy, but he continued: "I promise we'll look after him."

Obviously, she was not about to hand her son over to a total stranger. She thought, *You've got to be kidding,* but she responded more diplomatically: "No. That's very kind but we'll be done in a few minutes. Thanks anyway."

As if he did not hear her, the man said, "It would be no trouble, and since you're probably one of those overprotective parents, I'm sure Jess could use some time on his own."

When Marilee didn't respond to this, the man continued: "Kids are sure similar. Our son's tolerance for shopping is about fifteen minutes—unless he's shopping for lizards." To Jess: "He's got an amazing collection. I'm sure you saw the iguana at the pet shop downstairs—almost five feet long. Did you see it?"

Perusing a pile of assorted on-sale sandals, Marilee didn't really register how Jess responded. Though she'd never in a million years let some stranger take her son somewhere, she was relieved that Jess wasn't pestering her. As she continued shopping, she could hear the man talking with Jess, but their conversation took less and less of her attention. "My boy's name is Brad, like Brad Pitt. He's twelve. How old are you?"

And Jess answered. Then another question, and Jess answered. Marilee marveled that someone could actually have expected her to just turn her son over, even if he was a parent with a kid of his own. She looked at prices on shoes while another part of her mind asked, *Is that guy old enough to have a twelve-year-old?* Maybe the son is his wife's from a previous marriage. *Was he even wearing a wedding ring?*

She casually glanced over to get an answer to her question, but she'd moved a few displays down and the guy wasn't immediately within view. Neither was Jess.

Instant focus.

"Jess!"

No answer. Marilee rushed back over to where they'd been standing and looked around, scrutinizing every inch of that store. At the farthest corner, she saw Jess. He was with that man! She called out to him loudly but he and the stranger were at that instant passing through a door at the end of a hallway. Without knowing it, Marilee was running in that direction.

She assumed it led to a bathroom and was relieved that they couldn't get too far away, but in the hall leading to that door, she passed the bathroom, which was bad news. She blasted through the door she'd seen them go through and got more bad news. It led to the main mall, to a huge area congested with a thousand sets of people that looked just like Jess and that man. She had lost her son for an instant, and then for the day, and then for years.

Immediately, people judged her: A police investigator asked if she'd taken any drugs that might have dulled her senses; a news editorial described her as negligent; a caller on a radio talk show said she was stupid (she kept listening, though, hoping the kidnapper would call in).

As I write this, it has been nearly six years since Marilee ran down that hallway and burst through that door, years in which nobody's harsh opinions could even touch her own experience of regret and self-doubt. Our judgment about a mother we could say let down her guard at the wrong moment, a mother whose child was lost on her watch—well, our judgment is inconsequential. Whether or not we forgive her—and I do without reservation—nature has built in some predictable consequences to enforce the imperative that parents protect their children.

For Marilee, the depression came first, a melancholy so heavy that she didn't want to do anything, not even breathe. She did breathe, of course, but it was work. She developed a chronic flu that took months to shake. During the worst period, she had constant stomach pains and headaches. Within a year of Jess's disappearance, Marilee and her husband split. Well-meaning people kept saying things like "Any day now, you'll see," and "Don't give up hope," but she simply had to give up hope—and there was relief when she finally let it fly away. That was after all the comforting relatives had gone back home, after the news interviews were long forgotten, after the police detectives had moved on to other cases, after all the posters with Jess's photo had been taken down by shopkeepers. That was three years ago, and she is doing better now. The depression has lifted, her health has improved, and it's clear Nature has finally forgiven her.

·    ·    ·

With that difficult story, you have crossed the hardest bridge in this book. You have looked squarely at a thing you fear and you are ready to harvest the benefits: the survival signals that can alert you to a predator's intent.

The man who kidnapped Jess will be our teacher for a few minutes. There is some justice here (though not the justice we'd prefer): He who has caused so much pain to one family can help reduce risk and fear for other families. Though kidnapping by strangers is too rare to merit a whole chapter in this book, I'm exploring the strategies used on Marilee and Jess because they are the same ones used by any type of criminal who must persuade his target to cooperate. Once you've read what follows, you are likely to recognize these survival signals in every single story of predatory victimization you ever hear.

Think of violence as a process in which the early, subtle events are as telling as the dramatic events. A traffic signal does not turn red randomly; it is preceded by a yellow light, which is preceded by a green. Safety while driving requires that we know this sequence. Similarly, when predicting violence, there are *pre-incident indicators*—my firm calls them PINS. When we know the sequence, they can be as telling as the yellow light. Some misfortunes in life come upon us without obvious pre-incident indicators, seemingly unavoidable, but this book is about those misfortunes we can avoid.

There are two basic predatory types, the power-predator and the persuasion-predator. You'll recall that after leaving the movie theater, Holly was attacked by a criminal who used force in his attempt to control her. This describes a power-predator. The power-predator charges like a bear, unmistakably committing to his attack. He does so only when he feels certain he'll prevail.

Jess was taken by a persuasion-predator. This type of criminal looks for a vulnerable someone who will allow him to be in control. Observing Marilee and Jess, the man saw opposite vulnerabilities he could exploit: Jess was bored and wanted to be distracted; Marilee was busy and wanted not to be distracted.

Like a shark circling potential prey, the persuasion-predator approaches slowly and watches to see how people react (if at all). He begins a dialogue and with each favorable response he elicits, this shark gets closer. He makes a small initial investment so that he can easily call off the game at any point. His low-risk strategy allows him to test the waters and move on with nobody the wiser if things don't go well. He is a coward, a crafty one, but a coward nonetheless.

For sexual predators, which this man almost certainly is, there's another part to the selection process: attraction. This can be as complex and inexplicable as sexual attraction is for adults, with one important distinction: For most pedophiles, vulnerability is, all by itself, stimulating.

Just as in nature, human predators must separate their targets from the flock, so the man's first goal is getting Jess away from Marilee. Taking children from parents is rarely done with force; kids are not stolen at gunpoint. They are taken through a form of seduction, one that aims not at passion, but at trust—yours or your child's. Misplaced trust is the predator's most powerful resource, and we decide whether or not to give it to him. Your defense against such people is to recognize the survival signals—the PINS—in the very behaviors intended to put you at ease. Here they are:

# Survival Signals

- Forced Teaming
- Charm and Niceness
- Too Many Details
- Typecasting
- Loan-sharking
- The Unsolicited Promise
- Discounting the Word "No"

## Forced Teaming

This was shown by Jess's kidnapper through his use of the word "we" ("We're in the same boat"). Forced teaming is an effective way to establish premature trust because a *We've-got-something-in-common* attitude is hard to rebuff without feeling rude. Sharing a predicament, like being stuck in a stalled elevator or arriving simultaneously at a just-closed store will understandably move people around social boundaries. But forced teaming is not about coincidence; it is intentional and directed, and it is one of the most sophisticated manipulations. The detectable signal of forced teaming is the projection of a shared purpose or experience where none exists: "both of us," "we're some team," "how are we going to handle this?," "now we've done it," and so on.

Marilee did not recognize the tactic, so she couldn't apply the simple defense for forced teaming, which is to make a clear refusal to accept the concept of partnership: "I did not ask for your help and I do not want it. Please leave us alone." Like many of the best defenses, this one has the cost of appearing rude, a cost mothers must be willing to pay.

Safety is the preeminent concern of all creatures and it clearly justifies a seemingly abrupt and rejecting response from time to time. In any event, rudeness is relative. If while waiting in some line, a person steps on our foot a second time, and we bark, "Hey!" we don't call our response rude. We might even feel we showed restraint. That's because the appropriateness of our response is relative to the behavior that provoked it. When we view forced teaming as the inappropriate behavior it is, we can feel less concern about appearing rude in response.

Forced teaming is done in many contexts for many reasons, but when applied by a stranger, it's always inappropriate. Forced teaming is not about partnership or coincidence—it is about establishing rapport. That may or may not be all right, depending on *why* someone seeks rapport.

Generally speaking, rapport-building has a far better reputation than it deserves. It is perceived as admirable when in fact it is almost always done for self-serving reasons. Even though the reasons most people seek rapport aren't sinister, such as pleasantly conversing with someone you've just met at a party, that doesn't mean a woman like Marilee must talk with every stranger who approaches her. Perhaps the most admirable reason to seek rapport would be to put someone at ease, but if that is a stranger's entire intent, a far simpler way is to just leave the woman alone.

## Charm and Niceness

Charm is another overrated ability. I call it an ability and not an inherent feature of one's personality because charm is almost always directed toward a goal. Like rapport-building, charm has motive. To charm is to compel, to control by allure or attraction. Think of charm as a verb, not a trait. When the man gave a warm smile and a compliment ("My wife wasn't as patient as you've been"), Marilee could have told herself, "This person is trying to charm me" as opposed to, "This person is charming." Armed with this shift in perspective, you'll be able to see around charm. Most often, what you see won't be sinister, but other times you'll be glad you looked.

University of California at Los Angeles psychiatrist Leslie Brothers says, "If I am trying to deceive someone, that person has to be just a bit smarter than I am in order to see through my deceit. That means you have sort of an arms race."

The predatory criminal does all he can to make that arms race look like détente. "He was so nice" is a comment I often hear from people describing the man who, moments or months after his niceness, victimized them. We must learn and then teach our children that niceness does not equal goodness. Niceness is a decision, a strategy of social interaction. People seeking to control others almost always present the image of a nice person in the beginning.

If Marilee had explicitly rebuffed the unwanted approach, nice though it may have been, the man would have moved on, but I know it is difficult to do. Just as rapport-building has a good reputation, explicitness applied by women in this culture has a terrible reputation. A woman who is clear and precise is viewed as cold, or a bitch, or both. A woman is expected, first and foremost, to respond to every communication from a man. And the response is expected to be one of willingness and attentiveness.

Women are expected to be warm and open, and in the context of an approach from a male stranger, warmth lengthens the encounter, raises his expectations, increases his investment, and, at best, wastes time. At worst, it serves the man who has sinister intent by providing much of the information he will need to evaluate and then control his target. In this case, the man sought only to remain in Jess's environment so he could continue to circle his prey and exploit any opportunities.

## Too Many Details

People who want to deceive often use a simple technique that has a simple name: too many details. The video-game place is owned by a father and his son: too many details. The iguana in the pet shop is five feet long: too many details. His son, who has a collection of lizards, is named Brad, like Brad Pitt: too many details.

When people are telling the truth, they don't feel doubted, so they don't feel the need for additional support in the form of details. When people lie, however, even if what they say sounds credible to you, *it doesn't sound credible to them*, so they keep talking. Each detail may be only a small tack they throw on the road, but together they can stop a truck.

The defense is to remain consciously aware of the context in which details are offered. Think of context as the water we are swimming in, the circumstance in which things occur. Knowing context is the necessary link that gives meaning to everything we observe. You could watch two people argue, for example, and no matter how hostile they became, you'd feel no alarm if they were actors performing in a play. Context is always apparent at the start of an interaction and usually apparent at the end of one, but too many details can make us lose sight of it. Every type of con relies upon distracting us from the obvious. That's how a conversation evolves into a crime without the victim knowing until it's too late.

Marilee had so many details thrown at her that she lost sight of this simple context: The man was an absolute stranger. He used catchy details to come to be perceived as someone familiar, someone Jess could trust. But Jess knew him artificially, of course; he knew the con, not the con man.

No matter how engaging a stranger might be, you must never lose sight of context: He is what he is, a stranger who approached you.

## Typecasting

Marilee didn't bite for this one, but the man tried to label her in a slightly critical way, hoping she'd feel compelled to prove his opinion was not accurate. He said, "You're probably one of those overprotective parents," giving her a chance to cast off the mantle of "overprotective" by letting Jess go with him.

Typecasting always involves a slight insult, and usually one that is easy to refute. But since it is the response itself that the typecaster seeks, the defense is silence, acting as if the words weren't even spoken. If you engage, you can win the point, but you might lose something greater. Not that it matters what some stranger thinks, but the typecaster doesn't even believe what he says is true. He just believes that it will work.

## Loan-sharking

The man offered to help Marilee in order to place her in his debt. The fact that you owe a person something makes it harder to ask him to leave you alone. Also, people who offer to help us (or to help children) can be perceived as "nice," and this designation gives them an advantage with some targets. Like the more traditional loan shark, a person using this strategy gladly lends one amount but expects to collect much more. The defense is to bring two rarely remembered facts into consciousness: He approached me, and I didn't ask for any help. Then, though a person may turn out to be just a kindly stranger, watch for other signals.

It is important to clarify that forced teaming, too many details, charm, niceness, typecasting, and loan-sharking are all in use every day by people who have no sinister intent. For example, we are all familiar with the stranger who offers to help a woman with her groceries. It's still loan-sharking, though the debt he records in his ledger can usually be paid off quite easily; just a little talk will do it. The generous stranger and the sinister stranger have something in common: motive. Sometimes the motive is innocent, sometimes sinister, but since it's always there, we have to ask ourselves what it might be. Why does the man offer to help Marilee with her impatient son? Now we know.

## The Unsolicited Promise

When the man volunteered, "I promise we'll look after him," he gave one of the most reliable signals of trouble. Promises are used to convince us of an intention, but they are not guarantees. A guarantee offers some compensation if the speaker fails to deliver, but promises offer no such collateral. They are the very hollowest instruments of speech, showing nothing more than the speaker's desire to convince you of something.

Aside from meeting all unsolicited promises with skepticism

(whether or not they are about safety), it's useful to ask yourself: *Why does this person want to convince me?* The answer, it turns out, is not about him—it is about you. A person volunteers a promise because he can see that you are not convinced. You have doubt (which is a messenger of intuition), likely because there is reason for doubt. The great gift of the unsolicited promise is that the speaker tells you so himself.

In effect, the promise holds up a mirror in which you get a second chance to see your own intuitive signal. The promise is the image and the reflection of your doubt. Always, in every context, be suspicious of the unsolicited promise.

Here's the defense: When someone says, "I promise," you say (at least in your head), "You're right, I am hesitant to trust you. Thank you for pointing it out."

## Discounting the Word *No*

This is the most universally significant signal of all: ignoring or discounting the concept of *No*. When Marilee declined his offer to look after Jess, the man ignored it outright. Anyone who chooses not to hear the word No is trying to control you.

In situations in which unsolicited offers of assistance are appropriate, such as approaches by a salesman or flight attendant, it is simply annoying if you have to decline three times. With a stranger, however, refusal to hear No can be an important survival signal.

Declining to hear No is a signal that someone is either seeking control or refusing to relinquish it. With strangers, even those with the best intentions, never let the word go by without acknowledgment. If you let someone talk you out of the word No or ignore it, you might as well wear a sign that reads, "You are in charge."

A common response that serves the criminal is to negotiate ("I really appreciate your offer, but let me try to do it on my own first"). Negotiations are about possibilities, and providing access to someone who makes you apprehensive is not a possibility you want to keep on the agenda. I encourage people to remember that No is a complete sentence.

When Marilee declined the man's offer to take Jess to the video arcade, she did so with more politeness than she actually felt. I would have encouraged her to say what was in her head, because that would have been the response most appropriate to the situation. She was thinking, *You've got to be kidding*, but she said, "That's very kind, thanks anyway." If she had said "You've got to be kidding," the man would have had a more difficult predatory challenge.

Similarly, remember when Holly was in line at the movie theater with the other mothers and their daughters, and the man asked, "What's the idea, safety in numbers?" Holly just nodded, but she was thinking, *Bug off*.

First thoughts come directly from your intuition, so *say out loud a version of what you think*. Do or say something that communicates early and clearly that you are not an easy target (steely eyes, hold the stare, walk away, raise your voice). Marilee had the correct reaction to the absolute outlandishness of the man's approach, but she didn't communicate it to him. To borrow a popular line often spoken to children, I say to parents: "Use your words."

When a woman is approached by a stranger offering help in an underground garage, for example, if her shoulders tense slightly, if she looks intimidated and shyly says, "No, thanks, I think I've got it," she may be his victim. Conversely, the woman who looks right at him, raises her hands to the STOP position, and says directly, "I don't want your help," is less likely to be his victim.

If a man stomps off dejected, that's fine. In fact, any reaction—even anger—from a decent man who had no sinister intent is preferable to continued attention from a violent man who would use your concern about rudeness to his advantage. You cannot turn a decent man into a violent one by being momentarily rude, but you can present yourself as an ideal target by appearing too timid.

A mother in public with her child who feels she needs assistance is far better off choosing someone and asking for help than waiting for an unsolicited approach. (This same truth also applies to children alone in public, as I'll discuss later.) The person you choose is nowhere near as likely to bring you hazard as is the person who chooses you. It's highly unlikely that you'd inadvertently select a predatory criminal.

I encourage mothers to ask other women for help when they need it, and it's likewise safer to accept an offer from a woman than from a man. (Unfortunately, women rarely make such offers to other women, and I wish more would.)

I want to clarify that many men offer help without any sinister motive, with no more in mind than kindness and chivalry, but I have been addressing those times that men refuse to hear the word No, and that is not chivalrous—it is dangerous.

When someone ignores No, ask yourself: Why is this person seeking to control me? What does he want? It is best to get away from the person altogether, but if that's not practical, the response that serves safety is to dramatically raise your level of insistence, skipping right over politeness. "I said NO!"

When I encounter people hung up on the seeming rudeness of this response, I imagine the following conversation between a woman in an underground garage with her teenage daughter, and a man who has offered them assistance:

WOMAN: No thanks.

MAN: But I'm just trying to be nice to a couple of pretty ladies.

WOMAN: We do not want your help. Leave us alone.

MAN: What's your problem, lady, are you paranoid or just a bitch?

WOMAN: You're right. I shouldn't be wary. I'm overreacting about nothing. I mean, just because a man makes an unsolicited and persistent approach in an underground parking lot in a society where crimes against women have risen four times faster than the general crime rate, and three out of four women will suffer a violent crime; and just because we have to consider where we park, where we walk, and whom we talk to in the context of whether someone will kill us or rape us or merely scare us half to death; and just because these are life-and-death issues most men know nothing about so that we're made to feel foolish for being cautious even though we live at the center of a swirl of possible hazards, and just because I'm with my daughter and have a duty and a fervent desire to protect her as well as myself *DOESN'T MEAN A WOMAN SHOULD BE WARY OF A STRANGER WHO IGNORES THE WORD NO.*

Whether or not men can relate to it or believe it or accept it, that is the way it is. Women, particularly in big cities, live with a constant wariness, their safety literally on the line in ways men don't experience. Ask some man you know, "When is the last time you took a precaution for your own safety?" Most will not have an example in recent memory. Ask a woman the same question and most will say, "Last night," "Today," or even "Every day." Ask women for examples: "I had a friend walk me to my car last night"; "I lock the door immediately when I get in the car"; "I always carry pepper spray"; "I drive instead of walk to the store"; "I give out a voice-mail phone number, not my home number"; "I carry my cell phone in my hand"; "I use a PO box so no one has my home address"; "I park in inconvenient spots if they are well lit."

If you are a parent, nature has given you permission to choose whom you want around you and your child. Just as the man in the parking lot is free to make an approach and free to be persistent, so are you free to be insistent. Remember, it is he who escalated the rebuff by refusing to listen to No the first time.

The most common reason women are reluctant to appear rude is the fear that they'll cause someone to be angry. That fear is bolstered by a myth: that a man's anger equals danger. It does not. In the context of approaches by strangers in public, the anger you might cause is rarely a step toward violence. In fact, if perceived as a rude woman, you are far less attractive a target than a polite one. Bluntly put, putting things bluntly is safer.

One mother says it eloquently:

I am determined to teach my daughter not to be nice to every man simply because she is a female. That would be the equivalent of saying, "It is better to be hurt by a male than be thought unfeminine by the male who seeks to hurt you." As for me, I learned the hard way that the road to peace of mind is being armed within myself. I will not let anyone take away my openness to the world, but true openness is realizing that the guy across from me is not who I want him to be, but who he is.

•    •    •

Forced teaming, typecasting, the use of charm and niceness, too many details, and discounting the word No are not strategies of violence, but rather of persuasion. The violent or sexual assault comes elsewhere, so a predator's next step is to get his target to a place where victimization is possible. (This raises the importance of not allowing someone to take you to another location. He wants to do that only because where you are does not serve him as well as where he would take you. More on this point in Chapter 6.)

The defenses are all about not relinquishing control, which people do often. The human being is the only prey in nature that cooperates in its own victimization. Imagine an impala in Africa looking at a lion and thinking, "But this is a nice lion." Though people do just that all the time, you and your children don't have to.

In no viable form of self-defense does a person wait for a predictable attack to occur before responding. Not even the most spiritual martial arts master would tell students: "First, receive a substantial blow to the head so you know your adversary means you ill. Then respond."

If you don't make the mistake of waiting for clear signals to become memories you wish you'd acted on, then you can defeat most predators. When you don't trust someone who makes an unsolicited approach, when your intuition sends you doubt or suspicion, you've got all the information you need. People who never received permission to act on their intuition (and that's most people) may wait until they can construct a logical reason to act, but I encourage you to give up the old way. When you listen to the natural signals of danger, you are teaching your children to listen as well, and that will save them a lot of conflict and self-doubt.

Even young children do not inherently trust everyone. There are people they recoil from, and that reaction is something to cherish and to nurture, not something to force them to ignore (i.e., "Apologize to Mr. Ames for not being friendly," or "Give Mrs. Evans a hug right now"). Whom we trust and whom we fear is not an intellectual decision; thankfully, the defense system is smarter than that. Accordingly, when a child feels ill at ease with someone, that's an opportunity to explore why. Discussing these things with children can help them develop the skill they'll benefit from their whole lives.

•   •   •

Putting aside those cases where a persuasion-predator has been so effective that a parent has actually given him permission to walk off with a child, a criminal who takes a child in public needs three elements: First, access to the child, such that the criminal is closer to your child than you are; second, he needs cover, even a brief moment when you or other adults cannot see (or otherwise perceive) what is happening; and, third, he needs to escape. This might mean an easy way to get to his car or to a door or hallway that leads out of the public area. These three elements—Access, Cover, and Escape—can be expressed with the acronym ACE, and when someone with sinister intent has the ACE, it trumps all other cards.

I believe that parents naturally have a sense of proximity about their small children, so ACE is really just a way to bring into consciousness a resource that's already at work subconsciously. You can develop this sense such that you automatically evaluate each environment all the time in the exact same way an opportunistic child predator does it. If you are out with your child and the thought of ACE comes into your head, even for an instant, that means you've made it second nature to see yourself and your child as a predator would. ACE is not a signal of danger but rather a signal of vulnerability.

When you detect an environment or situation that could provide someone the ACE card, there's no cost associated with the simple precautions: Get closer to your child or get your child in view, and that alone takes care of Access and Cover. Place yourself between your child and the routes that lead away from public view, and that takes care of Escape.

Combining the favorable odds with the benefits that come from your understanding the concepts in this book, I can say to a near-perfect statistical certainty that *your child will not be kidnapped by a stranger*. You might decide to stop worrying about it altogether, which is fine, since intuition is likely to put it back on the agenda if necessary.

# CHAPTER FIVE

# TALK TO STRANGERS

No single maxim about safety has permeated our society so completely as the one spoken millions of times each year to millions of kids: Never Talk to Strangers. Perhaps because it seemed reasonable when we first heard it, this rule isn't often questioned. Let's question it now, along with the other culturally entrenched rules intended to keep children safe. We already know they don't work, so we can do this with an open mind.

## "Never Talk to Strangers"

Somehow we believe that if we teach this to our children, if we're certain they fully understand it, if they get it right every time we quiz them on it—if all that happens, they'll be safe. With some urgency, we implore, "You understand, right? Never talk to strangers. Tell Daddy again, okay?" In the world we cannot control, we can control at least one thing: Our children will know The Rule. Really, however, all we can be certain of is that they can recite it.

Children are taught The Rule when young, but the very week it's handed down, they see their parents violate it over and over. And they are themselves encouraged to violate it: "Say hello to the nice lady," "Answer the man's question," "Tell Mr. Evans your name." What children actually learn is: Never talk to strangers unless they are wearing a clown suit or a uniform, or they work at the bank, or they're registering us to vote, or they're seeking signatures on a petition, or they're handing out tasty samples, or they're nice.

Never Talk to Strangers, it turns out, isn't a rule after all, but a highly flexible and incomprehensible concept that only Mom and Dad really understand—if even they do.

The list of violently inclined predatory criminals defeated because a parent told his or her child not to talk to strangers isn't long enough to be called a list at all. More to the point, young children told not to talk to strangers *do* talk to strangers anyway. On a powerful segment of the *Oprah Winfrey Show*, children were successfully lured away from inattentive parents time after time. Ken Wooden, the author of *Child Lures*, is among the nation's most effective advocates for children's safety. He described his appearance on the program:

> Oprah's producers and I approached several young mothers in a suburban park to ask for their cooperation with our experiment. Each mother emphatically insisted that her child would never leave the park with a stranger, then watched in horror from a distance as her youngster cheerfully followed me out of the park to look for my puppy. On average, it took thirty-five seconds to lure each child away from the safety of the park.

(This Oprah Winfrey program, aired on September 27, 1993, can be ordered through Burrelle's Transcripts 800-777-8398. Title: "Child Lures.")

Clearly, the children lured away by this ploy were not ready to be on their own, and they were too far away from their mothers. I've observed people in public leave a small child farther away than they'd ever leave a purse or briefcase. Of course, a purse or briefcase isn't expected to protect itself, and herein lies the huge fallacy at the center of The Rule. It assumes that a small child has something to contribute to his or her own protection, and that's just not true.

Reliance upon a young child in such high-stakes matters is misplaced. Imagine selecting a five-year-old baby-sitter for your child. Many parents have done virtually that by placing part of the responsibility for a child's personal security on the child. I heard one parent say about The Rule, "We've told her a hundred times, but she just doesn't get it." Then think of that as your starting point: She doesn't get it. Maybe because she's too young, or maybe because she just doesn't get it, but listen to that fact. When we assume that a young child will reliably do what we say in our absence, or that doing it will keep him or her safe, we are choosing to share our duty with the least qualified person available. We'd actually find a more reliable guard for our children by choosing a total stranger.

Even if I believed in the effectiveness of The Rule it would be hard to endorse the ways it is often taught. Here's a passage from a children's book entitled *Never Talk to Strangers:* "If you are hanging from a trapeze and up sneaks a camel with bony knees, remember this rule, if you please—Never Talk to Strangers." The book goes on to discuss grouchy grizzly bears, parachuting hawks, a rhinoceros waiting for a bus, coyotes asking the time, cars with whales at the wheel, etc. With all due credit to the author, whose heart was surely in the right place, how effective can this be? Some people might judge effectiveness by a child's ability to recite the catchy rhymes, but that's a test of memory, not a test of the ability to protect oneself.

Even if a child fully learns and embraces the rule of not talking to strangers, many kids believe a stranger is an unshaven man in tattered clothes; neither the nice neighbor nor the guy at the check-out counter is one of those.

In addition to the fact that it doesn't work, The Rule actually reduces safety in several ways. One is that within the message Never Talk to Strangers (because they may harm you) is the implication that people you know will not harm you. If stranger equals danger, then friend equals safety. But the opposite is true far more often. First of all we are inherently more protected against a stranger; he must get around the defense systems of the parent and the child. The friend, conversely, is ushered inside the gates and given a pass. The friend has been gifted with what every other predator must work to gain: trust and access. So, the issue isn't strangers versus acquaintances; it is people who might harm your child versus people who won't, people who deserve your trust versus people who don't.

Until a child is old enough to understand what predatory strategies look like, old enough and confident enough to resist them, assertive enough to seek help, powerful enough to enforce the word No—until all that happens, a child is too young to be his own protector, too young to merit any of your reliance, too young to be part of the defense system, period.

Presumably, The Rule is intended to provide protection in the event the child is alone somewhere, because if a parent is present, then what difference does it make if a young child speaks with a stranger? The irony is that if your child is ever lost in public, the ability to talk to strangers is actually the single greatest asset he could have. To seek assistance, to describe one's situation, to give a phone number, to ask advice, to say No—all these interactions require the child to speak with strangers. If kids view talking to strangers as the threshold they mustn't cross, then when they do cross it (and they will), they have no further tools. Talking is just talking, after all, but since what we really want to avoid is our child going somewhere with someone, that's the thing to teach them about (more on this in Chapter 6).

Another way The Rule reduces safety is by providing unearned peace of mind; because of it, some parents don't take other precautions. But there's still another, more pervasive way The Rule reduces safety: Children raised to assume all strangers might be dangerous do not develop their own inherent skills of evaluating behavior. The Rule hurts all of us by producing generation after generation of people who fear people, mostly because they don't understand them. Fear of people is really the fear that we can't predict their behavior.

Recognize that for every person you encounter who might hurt your child, there are literally millions who will not. Does it make sense to treat everyone as if they are in the dangerous group? That's exactly what modern Western society has done. Ironically, adults end up being more loyal to The Rule than children: We, unlike people in many cultures, pass each other on streets and in hallways without acknowledgment.

Yet communicating with strangers is part of the test human beings are built to use to confirm that strangers are of good will. Just like animals, we have a complex system for evaluating the intent of those we encounter. In less fractured cultures, strangers exchange signals as they pass each other, signals that usually communicate, *I mean you no harm.* It might be a nod, a slight smile, a wave, or a greeting that puts both people at ease, but millions of Americans don't participate.

That's why being in the presence of a stranger can be uncomfortable or even frightening. You see, since we more than most species need to be reassured about the intent of others, that discomfort you feel in the elevator with a stranger is natural. Your body is waiting to be put at ease when the stranger passes a test. The tension is instantly broken when your nod solicits a smile, or when a comment initiates a cordial exchange of words.

Though this book focuses on violence, let's recognize that human beings are perhaps the most cooperative species on earth. Most animals live within a herd, flock, or hive, resisting contact with outsiders in their own species. In contrast, we spend much of our time in the presence of strangers, far from our home tribe. This works only because we can readily determine who is safe for us to be around and who is not. Human beings predict dangerousness (and far more often predict safety) automatically and with astounding accuracy—but not if we avoid the very things that inform our intuition. It is an individual's behavior, not merely his species, which might warn us of danger, and communicating is how we find our comfort and our safety.

Bottom line: *The issue isn't strangers, it is strangeness.* It is inappropriate behavior that's relevant: a stare held too long, a smile that curls too slowly, a narrowing or widening of the eyes, a rapid looking away. The muscles in the face are instruments of communication, resulting in an eloquent language that can put us at ease or give us the creeps.

University of California at San Francisco psychologist Paul Eckman says, "The face tells us subtleties in feelings that only a poet can put into words." One way to charm is with the smile, which Eckman calls the most important signal of intent. He adds, however, that the smile is also "the typical disguise used to mask the emotions." We know these truths naturally. Though the smile on its own might not reassure us, or might even be sinister in some contexts, I'd rather have it to evaluate than have nothing to evaluate. And we get something when we acknowledge strangers, most often by speaking with them.

Children who communicate with strangers are exercising their intuition. They learn what feels comfortable and what does not. That learning can be aided by a parent who watches a child communicate in a restaurant or store and then discusses the encounter afterward. "What did you think when that guy stood so close? I thought he seemed strange; I wasn't comfortable with him." Or, "I felt safe with that man at the next table who talked to us: Did you?"

Anna McDonnell is a remarkable woman and mother you'll hear more about in later chapters. She regularly encourages her seven-year-old son to approach strangers, giving him small challenges such as "Can you find out what time it is?" or "Can you get directions to the nearest frozen yogurt place?" Then she stands back and observes as he selects a person to ask. Afterward, they discuss why he chose who he chose, how the exchange went, if he felt comfortable with the

person he spoke with, if that person was comfortable with his approach, and so on. Her son has safely rehearsed all kinds of encounters with people.

Could it be that this boy who actually approaches strangers in
public is less likely to be a victim than someone taught never to talk
to them? Absolutely yes.

Though Jan is not a mother (and used to say she didn't want to be),
the thirty-two-year-old Los Angeles antiques dealer had a maternal experience with Andre, someone else's eight-year-old son. After spending the day at a swap meet outside Los Angeles, Jan couldn't get her
car started, making her one of a handful of people left in the huge remote parking lot. She was scared to ask anyone for help and scared
that it would get darker (which of course it would), and scared that
she'd be even more scared later.

Jan was about to be rescued by a child, though he had problems of
his own: Andre's parents had come to the swap meet in two cars. They
first decided his father would drive him home, but at the last minute
his father said he should catch up with his mother and go with her.
His mother pulled away just before Andre reached her car and by the
time he got back to where his father had been, he'd also driven away.
Those are the events that led Jan to be approached by the only person
in the parking lot that didn't scare her, and to hear the words, "My
name is Andre and I'm lost. Will you help me?"

She looked at his curly black hair, his glasses, his little blue
blazer—and she was hooked. "Where's your mom?"

Jan was amused and amazed by the small boy's answer: "I think
she's on the freeway behind someone who should get their eyes exam-
ined." Jan had no doubt a kid this clever would know his home phone
number by heart, and he did, but it didn't solve much. Her car phone
wasn't working (no electricity), and anyway Andre explained, "My
mom's not home yet and my dad's not home yet."

Jan asked where his parents might be going, and he knew

exactly: "My dad is going for a drive because he just needs to drive. My mom is going shopping because somebody in this family has to be responsible."

Jan had already fallen for Andre and would do anything to help him, but she needed help herself. When two men engrossed in a conversation walked by on the way to one of the last cars in the lot, Jan was way too intimidated to interrupt them. Andre wasn't: "Excuse me, do you have a portable phone I could borrow? Can you show me how to use it? Can you help that lady get her car started?"

The men didn't have a phone but they jump-started Jan's car, and that meant her car phone worked. Andre said, "If this is an emergency, you could call the police, or you could drive me to my house." That's the option Jan took, but to give Andre's parents enough time to get home, they stopped for dinner. Thus, Jan got the experience and the story she calls "My Dinner with Andre."

After they ate, Jan called Andre's house, reached his astounded but grateful mother, and then drove Andre home. That was two years ago and the friendship that was born because Andre knew how to approach a stranger is still going strong.

The capable communicator who can elicit and assert information is far less likely to be a victim than is the wallflower.

## "If You Are Ever Lost, Go to a Policeman"

Here's another popular rule that rarely enhances safety. Teaching this to a young child ignores several facts: All identifying credentials, insignias, badges, and nameplates are above the waist, but a young child sees a world of legs. In fact, many children get lost in the first place because of following legs (the wrong set): Legs aren't that distinctive when viewed from two and a half feet off the ground.

A young child cannot tell the difference between a policeman and a security guard, and you certainly don't want your child's first choice to be a security guard. (That's the employment pool that gave us the Son of Sam killer, the assassin of John Lennon, the Hillside Strangler, and more serial killers and rapists than you have time to read about.) Even if your child knows how to identify a police officer, it could take a long while to find one, and depending upon where the child is lost, it might not happen at all.

Some parents have taught their small children, "Go to the manager," but this poses the same problem of identification as with the policeman: That small name tag is several feet above the child's eye-line.

I don't believe in teaching inflexible rules because it's not possible to know they'll apply in all situations. There is one, however, that reliably enhances safety: Teach children that if they are ever lost, **Go to a Woman.**

Why? First, if your child selects a woman, it's highly unlikely that the woman will be a sexual predator. Next, as Jan's story illustrates, a woman approached by a lost child asking for help is likely to stop whatever she is doing, commit to that child, and not rest until the child is safe. A man approached by a small child might say, "Head over there to the manager's desk," whereas a woman will get involved and stay involved.

Is what I've said politically incorrect? Maybe so, but the luxury of not running for office is that I don't care if it's politically incorrect. The fact is that men in all cultures and at all ages and at all times in history are more violent than women—and facts are not political.

"If you are ever lost, go to a woman" works because it's practical (there will almost always be a woman around) and simple (easy to teach, easy to learn, easy to do). Finally, teaching children to choose someone rather than wait for someone to choose them will be a useful lesson their whole lives. It's the same advice I give to adult women.

I wouldn't call this next item a rule, but rather a commitment you can make to your child: "I will never send anyone you do not know to pick you up at school or anywhere else without telling you about it ahead of time. If anyone you did not expect ever says, 'Your mother or father sent me,' do not go anywhere with that person."

## "If You Are in Trouble, Go to the Nearest Police Station"

Some parents believe that children should know the location of the nearest police station and go there in an emergency. In many communities around the country, the nearest police station is not at all near, and until children are driving, it might not be useful for them to know. More to the point, I wouldn't want a child focused on getting to a police station when there might be actions that are far more practical and would be more effective, such as trying to call home or asking someone for help. They may need assistance, to be sure, but that doesn't mean passing up all adults who aren't cops. Think of your own response to an emergency. It is rarely "I've got to get to the police station" because that's not usually the most immediate or practical response.

## "No Place Is Safe"

This is said to children very often, presumably to make them more alert, but places are not inherently safe or unsafe; it is situations, not places, which might contain vulnerability and hazard. The seediest spot in town is not dangerous if you drive through it in a police car, and the police station itself is not safe if an officer uses excessive force. Sure, there are places we don't want our kids going, but that's not the key to their safety.

Danger is about the relationship between a target and a predator; telling children No Place Is Safe is telling them that it hardly matters what anyone does because danger is just waiting everywhere to get them. Not only is this inaccurate, but the hopelessness of the message discourages personal responsibility. No person is dangerous to your child unless your child is vulnerable to him. For most types of violence, if a predator does not have control of his target and does not have privacy, he is not dangerous. It doesn't matter where he is. As you'll see in coming chapters, every place is safe, if we make it so.

The final problem with the No Place Is Safe warning is that it quickly loses credibility. Imagine being told, "Every place you go contains a bag of diamonds." For a time, your brain would look for the diamonds, and then it would stop. Rather than looking for diamonds—which are rare—you could more constructively look for opportunities.

Similarly, when we warn children that no place is safe, they wait for danger as if it were an event that happens. Day after day, it doesn't happen, and they become desensitized to the real safety issue, which is the *process of being persuaded.*

## "Don't Wander Off in Public"

Saying this to kids makes plenty of sense—so long as we don't rely upon their compliance. Some parents expect their children to keep the parent within sight at all times, even though the parent has failed to keep the children within sight at all times. One father explained why it's his six-year-old's job to keep them together in public: "At a store, I can't always keep an eye on him; I'm busy shopping, but he's not. He can keep me in view because he'd got nothing else to do." Really? When I was six, I had a lot to do: touch everything, try to reach things that were too high up, pick off the small plastic price cards from the front of the shelves, read boxes of cereal in order to make a case for why we needed to buy them, and so on. No wonder I got separated from my parents so often.

One mother of five explained the anxiety she feels at every crowded mall or amusement park they visit: "I'm the only one not having fun because I'm suffering with fear about losing one of my kids." Though not directly relevant to violence, there are some practical steps parents can take to reduce anxiety in the event a child is lost. First is to dress small children in brightly colored, distinctive, easily describable outfits. Parents who remember what their children are wearing have less anxiety when they become separated. The small child in the brightly colored cap will be easier to spot in a crowd.

On vacations, parents and children are in unfamiliar areas where being separated is even more likely, so some parents bring along photos of their kids. Having a plan or agreement, such as "If anybody gets lost, we'll meet at the Ferris wheel" helps make reunions happen sooner. Nancy, a mother who often takes her two boys to Central Park, has taught them to go to the nearest food stand or pretzel cart if they are lost; then that's where she looks for them. This works well since kids take special note of those places that offer sugar and snacks.

It is inevitable that at some time every parent will lose sight of a child in public. In the overwhelming majority of these instances— and there are tens of thousands every day—it's the result of inattention or wandering on the part of either the parent or child, depending upon whom you ask. Soon enough they are back together, with one of them saying to the other (you guess which one): "I've told you a hundred times not to wander off."

Gabriel is the father of four children who all know how to talk to strangers. Over the years, each of them has been lost at some point, usually for a minute or two, and only a few times long enough to get some authentic anxiety going. Even though many parents panic, Gabriel says these situations typically passed "as if nothing had happened—because nothing really had." He adds an interesting irony: "Just as we finally got them to not wander off on their own, they reached the age where we started encouraging them to go off on their own."

# CHAPTER SIX

# THE CHANGING
# OF THE GUARD

Considering the number of books and pamphlets about safety that are addressed to children, it's clear some people believe that children themselves have a lot to contribute to their own protection. There's even one that claims it will teach them to "take responsibility for their own safety." Given that most kids can't take responsibility to feed the goldfish, I just don't see it.

Having said this, there does come a day when the people initially responsible for a child's safety welcome a new member to the team: the child. Parents may agonize over whether he or she is ready; they may even delay the day, but the day will come. Though it's at the end of a gradual process, your son or daughter will make that walk to school, or to a friend's house, or to the market. The eyes that used to casually take in the sights will have to detect, assess, perhaps even deter danger.

To be fully capable on their own, your children will eventually need information from every chapter of this book, but only you know what they are ready to learn and how to best inform them. I can offer a test of what children would ideally know before they are ever alone in public. (I am noting just those points relevant to violence and sexual predation, and I am leaving out obvious requirements such as knowing one's home address, important phone numbers, and other basics.)

# The Test of Twelve

*Do your children know . . .*

1. How to honor their feelings—if someone makes them uncomfortable, that's an important signal;

2. You (the parents) are strong enough to hear about any experience they've had, no matter how unpleasant;

3. It's okay to rebuff and defy adults;

4. It's okay to be assertive;

5. How to ask for assistance or help;

6. How to choose *who* to ask;

7. How to describe their peril;

8. It's okay to strike, even to injure, someone if they believe they are in danger, and that you'll support any action they take as a result of feeling uncomfortable or afraid;

9. It's okay to make noise, to scream, to yell, to run;

10. If someone ever tries to force them to go somewhere, what they scream should include, "This is not my father" (because onlookers seeing a child scream or even struggle are likely to assume the adult is a parent);

11. If someone says "Don't yell," the thing to do *is* yell (and the corollary: If someone says "Don't tell," the thing to do *is* tell);

12. To fully resist ever going anywhere out of public view with someone they don't know, and particularly to resist going anywhere with someone who tries to persuade them.

We've touched on several of these points in previous chapters, but there are a few that call for further exploration, particularly given that plenty of adults couldn't themselves pass the Test of Twelve. For example, many have never even considered that if a predator says "Don't yell," he is actually saying that yelling would serve you and silence would serve him. Too many people feel compelled to cooperate in their own victimization, in part because they assume they'll be hurt if they don't. In *Strong on Defense*, former police supervisor Sanford Strong says, when an intimidating criminal gives us an order, "Our intellect begins to analyze based on incorrect assumptions: 'If I do as I'm told, he won't hurt me.' "

On TV shows, when the tough guy says, "Keep your mouth shut and come with me," actors do just that. But in real life, when a predator says, "Don't yell," he is telling you what cards you hold, literally informing you of the way to mess up his plans. "Don't yell" should be heard by a child as "YELL." (It's probably obvious what a fun role-playing game can be used to teach this skill. It's called Don't yell/yell!)

The corollary guideline is that when people say, "Don't tell," your child should hear "TELL."

Item number 12 can take the most courage to apply. To resist fully is not easy, but if a predator orders you to go somewhere with him, he is really telling you that staying here is to your advantage and to his disadvantage. He wants to take you to a place where he'll be able to do whatever it is he can't do here. Since people often cooperate out of fear of being injured, it is essential to remember, as police expert Strong says, *"Initial injury is far from the worst consequence of a violent crime."*

(Note: It's true that in some armed robberies, safety can be best served by simply giving over what the robber demands, but I'm not discussing robberies here. My observations focus on crimes where the predator must take his victim somewhere.)

Item number 8 of the Test of Twelve requires a child to know that it's okay to strike, even to injure someone when that's appropriate. The best way I have seen to address this (and most of the other items at the same time) is through a training method called IMPACT FOR KIDS, where young students learn about actual physical confrontations. Male instructors wearing heavily padded outfits that can withstand real punches and kicks play assailants. Like IMPACT training (its counterpart for adults and young adults), IMPACT FOR KIDS teaches empowering, often life-changing skills with great sensitivity. (See Appendix #1 for more information.)

IMPACT FOR KIDS instructors teach children partly through setting up various scenarios. Many parents also use this approach, typically providing some details and then asking how the child feels about the theoretical situation. This can be done in reverse: provide the feeling, and then ask for the details that caused it. As an exercise to show that feelings are often based on small but important details, I recently met with a class of nine-year-old students at their school in Santa Monica, California. I described several scenarios, told them what they felt, and then asked them to tell me the details. For example: You are walking down the street and you see two sixteen-year-old boys. *You feel fear of them.* Tell me what they are wearing, carrying and doing.

ANSWER FROM A NINE-YEAR-OLD: They are wearing big loose jackets. They aren't carrying anything; their hands are in their coat pockets. They are staring at me.

GdeB: Okay, now you're walking down the street and you see two sixteen-year-old boys who don't scare you at all. Tell me what they are wearing, carrying and doing.

ANSWER: They're wearing T-shirts and they have backpacks with books in them. They are talking to each other.

GdeB: While you are walking down a crowded street, a car slows and the driver asks if you've seen a big white dog he's lost. You trust him because of something you saw him do before he talked to you. What was it?

ANSWER: I saw him ask other people the same question.

GdeB: You come home and find a uniformed police officer in your living room, but you don't trust him. Why not?

ANSWER: I didn't see a police car outside.

Though no answer is inherently right or wrong, all demonstrate that children connect their feelings of danger or safety to small things they perceive.

Science has much touted the concept of "fight or flight"—but it applies mostly to animals, and not all animals at that. Though many people believe that fight and flight are the only available responses to danger, human beings—including your children—have many more, including dexterity, agility, guile, negotiation, speed, cleverness, noise, strength, alliance, and the keen ability to predict behavior. Children who can pass the Test of Twelve have a more effective defense system than lions or tigers or bears. Even for these children, however, parents are the main component, because parents give them permission to protect themselves.

•   •   •

Anna McDonnell says, "A child doesn't magically at some predetermined age become confident, assertive, capable, and powerful." Ideally, it's a gradual process of ever-greater challenges wherein a child gains experience and autonomy. She describes teaching her own son when he was eight years old:

> Henry loved to get hot dogs from a vendor near his school. I started by buying them for him. Then I had him buy them with me standing there. Then I stood a little ways back when he went and asked for them. Then I parked the car in front of the vendor's cart and let Henry get out and buy a hot dog. Then I parked the car on the other side of the street, so Henry had to cross the street, go up to the vendor, buy a hot dog, get the change, and return across the street.

When her sons got to the age that they might be somewhere on their own, including visiting with other families, McDonnell developed a smart approach to ensure they could always contact her. She gave them laminated cards with all the needed phone numbers (home, office, pager). She taped fifty cents onto the back of each card so that wherever her kids went, they'd always have the money for a pay phone. This ensured they had the information, but also the autonomy to call home—even without the help or permission of an adult.

Allowing your child to be alone in public does not mean allowing him or her to make all the decisions about where and when, of course. Take walking to school as an example. You can decide the route, and you can even monitor the trip for as long as you feel necessary.

I suggest that you walk the route with your child, ten times if that's what it takes for you both to feel comfortable about it. Look at things from your child's height, for the view may be different. Together with your child, you can identify the safest places to stop and ask for help or refuge. The bookstore seems a better choice than the pool hall, and you can discuss why with your child. Go into the bookstore, introduce your child to the manager, get them acquainted with each other. Select several businesses or places along the way as safe refuges—and also point out those that are best avoided. You are choosing the route for its inherent safety advantages, not its directness, so try several ways to get from home to the destination. It's also good to have a second-choice route in case of construction or anything else that might make the primary route unworkable.

Stan, the father of three sons, has a system for when each boy reaches the age to walk to school: He gives his son the assignment of mapping out all the possible routes, literally using a map. Then they discuss the pros and cons of the various options. One of his boys, eight-year-old Will, jumped fully into the project, first highlighting the routes on a street map, boiling them down to three favorites, then getting his oldest brother to go with him as he walked along and made a videotape of each option. After a couple of weeks, he presented a movie-style review of the routes to his parents, complete with clips from his video. About his least favorite, he said: "Long blocks full of boring shops; people are unhappy because they know the route is boring and they have to work there. Two thumbs down."

About his preferred route, he wrote: "Lots of open stores selling things. They want me to be a customer when I get older, so they act nice. Two thumbs up."

Once you've selected the route, have an understanding with your child that they'll always stick to it. Explain that you might (particularly in the beginning) drive along and observe your child from time to time.

•     •     •

There are several high-stakes questions raised by the changing of the guard, but here's the one parents ask most often: *How can I teach my child about risk without causing too much fear?*

While kids want the freedom of walking somewhere on their own, most already are a little afraid. To give them the personal power to pass the Test of Twelve, we can think of fear as being like an antibiotic—great when you need it, but you wouldn't want to use it every day. That's because too much is toxic. Fear is the protection resource of last resort and having your kids afraid (of all strangers, for example) doesn't usually serve safety anyway.

Many parents think it does. When they want to underscore the importance of a given instruction, they attach some dreadful outcome to it: "Come right home; you don't want to get kidnapped," "Don't go there alone; remember, anyone could be a killer," and on and on. There are two likely results of trying to scare children:

1. It will work, and the child will be afraid.

Using fear to protect a child from sexual molestation, for example, gives the child one of the worst consequences of sexual molestation: being afraid and untrusting of people. In other words, they end up experiencing some of the very damage we mean to protect them from.

2. It won't work, and the parent will lose credibility.

The parent who loses credibility is not an effective teacher. How effective can it be, for example, to say, "Marijuana will kill you" when most kids know it won't? If children perceive parental warnings as a litany of outlandish dangers, they won't think any are important.

Children who are never afraid and children who are always afraid have something in common: Neither will get the benefit of fear when they need it. Since fear is a child's most powerful resource in an emergency, what can parents do to protect it?

One way is to show them that nothing is so terrible that it cannot be discussed calmly and explicitly. Children fear the unknown, so make the important things known. It's almost certain they've heard at least something about every topic anyway, and they probably know more about some risks than their parents do. In *What Should I Tell the Kids?*, Dr. Ava Siegler notes that "We are often called upon to manage problems we may never have envisioned, let alone encountered when we were growing up." Still, whatever it is can be discussed, and kids who are capable enough to be out on their own are also mature enough to learn about the world from their parents.

How and when they learn is as important as what they learn. Dr. Siegler says, "While the mind is capable of absorbing all kinds of new experiences—indeed even thrives on stimulation—too much too soon can heighten the child's fear of the unknown and prevent the child from developing a sense of security in himself and his world."

Would anyone want to destroy people's sense of security? Well yes, actually, there's a whole business right in your community that profits from doing exactly that: the local TV news. If allowed to, they'll show your young kids a world in which airplane crashes are frequent, fatal fires happen every day, children are always being kidnapped, men have their penises cut off by angry girlfriends, whole families are killed by fathers who then kill themselves, and young boys commit mass murders at school. Your kids will get to see dead bodies carried to the coroner's van and police snipers shoot and kill hostage-takers. All these things happen, of course, but if you don't want your kids believing they're likely to happen to them, I suggest that the local news be Rated R in your house.

All of us will have to experience calamities in our own lives; that's unavoidable. In the satellite age, however, we experience the calamities in *everyone's* lives—and that is avoidable. Constant depiction of a dangerous world leads children (and adults) to believe they are not competent to meet the challenges of life, and that belief can permeate the entire experience of life.

Parents trying to teach news-watching kids about safety have a tough job. That's because reasonable warnings will seem tame by comparison, and exaggerated warnings will seem like what kids see on the news anyway—only less realistic. In order to be effective, parents need credibility on the topic of danger; what they don't need is extra competition during sweeps week.

In millions of homes, the local newscaster is a guest who arrives in the afternoon full of frightening tales and gory pictures. He stays through dinner, enthusiastically adding grisly details, and he's still around at bedtime to recite a scary story or two. That's a huge daily dose of alarming images and manufactured urgency. The original town crier put us to sleep with the chant, "Eleven o'clock and all's well," but in the media age he bellows, "Eleven o'clock and milk causes crib death!"

Terror-provoking sensationalism takes its toll on parents too, of course. For example, 90 percent of adults feel less safe today than they did growing up. Since your children are very sensitive to your fears, let's take a look at that "safer" world of your youth. It was a world without airbags or mandatory seat belts, before the decrease in smoking, before early detection of cancer, before 911 systems showed dispatchers the addresses of people in distress. You remember those carefree fifties before CAT scans, ultrasound, organ transplants, amniocentesis, and coronary bypass surgery. Remember those oh-so-safe sixties when angry world powers postured for war and schoolchildren practiced monthly air-raid drills on how to survive nuclear attack.

The fact is that young people are more likely to survive childhood today than in 1960. Vehicle fatalities have dropped 25 percent since then, deaths by other accidents have been cut in half, and cancer deaths have been reduced by 30 percent. (As I'll discuss in coming chapters, only firearms deaths have increased.)

It's true that the violence we see today is far more gruesome than what we saw growing up—but that's the point: *the violence we see.* Parents and children clearly have a far larger catalogue of fears to draw upon, and I believe your kids will be safer and you will be more effective if you throw that catalogue out with the other junk mail. Consider teaching your kids my acronym for NEWS: Nothing Educational or Worth Seeing. It's accurate most of the time.

Some experts have recommended that parents actually compel their kids to watch the news: "They've got to know what the real world is like." This assumes that children don't live in the real world already, which of course they do. In addition to the good things in life, children live with disappointment, loss, confusion, pain, violence, alcoholism, sadness, death, and all the rest. Even those not old enough to understand events live with the consequences of their parents' troubles.

One father who advocates the use of fear told me, "You bet I want my boys afraid of strangers; it's the only way they can be safe." Actually, it might be the specific way they are victimized. For example, fearful children are easily exploited by sexual predators who threaten to harm parents, pets, or the children themselves. These predators use fear to control; they almost never have any intention of carrying out the threats. Children who are so afraid of strangers that they'll comply with any order cannot pass the Test of Twelve. Most predators are interested in children who will cooperate because they are afraid (and the same holds true for predators of adults).

Being afraid of others is actually the fear that we are unprepared to protect ourselves. Obviously, we cannot change or eliminate all the dangerous people in the world; what we can change is our ability to deal with them. That is most likely if you build a world for your children in which fear is a resource and not a daily drug.

. . .

We've talked about what kids ought to know before walking to school alone. But do they actually have to be completely alone? Some parents have said No.

If you visit Long Beach, California, on any school day, you might see a woman standing at the corner of 12th and Cedar, and another standing at the corner of 12th and Chesnut, and another at the next corner, and the next, for as far as you can see. They are members of the Mother's Brigade, a group of citizens who have volunteered to make sure their schoolchildren are safe from violent older kids, sleazy adults, and drug sellers.

Not far away, in Downey, California, there's a program called Safe Corridors. A hundred and fifty prescreened homes and businesses display a sign declaring themselves safe havens for schoolchildren. Retirees, mothers at home with younger children, people who work at home, and others stand ready to assist any child who is scared by a bully or a menacing stranger, or who might just be lost. Concerned citizens went door to door signing up people to help with Safe Corridors. By the end of the first day they had a hundred volunteers; a survey has since shown that six out of ten people would agree to participate if asked. If it's so easy to do, why isn't there a program in every neighborhood? One answer comes from a Temple University study: Half of America's parents say they don't know where their children go after school. Luckily, the other half does.

There's a group called Parent Patrol on the South Side of Chicago (where elementary schools used to lose as many as 40 percent of the students in waves of fear-induced absenteeism). There's one called Safe Walk Home in Escondido, California, that asks business owners to stand outside their shops for a few minutes every day as the school-children pass by. And I imagine there's one waiting to be organized in your neighborhood.

One of our closest relatives in nature, the Bonobo ape, long ago learned what these programs prove: that female alliances are the key to safety. When a female Bonobo is bullied by a male, other females will chase him off. The mothers I've discussed above protect their children the same way. Even in a neighborhood full of violent gangs, the gang of mothers can be the most powerful.

# CHAPTER SEVEN

# BABY-SITTERS AND NANNIES

*Who takes the child by the hand, takes the mother by the heart.*

—GERMAN PROVERB

Gail looked into Deb's eyes with relief. It wasn't just that she'd finally found a baby-sitter she liked, but also that Deb could start so soon. The attractive young woman had extensive experience with kids, had been a house sitter for some people whom Gail had once met, and best of all, she had lots of references. The following night, Gail and her husband Vince drove away from their house with hardly a worry; ten-month-old Vince, Jr., was in good hands.

Busy hands, too, for they spent a considerable amount of time going through Gail's closets and drawers, though that wouldn't be apparent for several months. By that point, Gail had trusted Deb a lot—with Vince, Jr., with the house, even with personal thoughts and feelings.

The job of a dishonest baby-sitter gets much easier as time goes on because once confidence has been invested, a family doesn't want to entertain the little feelings of doubt that intuition might send them. This isn't so just because of the inconvenience of replacing someone, but also because we may have to admit being wrong. And as much as we like to say, "I didn't have a clue," that's rarely so.

Here's the story Gail told me:

Some weeks after Deb started, she was going to take Vince, Jr., out for the afternoon. As they were leaving, I got a call canceling a meeting, so I had some extra time and decided to go with them for a while. When we arrived at the park, an unsavory-looking young man approached our car; he and Deb apparently knew each other well, and I guess he may have been waiting for her. When he asked how she was doing, Deb replied: "Staying out of trouble." I didn't think much about it at the time [though Gail obviously thought enough about it to register and remember it], but later what she'd said made me uncomfortable. Though she didn't introduce me to him, Deb told me later that guy was her boyfriend. A few other things started happening, like we'd get lots of hang-ups whenever Deb was at our house, and we didn't get hang-ups when she wasn't there. Then my watch was missing.

One night when Vince and I went to the movies, I called the house to check on Vince, Jr., and a man answered the phone. When I asked for Deb, the man hung up. I called again and Deb answered, so I just assumed I had dialed wrong the first time. I discounted each new thing that happened and was never willing to see what it all added up to—until that last night when it was obvious.

We'd gone to a friend's birthday party and left Vince, Jr., with Deb. When we arrived at our friend's house about a half-hour later, I realized I'd left the gift on the floor right near our front door. I wanted to go back and get it but Vince said we'd bring it over some other time. We argued because I was adamant about going back to the house to get the gift. Vince pointed out that going back home would make us more than an hour late, but I won, or really I guess our family won, because that's the night we found Deb's boyfriend and two other people going through boxes in our garage.

As Vince and Gail arrived, the three young men ran to a car and drove off. Vince got their license plate number while Gail went into the house and confronted Deb. She denied that she had opened the garage to admit the thieves, denied that her boyfriend was one of the people who'd run off, denied that she'd done anything wrong. All in all, she was fairly convincing, until Vince told her he was calling the police. Then Deb gave up the lie and showed her truest color: "You don't want to get me angry."

Gail is certain that her insistence on going back home had less to do with the forgotten birthday gift, and more to do with intuition. She now recalls that there was a hang-up call as they were getting dressed to leave. Also, Deb's pager went off and she didn't even glance at it to see who'd paged her. Gail had felt something wasn't right because something wasn't right.

There's no evidence that Deb was ever abusive to Vince, Jr. (though she was certainly negligent). She stole some replaceable property and some harder-to-replace peace of mind, but all in all, it was a low-cost lesson for Gail and Vince.

Speaking around the country, I sometimes ask for a show of hands by parents who've hired someone to watch their children while they are attending my talk. Of those who raise their hands, I ask: "Do any of you have someone caring for your children that you do not trust?"

Usually a few people will say Yes, and I tell them, "Go home." This might seem a glib response on my part, or a failure to understand how difficult it is to find good child care. But to demonstrate that it's possible to be confident in your baby-sitter's character, I then ask for a show of hands from parents who are completely comfortable with whoever is watching their kids. Many more hands go up. Parents in the second group usually have something in common: They describe their baby-sitters in glowing terms: "a remarkable woman," "kind, caring," "we love her," "an important part of our family," "would trust her with anything."

In contrast, those parents who don't trust their sitters are not specific about why: "You never really know about people," "You can't ever be sure," "People aren't predictable." With philosophies like that, it may be impossible to be comfortable with anyone. If you *never* really know about people, then even decades of superb performance wouldn't put you at ease. But here's the truth: It is possible to be comfortable with who you choose if you are comfortable with *how* you choose.

After the incident with Deb, Gail told me she wanted to undertake an honest exploration of her part in it. We started with the fact that she'd been impressed with the references Deb provided. Unfortunately, however, since Gail never tried to call any of the people, the references were little more than a list of names and numbers. The issue is not having references; it is *checking* references.

It was also perceived as favorable that Deb had worked as a house sitter for some people Gail had once met. "I figured that I'd have heard about anything serious in her history."

I asked Gail, "Did you call those people you'd once met who Deb said she used to house-sit for and tell them what happened?"

She shook her head No. "Then is it reasonable to assume they'd have somehow communicated something to you, particularly given that they barely know you and they didn't know Deb was working for you?" She shook her head No.

When I asked Gail if she and Vince approved of Deb having her boyfriend at their home, she said, "Of course not."

"Did you tell her that ahead of time?"

"Well, it's obvious that having your boyfriend over is against the rules."

"You provided her with some rules?"

Gail shook her head No. Like most parents, she had a substantial list of rules that were obvious to her, but which remained unexpressed to the very person expected to abide by them. The lesson? Establish and communicate house rules, best done with a guidebook. The list needn't include "Thou shalt not steal," but things like "Don't take the kids out of the house," or "Don't bathe the kids" must be communicated if they are your wishes.

(A good guidebook would also include the location and operation of fuse boxes and circuit breakers, policies for predictable occurrences, location of kitchen fire extinguisher, what to do if smoke detectors go off, child medical release form if you choose to have one, relevant phone numbers, etc.)

Gail conceded that she wanted so badly to qualify someone as a baby-sitter that she didn't really search for unfavorable information. She could have done worse. Some people take neutral, irrelevant indicators and treat them as favorable. Seeing an applicant stroke the family dog, for example, they might think, "She likes animals, that's a good sign." Or worse still, "Ginger likes her, that's a good sign." Choosing a baby-sitter is one process in which it's better to look for the storm clouds than to look for the silver lining.

•  •  •

Things would be so much easier if predictions about people were perfect, say, made with some high-tech chemical test. Just imagine, you could accept a ride from a stranger, ask a homeless person you'd never seen before to watch your house while you're out of town, or leave your baby with a "perfect" stranger.

In that easier future, Gail would hovercraft over to the park and look around for someone with whom to leave Vince, Jr. Using a device nearly everyone carries, she'd conduct an instant high-tech test on the first person she encountered. That woman would do a test on Gail at the same time. Let's say they both passed with flying colors. Then Gail wouldn't hesitate to ask the woman to watch Vince, Jr., for a few hours so she could skim over to a meeting. If the woman agreed, Gail would be off without any concern, because she'd have assured herself that this stranger is emotionally healthy, competent, drug-free and trustworthy.

The story sounds far-fetched, I know, but in our time we make every single one of these predictions about baby-sitters. We just don't do it as quickly—or as accurately.

With present-day technology, how much time would you have to spend with a stranger before she wouldn't be a stranger anymore? How many of your low-tech tests would a baby-sitter have to pass before you'd trust her? We undertake this common yet very high-stakes prediction by reviewing an application and asking a few questions, but let's really look at this process.

For starters, we wouldn't just interview a woman we met in a park. No, we'd want someone who was recommended by a person we know. That's because we like to rely on predictions made by others. Our friend Kevin is so bright and honorable, we think, that if he endorses somebody, well, that person must be okay. What often happens, however, is that we attach *Kevin's* attributes to the person he recommended, and we don't listen to our own uncertainty. As we drive away from home, leaving our child behind with someone we met just a half-hour ago, there's that tug that says, *You never really know about people.*

Just as some parents may feel more comfortable if a sitter is recommended by someone they know, so do many parents feel (unearned) peace of mind about a sitter or nanny referred by an agency. They may feel that since the agency sent the candidate, then no further background inquiry is necessary. They assume the agency is very familiar with the candidate and has conducted a full background check. That assumption will almost certainly be wrong. I often hear about how "reputable" an agency is, as if this says anything whatsoever about the candidate. I am told how long the agency has been in business, as if that matters. Understand that the agency isn't coming to your house and watching your kids. An agency is no more qualified to select a baby-sitter or nanny than you are. Further, the agency's commerce is served by qualifying a candidate, whereas you protect your child by disqualifying a candidate. Who would you rather have interviewing references and former employers: someone who pursues all information and is particularly alert to unfavorable information? Or someone who makes money only when it's good news?

In an interview with a baby-sitter candidate, parents watch attentively for any signs of . . . of what? Drug use? Well, that can be tested with great reliability. Tens of thousands of drug-screen tests are done every week by employers who have less at stake than parents do when hiring a baby-sitter. Though most people believe the drug question is a critical one, have you ever heard of a parent requiring a drug screen of a baby-sitter candidate? Or a Breathalyzer test to see if she's been drinking? Most parents don't even contact all the baby-sitter's references, so it's no wonder they drive away feeling you never really know about people.

I am not, by the way, suggesting drug tests or polygraphs for baby-sitters, but I am pointing out that we rarely bring even a tenth of the available resources to these high-stakes predictions. For example, the question people really want answered by a prospective baby-sitter is: Have you ever mistreated a child? But they never ask it. Why not? Because people feel that asking a question so direct would be rude, or ridiculous, since it wouldn't be answered truthfully by someone who had mistreated children. *Ask the question anyway,* and how it is answered will make you more comfortable or less comfortable with that applicant. Don't make it easy for someone who is dishonest by choosing not to ask a tough question—make them lie if they are going to.

Imagine you asked, "Have you ever abused a child?" and the applicant responded with "Define abuse," or "What have you heard?" (Bad answers, by the way.) It is entirely fair and appropriate to ask someone to whom you'll entrust your child to discuss the very issues you care about most. Good applicants will certainly understand, and bad applicants may reveal themselves.

Given the increasing incidence of sexual abuse, if you aren't 100 percent comfortable with the baby-sitter, you may want to skip the instruction given by millions of parents as they head out the door to the movies: "Do what the baby-sitter says."

•    •    •

The anonymity of modern society has lowered the consequences of bad behavior. In the small town of the past, the teenager's back talk at the general store wasn't so easy to shake off because his parents would hear about it. That element of accountability for our daily conduct toward others is gone in most lives today. In the South Pacific Republic of Fiji, where I wrote much of this book and where I observed how children can be raised without fear, the people live in small villages. They are born, get married, have children, and die all in the same house, surrounded by the same neighbors. You can be certain there is more focus on treating people well when you expect to spend a lifetime with them than if they will simply disappear into traffic.

In our culture of short encounters and little accountability, it is ever-more important to learn a lot about someone you bring into your life, particularly someone who'll be alone with your children. Information helps you evaluate someone's suitability for the job, of course, but there is a deeper benefit. The more you know about someone, the more you reduce that person's anonymity. If you have talked to five of the candidate's references, that's five more inhibitors against bad conduct, five people whom you and the baby-sitter *know* in common, five people who could hear about a misdeed. When you have many inroads into a person's life, you raise the consequences of bad behavior.

Preemployment questions are low-tech, easy tests you can perform when screening someone to take care of your kids. They are designed not just to elicit information, but to put important subjects on the agenda.

Among the questions you might ask (after having someone fill out an application):

### What is your philosophy about discipline?

Exploring this topic will reveal their opinions, and also serve as an ideal segue for you to set forth your house rules on discipline. If you don't want the baby-sitter spanking your child, this is the time to say so.

### Have you ever suspected that a child in your care was being sexually molested by someone?

This question is designed as a bridge into the topic of sexual abuse, but also as a way to test denial—and you do not want a denier as a baby-sitter or nanny. People caring for children have a duty to acknowledge and recognize reality, even hard reality, and denial is an evasion of that duty. When evaluating a baby-sitter, put sexual crimes against children squarely on the agenda. If the person you are talking with is a denier, you'll know it quickly ("Things like that don't happen around here"; "I've never even considered such a thing"; "I've worked only with good families").

*What discipline method did your parents use?*

The one used on them may be the one they believe is best. In any event, you'll gain further insight into the topic.

*Do you have children of your own?*
*Do you have younger siblings?*

It may be a plus when they answer yes to either question. In any event, the topic allows easy transition to several other areas: Did you take care of siblings when you were growing up? How old were you when you first stayed with them alone? How young do you think is too young?

*Why do you do this work?*

The answer might be "For the money, "It allows me time to study/read," "I love children," "It's easy," or "I dunno," but whatever it is, the answer will inform your intuition.

*Have you ever been in an emergency situation while baby-sitting? Have you ever been in any emergency situation?*

These questions can reveal the applicant's thought processes about emergencies. One parent I know asked this question of a baby-sitter candidate (a boy of eighteen) and was told the following story:

> I was watching these two eight-year-old twins and the lights suddenly went off. I thought maybe some burglar had cut the power so I got a big knife from the kitchen and then woke the kids and took them into the garage. I locked them inside the car and then ran home to get my brother's rifle. I lived just two blocks away so the kids weren't alone more than five minutes. They were safe when I got back, and I stayed in the garage with the rifle until their mom got home a couple of hours later. She was able to get the lights back on by doing something with the fuse box.

Imagine the experience for those terrified children, or for the mother who came home to a dark, empty house, searched in a panic, and then found her children inside the garage with the heavily armed baby-sitter.

### What is your opinion of drugs and alcohol?
Many parents look intently at applicants, hoping somehow to determine if they are drug or alcohol abusers. There's a greater likelihood of learning something valuable about the topic by discussing it explicitly.

### Describe a problem you had in your life where someone else's help was very important to you.
Is the applicant able to recall such a situation? If so, does he or she give credit or express appreciation about the help? This may seem a personal inquiry, but with a moment to think about it, most people can think of a situation they'll be comfortable sharing. Anyway, you are considering whether or not to make the most personal possible investment in this person: the investment of your trust. A friend of mine who was interviewing sitters for her nine-year-old daughter received this answer to the question:

> I was breaking up with this guy after two years. He lied and said there wasn't another woman. I had her name but I couldn't find her, so I started dating this other guy who I didn't like too much, since he was a private detective and I thought I could get him to help me find that woman. He eventually got me her phone number, which she promptly changed after I started calling her, so he got me her new number too. I'm not even going out with him anymore but he still helps me with stuff like that.

This was not the kind of life-ethic my friend wanted around her daughter.

*Who is your best friend and how would you describe
your friendship?*
While many people will name several friends, there are, believe it or
not, some who cannot think of a single person. Another benefit to the
question comes if an applicant gives a name that was not listed as a
reference (which happens often). Ask why the person wasn't listed;
ask if you can now have the contact number.

*Describe the best child you ever baby-sat for. Describe
the worst child you ever baby-sat for.*
This is a powerful inquiry that can reveal important attitudes about
children and behavior. If the applicant speaks for just a moment
about the best child, but can wax on enthusiastically about the worst,
this is telling. Does he or she use unkind expressions to explain the
trouble with a given child ("brat," "little monster")? Does the applicant take any responsibility for his or her part? A follow-up is: "Could
you have taken another approach?" Is the applicant capable of some
understanding about the child?

Consider asking applicants to give you examples of problems
they've encountered with children in the past and how they've handled them. You might ask how they'd react if they saw your child
fondling himself, or what they'd do if your child asked them to keep a
secret from you, or how they'd handle fights between siblings.

During your interview, few things are as powerful as silence. When
someone finishes an answer you consider incomplete, don't just accept it and go on. Instead, wait silently; he or she will start talking
again and give you more information to evaluate.

Some parents ask about medical conditions that could be relevant,
and some even ask baby-sitters to pass medical examinations or drug-
screen tests. Some require special skills, such as CPR. (Remember
that CPR for infants requires training beyond regular CPR.) Safe
Sitter is an excellent national program that offers an intensive two-day
course in the prevention and management of accidents. Founded by

Dr. Patricia Keener, Safe Sitter teaches baby-sitters (as young as eleven years old) about medical emergencies in addition to the basics of child care. Students must pass a rigorous written and practical exam. (Safe Sitter: 1-800-255-4089.)

Some people who live in predominantly English-speaking communities have concluded that baby-sitters for their kids need to be able to speak English. I agree, particularly if the sitter is going to be out in public with your kids. This is important because just as a child must be able to describe his or her peril, so must an adult caretaker. Understanding what people say is a key part of understanding their intent.

However you do it, the sitter should know some basic safety skills (that many people don't know), such as: Do not open the door to anybody. Do not fall for a con ("I'm here to give an estimate for the new roof"). Assure baby-sitters that you won't be angry if they don't admit a person you forgot to tell them about, even if you later wish they had.

I'm addressing solely those topics relevant to protecting children, but I know there are many other issues you'll need to communicate to a baby-sitter. Given how many there are, you don't want to rely upon memory as you run to the door (late) while the baby-sitter frantically takes notes, jiggles the crying baby, and tries to make friends with the barking dog. Parents who organize these issues in writing ahead of time benefit from knowing as they drive away that all the issues have been communicated.

Some parents ask applicants to provide copies of their driving record and credit report (both are easy to get). Stacy, who has two sons and a daughter, told me she always makes this request: "You'd be amazed how many applicants we've had cancel or just not call again simply because we asked them to bring these records. If they weren't willing to go through that small chore to help put us at ease, then they don't understand what we need for child care."

Some parents can afford to conduct full-scale background investigations of sitters before they hire them, but whatever you do, much as we require people who are sitting in the exit row of a passenger jet to be capable of certain tasks, it is reasonable for you to satisfy yourself about every aspect of a person's readiness to care for your child.

.    .    .

Once your preemployment questions have been answered, it would be helpful to ask the candidate if he or she has any questions for you. What a candidate asks will provide you further insight and may introduce topics that weren't discussed. An applicant might ask if your child has any special medical conditions, or if you have policies about what they watch on TV. While these and other things would probably be covered in your guidebook, the fact that the applicant asks is favorable. Conversely, if an applicant seeks permission to take an occasional drink from your bar, or asks to date your teenage daughter, better to learn about it now than later.

I suggest you tell the applicant you will call him or her after you've reviewed the application and spoken with the references. Hiring anyone at the time of the interview robs your intuition of the wisdom that comes from reflection. In any event, you need the time to contact references, because this is an absolute requirement.

References on a list are valuable only if all the information needed for you to contact them is provided. Consider it a small red flag when an applicant puts a name only, without full contact information. Similarly, don't let an applicant say, "Well, I don't know how to reach her now," or "He's moved, I think." If the person can't readily be contacted, then that name should not be using up space on an application.

One of the most valuable results you can get from interviewing references is gained by asking each this question: "Do you know anyone else I might speak with who also knows Sally?" If they give you a name and number, you have got what professional investigators call a "Developed Source," a person who knows the applicant but who was not briefed to expect your call. If the reference can't put you in touch with anyone else who knows the applicant, that indicates a reference who is not that close to the applicant. You can also ask references, "Did you know her when she worked at [some former employment listed on the application]?" This is a way of confirming information the applicant listed while also determining how well a given reference knows the applicant.

Having used the word *applicant* throughout this chapter and re-ferred several times to an application, it's probably clear that I suggest using one. Applications require candidates to commit to the accuracy of information they provide, and they make screening far easier for the parent.

The process of checking the accuracy of information on applica-tions and checking someone's references is easier with young ap-plicants because they have a shorter work background. By the same token, however, there is less history to help inform your hiring de-cision. The fourteen-year-old neighborhood girl isn't likely to have served time in prison for bank robbery, but she also isn't likely to have proven her reliability over several years. Young baby-sitters are popular, perhaps because we tend to fear them less (the teenage girl isn't going to be a depraved molester), but choosing a baby-sitter on the basis of few negatives often means settling for few positives.

This raises the question of how young is too young for a baby-sitter. I committed at the outset of this book to avoid judging parental deci-sions, so I am not expressing an opinion about what age is too young (or potentially just as important, too old). Many factors might be weighed in each case: Does the teenage baby-sitter have younger sib-lings (and, thus, some experience with children)? Have you known her or her family for a long time? Does she have strong family ties? Do you believe her to be a mature and responsible person? In decid-ing if a candidate is too young, parents must take into account what the baby-sitter might be called upon to handle: fire, intrusion, injury.

Most people wouldn't have a twelve-year-old house sitter, yet many have twelve-year-old baby-sitters.

Last year, a twelve-year-old boy in New York City was accused of killing a toddler in his care. The baby had been left by his parents in the care of the boy's mother, who'd been a close friend of the family for decades. She was there most of the day, but asked her son to watch the younger child when she went out for a while. Prosecutors alleged that as the baby was sitting on a tricycle, the boy repeatedly rammed it against a wall. After that, he put the toddler into bed, apparently thinking he was asleep, but the baby died of head injuries.

Instances of children dying while in the care of other children are not unique, but what makes this case remarkable is that the mother of the twelve-year-old was charged with endangering a child's welfare because she left the toddler in his care. Think about it: This mother was prosecuted for doing what thousands of parents do every day. Don't many leave their younger kids in the care of a twelve-year-old sibling? And the prosecutors weren't claiming the mother was negligent because of some special knowledge that her son was dangerous. To the contrary, the boy was widely perceived as a good, well-mannered kid, and the case against him didn't allege that the death was intentional.

If a mother can be prosecuted for leaving a baby in the care of her own twelve-year-old, what about parents who leave their child with somebody else's twelve-year-old? The New York case appears to be about rough horseplay that turned deadly, but it's also about a boy who didn't detect the medical emergency. We're asking a lot of some twelve-year-olds, it seems.

How a baby-sitter might handle a medical emergency is a bit off my topic, beyond this: If you doubt a sitter in that area, you certainly don't want to rely upon them to deal with an intruder or a con man. Young female baby-sitters may be the least likely to hurt your child, but at the same time, they may be the least able to protect your child. If the young baby-sitter is to be out in public with your child, she herself is a predatory prize and thus needs to be a capable self-protector. (See IM-PACT courses in Appendix #1.)

When hiring a teenage girl as a baby-sitter, parents must also consider whether she has a boyfriend, and if so, the nature of their relationship. Is he going to be calling and distracting her? Is he going to be coming over?

A father of six-year-old twin boys told me about phoning his home to check on the kids: "Instead of reaching the teenage girl who was supposed to be baby-sitting, I reached some girl I'd never met. It turns out our baby-sitter had [hold on for this one] hired a baby-sitter of her own because her boyfriend insisted she go out with him somewhere."

What about teenage boys as baby-sitters? This immediately raises the specter of sexual molestation and brings us to the complex topic of men versus women in child care. I call it a complex topic mostly because of the politics; otherwise, the facts are stunningly simple: Men are more likely than women to sexually abuse children.

Is this antimale on my part? No, it is antiillusion. If I were evaluating the history of engineering or architecture, men would come out way better than women, but I am talking about violence, where they don't. Many of the advancements in gender roles over recent decades fall under the heading of feminism, which I believe is a key part of our evolution as a species. While men may have made adjustments to accommodate this evolution (or revolution), the changes have been cultural, not anthropological. Men are ruled by male biology.

Given that we all know this, men are doubtless subject to discrimination in child-care professions. Most parents are more comfortable with women in these roles. Those who disagree may cite horror stories of female baby-sitters accused of harming or killing children, but no anecdotes will change the answer to this question: If you have two candidates who are in all other ways identically qualified, but one is a man and one is a woman, who do you hire as a baby-sitter?

Most parents would choose the female candidate and most of the time, I think they'd be right to do so, if for no other reason than the need to satisfy their own comfort level.

I am not suggesting you avoid hiring some particular male baby-sitter or nanny—that's your call. There are many men in child care who contribute enormously to the welfare of children. On a personal note, one of the most favorably influential people in my life was a male teacher with whom I frequently spent time alone when I was ten. Mr. Conway gave me an alternative design for self-image, not just the one I'd logically deduce from the violence and chaos at my home (*If this is how I am treated, then this must be the treatment I deserve*). He is doubtless one of the reasons I am able to write this book as opposed to being a sad story in someone else's book. But even with that in my heart, I believe when it comes to child care that male applicants require more scrutiny than women, perhaps much more. And if hired, they require more supervision.

Some people have vocally opposed homosexual men working as teachers or in child care, but statistics indicate they are far less likely to sexually abuse children than are heterosexual men. Whatever one's gender or sexual orientation, however, the challenge for parents is to ask enough, explore enough, evaluate enough so that you feel comfortable with the person you choose.

●    ●    ●

Just as gender alone doesn't offer assurances of anything, neither do references or fancy agencies. When Loren and Clark needed a nanny for their seventeen-month-old son Donovan, they found her through a Beverly Hills agency. Those words—Beverly Hills agency—sound reassuring, but they meant a lot less than Loren's gut feeling that something wasn't right. After they'd hired the nanny, important information started coming from an unexpected source: the baby Donovan, who communicated in the best way he could.

The toddler started acting in ways he never had, for example, intentionally banging his head against the floor. When Loren called the doctor about this, a nurse assured her that it was normal—but Loren later said, "I just knew it wasn't normal for my son, though I was lulled into a sense that it must be okay."

Donovan next contracted diarrhea that didn't go away despite changes in his diet. Finally, the boy stopped talking. Loren knew the nanny was the problem, but since she couldn't say how she knew, it wasn't good enough. After a month of disloyalty to her own intuition, Loren decided to have a concealed video camera installed in her home.

The videotape clearly proves what intuition had already established. The nanny can be seen dragging Donovan through the living room, hitting him on the head with her shoe, forcing him to stand in one place for hours at a time. The tape shows Donovan sitting silently beside the nanny. Periodically, with no apparent connection to anything, she hits him on the head.

Loren is brave enough to acknowledge: "Had I followed my intuition, I could have spared my son the worst month of his life."

This story may seem like quite an endorsement for having a hidden camera in the home. It isn't.

Parents who place a camera in the home because they actually *expect* to catch the baby-sitter or nanny abusing their child are conducting an awfully high-stakes experiment with their own baby. Imagine you obtain a tape of your child being abused. Do you think he will someday thank you? "Sure I wish you'd just prevented the abuse, but at least we've got that tape."

If you are suspicious enough to install a hidden camera system, get rid of the baby-sitter. The proverbial nanny-cam could be sold at a chain of stores called Procrastinators R Us, because according to a survey by *Child* magazine, if you install one, you're going to change sitters anyway. Why not just do it now?

Let's go a little deeper. Suppose you suspect abuse by your baby-sitter and you place a hidden camera in the kitchen. You review the videotape and to your great relief, there's no abuse. What have you learned, really? Only that there was no abuse at that time in front of that camera. Are you suddenly over your feelings of suspicion about the baby-sitter? What about every other room? What about every other day?

Most parents who've decided to install a hidden camera already wanted to fire the baby-sitter or nanny but didn't have the courage to do it without proof—as if the fact that they felt uncomfortable about their child's welfare wasn't grounds enough.

Other parents have a whole different story. They *don't* want to fire the sitter—they want their suspicions to be disproved, to just go away. Lo and behold, the tape shows no abuse and they get to say, "Weren't we silly to be so untrusting?" And everything's back to normal, and this is how a hidden camera can actually reduce the safety of a child.

I don't oppose all uses of hidden cameras. If parents want to video-tape a baby-sitter or nanny in order to observe the quality of care or to be sure that instructions are being followed, that's a fair goal. A video can confirm what appears on the tape; it can prove what occurs in its view, *but it cannot disprove anything*.

Many parents delay changing baby-sitters because they feel it would be hard on their children. Here is where Anna McDonnell can help. She designed the Parenting Packs Web site that includes innovative ways for parents to help their children through common but often difficult life experiences. Such events can be an opportunity for a child to learn from life's greatest teacher: change. The Web site offers guidance on helping children through the death of a pet, the arrival of a new sibling, a move to a new home, a trip to the hospital, separation of parents, a change in child care, parents going away on trips, and so on. McDonnell designed kits used to help hundreds of military families through relocation. Each kit contains postcards kids can give their friends, a child's calendar that shows how life goes on before, during, and after a move, pictures that have been drawn by other kids expressing what they felt through the same experience, and all the material needed to put together a "Moving Book" that helps the child express and understand his or her experience. (The Parenting Packs Web site can be seen at *www.parentingpacks.com*.)

McDonnell says:

> You don't have to read a 200-page book on every problem and you don't need a Ph.D. You do need to know your own child. With the right intentions, information, tools, and a little time, we can all do an expert job of helping our children learn how to adapt to change and transitions.

However difficult a change in child care may be for you or your child, it will be easier than living with your suspicion—and far easier than living with guilt if there is abuse that could have been prevented.

Loren's experience also raises the issue of seeing how your child (or even infant) reacts to a prospective baby-sitter before making the hiring decision. This practice is touted in several parenting books, but I'd like to add a caveat: Yes, it can be meaningful if your child has a terrible reaction to a particular person, but if the child has a good reaction, that fact is absolutely irrelevant to safety. Remember that many predators are exceptionally good at gaining trust and putting children at ease. Accordingly, *your* intuition—which is informed—is far more significant than your child's. "But Bobby really liked that sitter" will not be a viable excuse for hiring the wrong person.

There is a postscript to Loren's story. She turned the tape over to the police and Donovan's abuser was eventually tried and convicted. The most remarkable thing in court wasn't the alarming video; it was the testimony of another mother who'd used that nanny in the past. Even having seen the video, this witness said she would still be glad to have the defendant care for her kids in the future. Denial is not just a river in Africa.

. . .

Having presented a case of an abusive nanny who is a woman, there is one involving a man that also teaches important lessons.

The socioeconomic opposite of finding a sitter through a Beverly Hills agency is, I suppose, finding your sitter at McDonald's, or more accurately, having just left his job at McDonald's. That's where Kathy and Michael Parker found Robert Gordon.

The Parkers allowed the twenty-four-year-old Gordon, whom Kathy had worked with at McDonald's, to move in with them. In return, he baby-sat their two kids, Michael, Jr., four, and Nicole, eight. Gordon had a son of his own, but he wasn't allowed to see him. Imagine you were to ask a prospective sitter if he has children, and he replied, "Yes, I have a son, but his mother won't let me see him." I don't know if Mrs. Parker ever learned this, but Gordon's ex-girlfriend must have had some reason for keeping Gordon out of her son's life.

Whatever her reason, she was proven right—horribly right—the last time the Parkers left Gordon to care for their kids. Returning from church bingo, Mrs. Parker found both of her children shot in the head. Their mouths and legs were bound with duct tape. The Parkers' eight-year-old daughter survived but their son died before reaching the hospital.

Robert Gordon was also found dead, having self-administered justice with a shot to the temple. Earlier that evening, he had gone to the home of his own son, but was unable to see the boy or his mother. If he had seen them, it likely would have been a very dangerous visit.

One might call my choice of stories unfair because the female nanny I discussed merely abused a child while the man committed murder. Of course, there are women who do the same—sometimes even mothers—but I recounted the story of Robert Gordon for a few reasons. First, men are far more likely to have guns than are women, and they are far more likely to use them destructively. Second, young men and teenage boys are twelve times more likely to murder than are young women or teenage girls. Finally, if a prospective baby-sitter is prohibited from seeing his son, or is in some dramatic relationship turmoil, that's reason for concern all by itself.

Yes, there are plenty of divorces where access to a child is withheld in order to punish an estranged spouse, but often parents in these disputes make tough decisions in order to protect their children. Parenting itself could be described as a succession of tough decisions, and I'll close this chapter with the story of a couple that made a good one.

· · ·

In the summer, Ally and Bill both worked long hours to meet the obligations of their sporting goods business. Their success would have been impossible without Marta, the only person they had ever trusted to watch four-year-old Callie. Marta fled Cuba with her two tiny children in 1988, leaving behind an abusive husband who beat her whenever he got drunk, which she said was often. Trouble seemed to follow her, though, her second husband, whom she was trying to get away from, sounded almost as bad.

Though Bill always said don't get involved, Ally encouraged Marta to talk about whatever drama was going on at home. One example sounded particularly unjust: When Marta's ten-year-old son, John, got a fairly serious head injury falling off a skateboard, it became part of her husband's campaign against her. He filed a report saying Marta had caused the injury. Driving to work one morning, Ally discussed it with Bill: "For God's sake, this woman is a hero who gave up everything she had for her kids, and now she's being accused of beating them. It's not possible, is it?" This type of question isn't really seeking information but rather reassurance. Thankfully Bill was unwilling to deliver. "Of course it's possible, Ally. We don't have any idea how she treats her kids."

"Well, I won't believe it," Ally decided, driving right past one of the clearest signals of denial: refusal. Bill got them back on course. "I'm not saying I don't trust Marta, but she's alone with Callie a lot and we should watch this closely."

A few days later, Marta showed up for work crying. Her pride made it almost impossible for her to explain what had happened: "I've never been in trouble in my life, and now they've taken my children away." What's more, the Child Protection Agency was insisting that she—and not her husband—attend classes in anger management. When Bill heard about this, he said Marta had to leave—at least until the matter was resolved favorably. Ally began to float the idea that just because someone's been violent toward her own kids doesn't mean she'd be violent with Callie, but Bill cut her off. "That's not an experiment I'm willing to do with Callie."

Ally wasn't ready to let go of her image of the woman she'd come to care for deeply: "What if we install a video camera in the house and then—" but she stopped herself when she saw the look on Bill's face. Though it was a tough decision for Ally, they said a tearful goodbye to Marta that very afternoon.

Bill didn't go to work for the three full days he spent finding and screening a day-care service they liked. The process made Ally miss Marta even more, and the first morning she dropped Callie off at day care, she resolved to do the thing Bill advised her against: get involved. She spent her lunch break on the phone with an assortment of bureaucrats trying to get someone who knew about Marta's situation. She intended to explain that Marta was the victim of an angry husband's vendetta.

Ally finally reached the right person but what the case agent said stopped her cold. "I assume you were referred to me by Marta's probation officer." *Probation officer?* "Would you be willing to speak with the prosecutor?" *Prosecutor?* "People are reluctant to get involved, I know, but it would really help, particularly if you've got information on the injuries." *The injuries?*

Though the case agent was unwilling to disclose Marta's history, it was clear this wasn't the first time she'd been investigated for child abuse. In the current instance, Marta's son John had gone to the hospital with a fractured skull, an injury he first said was an accident, but later admitted had been inflicted by his mother's hitting him with a large soda bottle. The young boy assured the nurses he'd be fine: "The bottle didn't even break and I have a strong head."

The tough decision Bill and Ally made would have been made for them in another month anyway, when Marta was arrested for felony child abuse. She pled guilty to the lesser charge of child endangerment, and was sentenced to one year in prison. It was the second conviction for the proud woman who said she'd never been in trouble.

Callie loved going to day care, and Bill and Ally came to trust and respect the people who ran the service. They were glad they'd put so much effort into checking the place out, because it gave them greater confidence. Of course, that's not the experience of all parents.

# CHAPTER EIGHT

# CHILDREN AWAY FROM HOME

*Fifty percent of working parents of young children are having to leave their children in care you or I wouldn't trust—nor do they.*

— DR. T. BERRY BRAZELTON

"A *world of butterflies and blueberry skies*"—that's how the planned community of Country Walk, Florida, was described in its promotional material. Tranquil neighborhoods need tranquil day-care centers, and the one you'd find advertised in the Country Walk newspaper was run by Frank and Ileana Fuster out of their neat three-bedroom home. They had gained a lot of confidence among the parents whose children went there, including two Miami police officers.

Before deciding to use the service for his three-year-old daughter, Lt. Vince Landis spent nearly an hour talking to Frank and Ileana. He was impressed with how well organized things were. He noted that the Fusters gave him health cards to take to his daughter's doctor before she would be accepted and that they told him they were licensed by HRS (Florida's Department of Health and Rehabilitative Services). All in all, Lt. Landis came away feeling everything was in order, describing Frank and Ileana Fuster as "very well-mannered people."

True, Ileana was very young, only eighteen, but that doesn't necessarily mean she wasn't capable. The parents probably didn't know that Frank had once been ordered by a judge to have a year of psychiatric counseling, but that certainly doesn't disqualify someone from looking after children. He'd once killed a man in a traffic dispute, but that on its own doesn't mean he shouldn't have been running a day-care center. Frank had also been convicted of fondling a nine-year-old girl while she sat in the driver's seat of his van, and that *does* mean he shouldn't have been running a day-care center.

Given all this, how in the world did the Fusters ever obtain a license to provide child care? The easy way: They didn't. They just said they did.

Frank's conviction for child abuse required monthly visits to his home by a probation officer, but apparently the probation department failed to recognize that Frank and his wife were running a day-care center.

The service so many parents raved about might still have been in business today but for the young boy who came home from day care and asked his mother, "Would you kiss my pee-pee?" He advised his mother that Ileana Fuster had done that. It later emerged that children had also seen the Fusters having sex and had been terrorized by Frank, who donned frightening masks and threatened to kill the children's parents if their behavior was ever revealed. Were it not for the willingness of one mother to believe the unwelcome truth offered by her child, we wouldn't be exploring this—rather, the children would still be living it. Thus, this is partially a success story and partially a horror story.

In the end, Ileana claimed she was forced by her husband to

participate in the abuse, and testified against him on all counts. He was found guilty of fourteen child-abuse offenses, including performing oral sex on toddlers and killing animals to scare the children. Since Frank Fuster has now been sentenced to six consecutive life terms in prison, his part of the story is over, but I didn't present all this for insight into him. Rather, the events at Country Walk provide insight into the parents.

Amazingly, not one had ever asked to see Country Walk's license or tried to confirm the license existed. And many of the parents had denied their intuition, later reporting, for example, that they never saw any toys at the day-care facility and that the Fusters always took a long time to answer the door.

•   •   •

Stories of abusive child-care workers go right to the heart of a conflict most parents wrestle with. Should they personally care for their children all the time? Are they wrong to have their kids in the care of others? Parents are substantially divided on this, one father explaining to me: "We live in a curious era where lifestyle and parenting decisions are almost as difficult to discuss as religion. Unless you like arguments at social events, it's usually best to stay away from this topic entirely."

The comparison to religion is not far off, for people religiously defend their positions about raising children. Some believe that children should be raised solely by parents; others believe both parents should work. A father named Glenn finds his answer in the stark reality of the animal world:

> A doe will not leave her fawn with other deer, and a monkey doesn't send its young offspring into the rain forest with words of caution. Even the keenly honed instincts of a wild animal can-

not protect that animal if it isn't physically developed, and it certainly can't protect itself against larger members of its own species. Violence occurs against the weak because they are vulnerable. All we can do is physically protect our children and never let them out of our sight. What works in nature will work for us parents.

Glenn doesn't believe in relying on rules, explaining that even if his five-year-old could be taught to reliably follow them, it wouldn't help with "gradual danger," danger that builds as children develop trust in people they know. Only parents staying with their children, he believes, can ensure safety.

An opposite view comes from Michael Gurian, author of *The Wonder of Boys*. Quoting a parent who says "God didn't give me kids to let other people raise them," Gurian notes that whether it springs from religious beliefs, traditional beliefs, or fear, most people hold a variation of this opinion. Thus, most parents have strong feelings of guilt when they rely on others to care for their kids. Gurian wants to discourage that guilt, for not only does he see nothing wrong with having others care for your children, he feels if done wisely, it's a benefit in their lives: "When parents and day-care providers work together to form a relationship among themselves, they create a community spirit in which their children feel like they are moving between first and second families in a blend of loving attention."

Strictly from a safety point of view, Glenn may be right, but even the best parents (including Glenn and his wife) don't raise children "strictly from a safety point of view." Parents are not merely guards, they are caregivers who must weigh many issues every day—safety is but one of them.

While I understand Glenn's point, he isn't entirely right about the animal world, as parents in several species give over care of their young to others. The tiny African meerkat regularly leaves its offspring in the care of "aunties." If a predatory bird soars overhead, an auntie will throw herself over her young charge. Elephants, too, choose competent aunties from the herd. The European cuckoo goes the farthest: She literally places her eggs in the nest of another bird and lets that bird hatch and care for the offspring.

Glenn also isn't entirely right when he says what works for animals in nature will work for us, because in fact, it doesn't work all that well for animals. Almost every species on earth loses more young offspring than we do, so we're already the most successful protectors on earth.

Glenn is, however, absolutely right that there is much to learn from a comparison to the animal world, particularly if we want a strong foundation for assessing child care.

Among all creatures, human beings parent offspring the longest. In fact, some species don't actually parent at all; they give birth and then abandon. Some are even as likely to eat their young as to protect them. In species where care is not practiced, nature's answer is overproduction: thousands of eggs out of which only a few will survive. But humans have gone the opposite route: Usually we have one child at a time, and that one gets extraordinary care (compared to most animals). In A *Natural History of Parenting*, Susan Allport says, "Our species has truly traded quantity for quality. This has been our reproductive bargain, our way of ensuring that our young survive."

Given how long it takes to raise a child, few human beings at any time in history did it all on their own. Mostly, they got help from family members, but that's changed in modern America. For most of our history, parents and children worked together on the farm to support themselves, so child care was not an issue. In the forties, fathers left the farm for industrial jobs. Then, with the advent of child-labor laws and compulsory education, kids went to school and mothers were freed up to work.

By the fifties, both parents were following the good jobs; that meant moving away from grandmothers and aunts. It proved to be a popular trend, for today, children in our country raised solely by family are in the minority. Between 1940 and 1989, the percentage of children under six who needed alternative child care rose from 8 percent to more than 50 percent. So though the question of whether parents should do it alone is moot, that doesn't stop millions of parents from agonizing over it. Even when couples leave their children with relatives they still experience parental anxiety, though not what Gurian describes as "the gut-wrenching fear we feel when we give our kids over to the care of strangers." Glenn's approach certainly helps with that, because parents worry less when they personally care for their children.

I've provided this bit of human history to help lessen the guilt of parents who do the most natural thing in the world: seek help with raising their children. At the same time, I want to discourage parents from doing the most unnatural thing in the world: leaving their children with strangers. This applies to professional day care, family members with whom we leave our kids, and families where we allow sleepovers and play-dates.

My friend Paul is the father of three kids; the oldest is sixteen-year-old Erin. Not long ago, when she wanted to sleep over at the home of her friend Lisa, Paul asked if there'd be an adult there. Erin chose to answer with the three words most popular to American teens: "I don't know."

PAUL: Well, we'll have to find out. I'll call Lisa's father.

ERIN: Come on, Dad, that's so embarrassing. Anyway, I know Lisa's brother will be home because he's having a party that night. And he's seventeen, so it'll be fine.

PAUL: If that's supposed to make me feel better about the sleep-over, it doesn't.

ERIN: But don't you think with a party and everything, at least one of her parents will be there?

Paul took this perfect opportunity to use those familiar three words, "I don't know," and he called and left a message for Lisa's father.

On Thursday, the night before the hoped-for sleepover, Lisa's father called back and answered the question: "We're in New York seeing some plays; we'll be back in Los Angeles on Monday."

"Oh," Paul asked, "so you won't be here for the party on Friday."

"What party?"

That question told Paul all he needed to know; Erin would not be sleeping over. "My daughter said your son is having a party on Friday night."

Lisa's father couldn't have responded more casually: "Well, I'm sure it'll be fine and they'll have fun."

"Will there be an adult there?"

"Nope, but you know the kind of party a seventeen-year-old has; they wouldn't want us around. Look, he won't be doing anything you and I didn't do at his age."

That wasn't reassuring for Paul. "Brad, we're talking about my daughter."

"Okay, okay, don't worry. I'll call my boy and tell him no party, okay? Listen, we've got to be at *Cats* in a half-hour so I gotta go."

Erin was disappointed to spend Friday night at home, a fact she worked into conversation each time she could, like when Paul called into her room to get her to turn down the music: "If you had let me sleep over at Lisa's, I wouldn't be here and you wouldn't be bothered by the music."

To give the issue a full airing and to quiet his daughter's complaints, Paul offered to drive by Lisa's house and see if there was a party after all. "I'm sure there's no party, Dad, but just in case, don't stop in front of the house. I don't want anyone to see us. Just drive right by." That turned out to be impossible because there were so many cars and teenagers jamming the street. "Hey Erin," a drunken boy called out, waving a beer bottle. "You missed the best part. The cops were just here; it was cool." Paul snaked the car through various groups of teenage boys acting as they might in a father's nightmare. The scene was bad enough that even Erin appreciated Paul's decision to prohibit the sleepover.

Before allowing a sleepover, most parents want to learn something about the home their child will be staying at. My friends Jackie and Michael, the parents of three, have an excellent system for when their nine-year-old son asks to sleep over at a friend's: "Before you can get permission to sleep over at a friend's house, that friend must sleep over here." This method allows them to acquire some information about the other child and his family, mostly through observation and a bit through casual conversation. If you learn that the child has teen siblings, for example, you'll want to be sure the parents don't go out and leave teenagers to look after the kids.

Perhaps the most telling thing Jackie and Michael learn is the extent to which the other family is cautious about the sleepover. Do they call and ask questions about whether adults will be home during the sleepover? Do they call to give contact information? Do they ask to come over and see the house and meet you? Does a parent even call to introduce him or herself? Many don't. Such a low degree of parental participation in the decision leaves the least qualified participant—the child—to decide where he spends the night. Your son may have chosen to sleep over at his friend Matt's house because Matt's parents are never home, or because Matt does stuff you'd never allow.

Before allowing their son to sleep over at someone's house, Jackie and Michael make contact with one of the parents. Jackie usually asks, "Would you like me to stop by and introduce myself?" If the other parent says Yes, she'll be able to observe several things at the house. She can be certain there are smoke detectors, ascertain that there are no vicious dogs, and she can see how the parents interact with their children and other family members. Jackie asks what the family expects to be doing the evening of the sleepover. Jackie always asks if the other family has a gun, and if so, she needs to be satisfied that it is kept locked. One father told her, "We don't keep it locked, but no need to worry, our son [ten years old] knows all about how to handle a gun." That wasn't much reassurance for Jackie, who didn't allow the sleepover. She explained that her son is not familiar enough with guns for her to be comfortable.

Jackie and Michael have an agreement with their children: If you are ever at all uncomfortable, or you just want to talk, you can call home at any time. You don't even have to ask permission to use the phone if you don't want to; you can just call home.

On picking up a child after a sleepover, a parent typically asks, "Did he behave?" This acknowledges that misbehavior is a possibility, so it's worth establishing a policy with the other parent for what you want done in that event. Jackie says, "If you feel my son is misbehaving, please do not handle any discipline yourself; just call me, no matter how late."

I suggest talking to your kids as soon after a sleepover as possible. Ask how it was, what your child did, who was home, and so on. What you are told about your child's experience during a sleepover—combined with what you intuit—will make the decision easier the next time he or she wants to spend the night with that family.

A family you might allow your child to stay with overnight requires at least as much scrutiny as you'd apply to a baby-sitter, though the strategies for gaining information are clearly different. Given how much you would ideally know before approving a sleepover, it's clear that knowing the other family well is the best course. This may reduce the number of homes you allow your kids to sleep over at, but given the stakes, that's okay.

All the people we entrust with our child's safety and well-being must cease being strangers—but how? The same way others become people we select for inclusion in our lives: We learn enough about them, they pass several of our tests, they lose their anonymity, and we discover an acceptable degree of shared values. The price of real peace of mind is not just comfort with whom we've selected, but also with how we've selected them. Every parent who has ever worried knows that real peace of mind is a bargain at that price.

·    ·    ·

Recall the story of Frank Fuster and the Country Walk Daycare Center. Much like kidnapping by strangers, abusive day-care workers are rare, and parents can make them even more rare if they insist on—and confirm—the highest standard of service. That didn't happen with Country Walk. For example, not one parent whose children attended sought to confirm that the place had a license. It's likely most parents fail on this point, either assuming some other parent must have done it or assuming a business would be caught by the authorities if operating without a license. So that you are not one of those parents, I suggest that confirming licensing be the first step when you are screening a day-care service. (For more information, you can call Child Care Aware, which is sponsored by Cheerios. They're able to provide the phone number of an agency that can explain licensing in your area: 800-424-2246.)

Once you've confirmed licensing, the screening and evaluation of a day-care facility is mostly an assessment of how the owners screen and evaluate their employees. For you to be satisfied, they must have an effective process, and one that can be demonstrated. You won't accept merely, "We're very strict in our hiring."

You'll want answers to several questions: Is an outside investigator used for background checks? Is there a written report in each personnel file? Is every reference successfully contacted? If not, are others requested? Is every former employer contacted? Is the information on each application verified? Is a criminal-background investigation conducted? What in someone's history will disqualify a candidate? What problems in someone's history will you tolerate?

If the center has any volunteer workers, ask how they are screened. A federal study of thousands of youth-serving organizations found that nearly 90 percent elected not to conduct any type of criminal-records check on volunteers. Almost half didn't even check the references of volunteers. When you ask why they screen volunteers less effectively than regular employees, they might explain, "Volunteers are always supervised; they're never alone with kids, so we have less concern." To which you can say: "Volunteers elected to work for free in an environment where there are young children, so I have *more* concern."

### Is each person checked against the list of registered sex offenders (in states where this is available)?

Not even 10 percent of day-care facilities will be able to say Yes. Actually, 100 percent will be able to *say* Yes, but fewer than 10 percent will be able to demonstrate that they really do it.

### Do you ask applicants to bring in a copy of their driving record?

In most states, it is very simple and inexpensive for anyone to obtain his or her own driving record. A day-care facility can review it for indicators such as citations for reckless driving, drunk driving, failures to appear in court, etc.

### Do you obtain fingerprint-based background information on all employees and volunteers?

Any business that provides care, treatment, education, supervision, or recreation to children can obtain fingerprint-based national criminal-history background checks of their employees and volunteers. Many organizations don't know they are covered under the recent Volunteers for Children Act and the National Child Protection Act of 1993 (also known as the Oprah Winfrey Act because of Winfrey's effective advocacy and senate testimony).

### Are you familiar with and do you apply the U.S. Department of Justice Guidelines for the Screening of Persons Working with Children?

This project was undertaken to provide a model for screening employees who work in settings with vulnerable people, most notably young children. Thus, the question will be relevant several times in your child's life: schools, community recreation programs, camps, and organizations such as the YMCA, Boy Scouts of America, Girl Scouts USA, Big Brothers, Big Sisters, etc.

The guidelines advise that wherever employees might be alone with young children for substantial periods of time, work without direct supervision, have frequent contact with children, or might be with children at remote or nonpublic areas (classroom, camp, bus, etc.), then "supplemental screening practices" are appropriate. These might include criminal-records checks, drug testing, driving history, and so on.

If a day-care service you are using or considering hasn't heard of the guidelines report, you can inform them (and impress them) with this knowledge: It is available through the Office of Juvenile Justice and Delinquency Programs at the U.S. Department of Justice; published April 1998; project director Noy S. Davis, Esq. Ask that the day-care service get back to you after they've reviewed it with an answer to your initial question: Do they apply the guidelines?

### Have you ever suspected that one of the kids in your care was the victim of child abuse at home?

As with baby-sitters or nannies, this question puts the topic on the agenda and helps you be certain that you aren't leaving your child with a denier. If they ever suspected that a child was abused, ask why. If they *never* suspected that a child was abused, ask why not.

These questions lead to: May I see a copy of your policy book? Some smaller facilities might not have one, but your question may encourage them to change that. The process of developing and documenting policies requires a facility to consider the many issues you would want them to consider, and you'll be helping them if your question gets them to develop written policies.

*Do you inform parents if an employee here is suspected of sexual or other abuse? (And by the way, I want to be informed.) What are the laws that govern your actions insofar as notification when you become aware of abuse or suspect abuse?*
The laws are of some interest, but more important is that the child-care professional be familiar with them. Do you feel these laws are effective? Their opinion is not so important, but you want them to have one.

The answers to all these questions will either enhance your confidence or lessen it, and like everything you observe and intuit, it's all part of your selection process. For example, when you request a photocopy of a facility's license, fast compliance will reassure— hesitation will not.

After you've made your selection, I suggest seeking contact and open communication with all the other parents whose children attend the day-care facility. It can be done with a letter:

Dear Parent:
My name is Holly Jason. Like you, my husband Ryan and I have selected the Building Blocks Daycare Center for our daughter Kate, and I asked them to deliver this letter to you.
I'm writing to introduce myself and suggest that we parents whose children attend day care together will benefit from the

ability to easily reach each other should any of us ever find that necessary. I've provided our phone number and email address below, and if you share your contact information with us, we'll retain it. Then, if any of us ever wants to reach other parents, it'll be easy.

We look forward to meeting you sometime.

Sincerely,
Holly Jason

When you ask the administrator of the day-care facility to distribute your letter to the other parents, agreement will reassure—refusal will not.

One of the most important things you can do is visit the facility often. Aside from improving your relationship with the people there, what you perceive will update and inform your intuition. Sometimes opinions are formed instantly on the basis of just one thing; other times they are cumulative. The more often you observe the people and the place, the more valid your opinion will be.

On this point there's a use for cameras that I fully endorse. More than a hundred child-care facilities nationwide now have Internet-wired camera systems that allow parents to "look in" at any time. While it's no substitute for an actual visit, it does add a lot more than would otherwise be available. At Kids 'R' Kids in Marietta, Georgia, for example, parents pay $10 a month to be able to view password-protected images from sixteen cameras. Aside from gaining peace of mind and a greater feeling of connection to their kids' experience, parents can share the password with friends and family who rarely get a chance to visit. Employees at such facilities know that they can be viewed at any time, meaning the children are not the only witnesses to what goes on.

All the clients of a day-care facility can join together in asking for installation of such a system. The parents may even choose to share in the cost of the installation. If so, it gets very hard for a day-care business to say No.

.    .    .

Clearly, a society where most parents are working needs government to provide preschool in addition to regular school. About 400 public schools in 13 states have implemented day-care services caring for three- and four-year-olds within the existing educational system. Most public schools use their buildings for only part of the day, nine months a year, but those known as 21st Century Schools (or 21C for short), operate from 6:00 A.M. to 6:00 P.M., some even until 10:00 P.M. According to one study, many of the 21C schools are able to operate profitably on the basis of the school district's support and small parental fees for the child-care services.

It's obvious that we need inexpensive and safe care for young Americans; this was clear to Congress nearly thirty years ago when it passed the Child Development Act of 1971. This act would have created a national network of child-care centers with parent fees set according to income. Here's why I say *would have*: Though busy with the Watergate scandal and the impending loss of his job, President Nixon somehow found time to veto the Child Development Act.

While we're waiting for Congress to get back to this issue, there is one approach that addresses more of the safety concerns surrounding child care for working parents than any other: It is employer-sponsored day care. There are so many reasons this is ideal, but the one most relevant to safety is that parents are nearby (at work) and able to drop in at any time. Further, child-care services at work have something typical services do not: All the parents know each other and can easily communicate. This brings a collective look at the quality of personnel and procedures.

One parent observing something disconcerting might rationalize: "Well sure, day-care workers will get impatient from time to time. You have to expect them to treat a child with less than ideal restraint at some point." But a group of parents seeing the same thing is more likely to say: "These are professionals, paid to be at their best. A parent might get impatient in a 24-hour day, but we must hold day-care workers to an even higher standard. Their patience is part of what they sell."

With all the parents knowing each other, there is less chance for secrets, less opportunity for child-care workers to conceal a pattern or to hush a complaint.

For the purposes of arming you to encourage your employer in this direction, here are a few points:

- The National Conference of State Legislatures has found that the overwhelming majority of employers who provide child-care programs enjoy a measurable increase in productivity, morale and loyalty, and a decrease in absenteeism, turnover, and tardiness.
- A *Fortune* magazine survey reported that the need to care for children might account for *more than half* of all absences from work. In other words, a sick day is most often a "my-kid-is-sick" day.
- Researchers estimate that businesses lose nearly $3 billion a year due to child-care-related absences.

Employee turnover is dramatically reduced for firms that provide child care. For example, Neuville Industries, a North Carolina firm, opened a day-care center for thirty-nine children. During the first two years, the job turnover rate for Neuville was 5 to 8 percent, compared with 50 to 100 percent for the rest of their industry.

Many firms end up with child-care programs so successful that they sell services to others in the community, as does Northridge Hospital in Northridge, California, where about half of the customers work at the hospital and about half do not. Parents are welcome to join their children for lunch, and to observe or participate in activities. The program at Northridge aims to make their child-care center "a new neighborhood where family friendships and support systems can develop to the benefit of not just the children but their families as well."

Even small firms can get these benefits: One with seven employees had four of them expecting babies around the same time. Since they all planned to continue working after giving birth, the company hired a nanny and converted some office space for the children.

I know of three friends, all working, who became pregnant around the same time. They made a pact that one of them would leave her job and take a new job, that of looking after all three kids during the workweek. The other two mothers pay her salary. That's not so far from the method of those species that choose aunties to look after offspring.

●    ●    ●

If you go with traditional day care, and this assumes that you'll have found one you are comfortable with, I suggest you document your wishes and expectations in a letter. In our outrageously litigious society, few things stimulate action like a letter.

Ms. Cindy Ames
Director
Building Blocks Daycare Center

Dear Cindy:
Thanks for the time and energy you provided during our recent meetings. Our family is happy to have selected Building Blocks

to care for our daughter, Kate, and we welcome your role as an important part of her life.

We're writing to set forth a few of our expectations, as well as our commitments to you.

We'll expect that Kate will be allowed to contact us at any time she wishes to. By the same token, we'll always keep you informed of how to reach us, and we encourage you to call anytime you wish.

We recognize that different families have different levels of interest in the goings-on at day care. Our interest is very high, and we're relying upon you to keep us informed of anything that might be relevant to Kate's safety or well-being. For example, we're relying upon you to inform us if you ever have reason to suspect that Kate or any of her peers have suffered sexual or other abuse.

We recognize that you may feel bound to confidentiality in some matters, so we'll welcome even partial information if that's all you feel you can share. Kate's doctor, William Smith, is also available to talk to you at any time (555-5555).

Your intuition about Kate's health and well-being is of interest to us even if you can't cite specific evidence in a given situation. By the same token, we commit to share our intuitions with you.

We are relying upon you to screen and supervise your employees effectively, and to follow all available "supplemental screening practices" set forth in the DOJ Guidelines for the Screening of Persons Working with Children. We'll expect to be advised if you ever have reason to suspect (or learn that others suspect) one of your employees is or has been involved in behavior that could be detrimental to Kate or any of the children. We commit to treat any such information in a calm and mature manner.

We recognize that some parents may have unreasonable expectations of a day-care facility, but we expect only that you meet the standards of your profession. Just as we hold you to your duties, we ask that you hold us to our duties as parents. We are willing to do our part, and as you do yours, we're sure the confidence we've invested in you will be re-earned for many years to come.

[Specific issues they need to know about, such as custody, who will pick up child, medical conditions, special situations, etc. End text as appropriate.]

> Sincerely,
> Holly and Ryan Jason

Steve, the father of a three-year-old girl, told me he and his wife would be reluctant to send such a letter to the prestigious preschool that had just accepted their daughter. After the difficulty of getting her in there, he didn't want to rock the boat. He recounted the story of a group of parents who asked that a back gate be kept locked during the day. The preschool responded by saying to the mother who spoke for the group: "Maybe we're not a good match for your family."

Steve said to me, "I don't want to send that letter and then have them say they're not a good match for our family."

"You mean, not a good match for parents who express opinions about the safety of their children?" I asked him. "It seems to me if that's the case, it would be better to learn it now than to learn it later. You chose this place, which means you believe in the people who run it, so why not give them the credit of expecting them to react professionally?"

Steve decided to send the letter. A few days later, the director of the preschool called him at work. When she began by saying, "In fifteen years, I've never received a letter like yours," Steve braced for the worst. She continued: "I wish all parents were as clear and as willing to discuss sensitive matters as you've been." She agreed to every item in the letter, and ended the call with some of the exact words Steve worried he'd hear, only not in the same order he expected: "I'm glad you've decided we're a good match for your family."

# CHAPTER NINE

# SEXUAL PREDATORS

A mother named Carla told me of taking her six-year-old daughter, Juliette, to the small fenced playground at their local park. Most of the children there were brought to the park by a parent, a few by baby-sitters or nannies, one by a grandparent. After a short while, Carla had intuitively connected each child to his or her guardian. In one case, it was because they resembled each other; in another, she saw a child run up and say something to an adult. She heard one man call out some encouragement to a boy who was hesitant to let go at the top of a slide; she heard another parent warn her daughter to stop hitting a smaller child. Soon enough, Carla had accounted for every adult in the playground but one man, one man she didn't like.

He was about forty, clean-shaven, with short hair. He was sitting on a bench watching the children play, but not focused on any particular child. He had nothing with him, while most of the other adults had something they were keeping an eye on: a doll, a toy, or else a whole bag of things parents seem always to be carrying around when they go out with their kids. When Carla saw the man leave the playground alone, she was relieved he'd gone. Sure, he might have stopped by just to get the joy most of us feel in the presence of children playing, but she didn't think so: *I don't trust him. What was he doing here anyway? Glad he's gone. I'll watch for him in the future. He seemed like a child molester.*

Seemed like a child molester? On the basis of what? This is an outrageous and unearned condemnation, a secret discrimination so intolerant that it would be illegal in any other context. When the man came back to the playground a few minutes later and Carla saw his son run up and hug him (she'd misconnected the boy to another adult), she quickly forgave her own prejudice. After all, she told me later, "I was just protecting my child."

I asked if she felt bad for having falsely accused the man in her mind. *Nope.* Did the experience make her reluctant to judge people so quickly in the future? *Nope.* Even though he turned out to be just another parent, did she regret her suspiciousness? *Nope.*

I praised her for her self-confidence and pointed out, "To effectively protect Juliette, you'd need to be just as willing to entertain suspicions about people you know."

"That's not quite as easy," Carla responded, "because then I'd feel terribly guilty."

That misplaced guilt is a problem because Juliette, like any child, is far more vulnerable to someone the family knows than to a stranger. And Carla, like any parent, is far more resistant to suspecting someone she knows. Those people we are willing to suspect are inherently less dangerous than those we refuse to suspect. We may suppress an objectionable thought about a friend, but the only way to really banish a thought is to consider it. In fact, we are treating our friends with greater respect and ourselves with greater integrity and our children with greater love when we are willing to consider any thought.

I am not saying you ought to distrust a man or teenage boy merely because he has access to your children, but rather, be willing to listen to yourself when you do feel distrust. It makes sense to pursue suspicion rather than immediately abandon it since it's a fact of our species that some of the adult males molest children. Expecting those particular males to look glaringly different from all others has proved to be an ineffective strategy for preventing sexual abuse. Popular, but ineffective.

.    .    .

When it comes to the safety of children, I've just about concluded that the difference between parents and experts is that parents say "I guess" more often—as in "I guess these molesters hang around places frequented by kids." And parents end their statements with question marks: "Kids are less vulnerable in pairs, right?" The information remains roughly the same no matter who offers it. Quite often, my greatest contribution to solving the mystery of aberrant behavior is my refusal to call it a mystery. Rather, it is a puzzle; I have seen the pieces so often that I may recognize them sooner than some people, but my main job is just to get them on the table. As we explore the pieces of the sexual abuse puzzle in this chapter, I'll show you their shapes and their colors. You'll see that most of them are already familiar to you. Above all, I hope to leave you knowing that you never have to wait for all the pieces to be in place before you act.

Last year, I met with groups of parents around the country to discuss my plans for this book. I was at each gathering to learn what concerned them as fathers and mothers; they were there to have an expert on violence answer any questions. Groups like this assume that I have information they don't have, so I show whenever possible that what people think the answer might be is, in fact, exactly what it turns out to be.

About an hour into one of the meetings, the mother of an eight-year-old boy turned the questions from the requisite topic of kidnapping by strangers to the far more pressing matter of sexual abuse.

*What are the signs that a child is being abused?*

I responded with a question: What do you think the signs are?

*I don't know.*

If you did know the answer, what would it be? (This almost always stimulates an answer from the very person who just said I don't know.)

*Well, I guess sleep problems. Maybe the child's behavior changes— but other than that, I don't know.*

You mean that other than knowing, you don't know?

*I don't know.*

(Oh geez.) If you did know, what other signs might there be?

*Acting sort of sexual with other kids? Drawing pictures about sex? Doing sexual things? I don't know.*

Right on all points, of course. If you add hyperactivity, fear of being alone with certain adults, unusual or exaggerated interest in people's bodies, wearing excessive amounts of clothing, and inappropriate affection toward strangers, you'd have the most common behavioral signs.

In some cases a child's body will clearly say what's happened, and those clues are far harder to miss. This list tells the story so starkly that it hurts your heart to read it:

- Stomach and digestive problems
- Difficulty walking or sitting
- Torn, stained, or bloody underwear
- Blood in urine or stool
- Unexplained genital contusions
- Sexually transmitted diseases
- Pregnancy

Lists like that are part of what makes this a topic nobody really wants to think about, but here's why I have to stay with it for a while: Of all the serious harms that could come to your child, sexual abuse is the one that most needs your attention and your intuition. And, unfortunately, the odds are getting worse, not better. More mothers are working, so more children are spending their days in child-care facilities. Divorce is on the rise, and the increasing number of remarriages means more sexual abuse by stepfathers in the home. Sexual crimes against children are also increasing of their own accord as the abused grow up and become abusers themselves. Because these predators so often molest more than one child, the number of victims is increasing exponentially.

So here we have a risk that is not at all rare: One in three girls and one in six boys will have sexual contact with an adult. Sometimes it's a neighbor and sometimes it's a day-care worker, but a family member is still most likely to be the sexual abuser. In about 20 percent of the cases, the abuser is an adolescent. According to a study by the National Institute of Mental Health, the average molester of girls will have about fifty victims before being caught and convicted; the average molester of boys will have an astonishing 150 victims before being caught and convicted. Most will have plenty after being caught as well, some even victimizing as many as 300 children during their "careers." In addition to what we usually think of as molestation, children are victims of rape more often than most of us have ever imagined. The Bureau of Justice Statistics reports that fully 15 percent of rape victims are younger than twelve.

Who are the offenders in these crimes? Nearly 100 percent are heterosexual men. All of them have a process by which they gain access to and control of a child. We'll call it the predation process. Thankfully, there is also a protection process.

# The Protection Process

1. **Detect evidence that sexual abuse has occurred;**

2. Detect evidence that it's likely to occur;

3. Make careful, slow choices about the people you include in your child's life—and fast choices about the ones you exclude from your child's life;

4. Teach your child about touch, the body, boundaries, communication, assertiveness, and sovereignty over the body.

## 1. Detect evidence that sexual abuse has occurred:

On this one, you have a partner: your child's doctor. When a child is sexually abused, his or her body may try to communicate what has happened; a good doctor can help you break the code.

Your child's doctor is obligated by law to help, but you are the one obligated to choose a good doctor. Here, as with baby-sitters, your comfort level will be influenced not just by whom you choose, but by how you choose. Like much of what we were taught as children, "The doctor knows best" still lingers somewhere in our consciousness, even if we've seen plenty of exceptions.

David and Rita Boyd are a remarkable set of parents whose experiences help put the expertise of doctors into perspective. Most of their fourteen children (yes, you read correctly) were born at home. In those instances, the Boyds assumed full responsibility for their child from birth on, and David feels that foundation carried over into all other aspects of their parenting.

Though the Boyds recognize that most will choose to have a

hospital birth, they suggest that every family at least consider a home birth. Their reason: It compels the mother and father to learn all about the topic. Then, even if the couple ultimately uses a hospital, the better-informed parents will be participants and not mere followers in the process. Doctors, Boyd says, cannot easily intimidate parents who are well informed.

Choosing a pediatrician starts with knowing that the doctor is not the expert on your child—you are. Remember that among doctors—just as with every profession—some are jerks, some are drug addicts, some are incompetent, some are lazy. (A few are lazy, incompetent, drug-addicted jerks.) Thankfully, most are capable, caring professionals who dedicate themselves to the well-being of their patients; your job is to find doctors in that category and avoid doctors in any other.

If you must have your child treated by someone you feel uncertain about (because of an HMO, for example), then supervise more closely. The best possible outcome, however, is to invest your confidence in someone who earns it and not give it away for free just because they hang a diploma on the wall. Some parents carry around a needy uncertainty and look for a professional to soothe it, but this is one choice where it's better to carry around a healthy skepticism and look for someone who dispels it.

Interview the doctor. Ask questions and get full, understandable answers. Some professionals use the terminology of their particular field as a defense against scrutiny—they want you to be discouraged by how difficult it is to understand. Accordingly, when an answer is unclear, that's a signal to intensify the inquiry. If the doctor takes a deep breath and feigns a valiant effort to help us understand, most people pretend to get it instead of saying, "No, you're still not there, Doctor. Try again." Remember, the doctor is the one choosing to speak in a foreign tongue, not you.

There are some valuable questions to add to those you might normally ask when selecting a pediatrician. Rather than tell the doctor you have questions to ask him, just begin:

*Have you ever suspected that any patient of yours was being sexually abused?*

*What signs of sexual abuse do you find most significant?*

It's possible the doctor's own intuition will appropriately kick in and she or he will take your inquiry as a signal to ask *you* some questions ("Why do you ask?" or "Are you concerned that something may be going on with your child?"). At that point, you can explain that your questions are to help you meet your duty to select the best possible pediatrician. Ideally, the doctor will be willing to take a few minutes to participate and you'll continue your questions:

*Are doctors required by law to make certain notifications when they suspect sexual or other child abuse?*

The answer is Yes; the law in your state requires notification and your doctor should be closely familiar with the statutes.

*Do you think such laws help to bring intervention to cases where it's needed?*

Neither Yes nor No is the correct answer, but you want an answer that indicates the doctor has thought about the topic. The idea here, as with selecting a baby-sitter, is to place important issues on the agenda and give your intuition plenty of material to evaluate. A good feeling about a particular doctor is great; it's better still if your intuition has a lot to go on.

*Is sexual abuse of children common?*

There can be different interpretations of the word common, but what you are looking to be certain of is that this doctor is not a denier. The American Academy of Pediatrics long ago recognized in its policy statement that the diagnosis of sexual abuse "will depend upon the pediatrician's willingness to consider abuse as a possibility."

*When children tell you about symptoms or about how they feel, I imagine it's hard to determine what's credible and what isn't. How often are the things kids tell you actually helpful to your diagnosis?*

A good answer will show respect for children. It may include observations about the reduced credibility of younger children, or about kids who make things up, but the overall theme would be that the doctor believes there is important information to be derived from what children say.

*How do you deal with a child who is afraid of you?*

Good answers might be that the doctor acknowledges the child's fear and tries to soothe it (with gentleness, humor, involving the parent more, taking a little extra time, explaining what's going on, etc.).

*Have you ever become aware of a doctor who molested a child (or even heard of a case)?*

The answer may well be No, because such abuse by doctors appears to be very rare. Still, the question tests the doctor's attitude about whether such a thing is possible. If he says, "Of course not; it never happens," that reveals a mind closed to the topic.

*Doctor, I know you'll understand why I'm asking a few tough questions: Have you ever been accused of malpractice or sexual misconduct?*

You might feel a doctor would never admit to such a thing if true, and that's possible. But however he or she reacts will inform your intuition and make you more or less comfortable with this doctor.

With private practitioners: *Do you conduct background investigations on your staff? Do you confirm credentials?*

Perhaps you'll be surprised to learn that I'm not a strong believer in referrals about pediatricians. If you ask friends about the doctor they chose for their children, the almost guaranteed response will be praise; doesn't it have to be if they're investing their confidence in a given doctor? And you don't want to rely on their opinion, particularly since they likely relied upon someone else's anyway. Automatically selecting a pediatrician because others recommend him can be a protection against later regret, i.e., "Steve and Tanya liked him." It can be a way to avoid being wrong (if you never make a decision, you can't make a mistake). It's my belief, however, that parents who don't make independent decisions on high-stakes matters are automatically wrong—for even if everything works out well with a given doctor (as odds are it will), responsibility was still avoided.

One couple I know, Michael and Jackie, interviewed a pediatrician they'd heard a lot about. He was a member of their church and several of their friends had raved about him. Still, they both came away from the meeting with little confidence in him. When friends learned that Michael and Jackie didn't choose the doctor they'd recommended, that led to several discussions. Three of the couples whose kids went to that doctor admitted to also feeling uncomfortable about him ("but he came so highly recommended, we just kept going to him"). Since then, every one of the people that praised that doctor to Michael and Jackie has selected other pediatricians for their children.

Imagine the pediatrician you choose has several patients you know personally. We tend to use such information to make ourselves more popular with the doctor: "Jane and Steve Keller are good friends of mine," to which the doctor says something predictable like "Oh, the Kellers are a fine family." I suggest a different approach. Use the names of people you know are patients to make clear that anything other than the best performance will have consequences for the doctor: "I often speak with Jane and Steve Keller, and with Arlene and Bob Jones, and with Marsha Harris. I'll pass on your regards to them." Remember, you are not auditioning for the doctor; he is the paid professional and you are the customer. As you would with any professional, take the steps most likely to stimulate the best service. (This strategy can also be applied when interviewing the owners of day-care centers.)

I suggest keeping a full copy of your child's medical records at home. As each record is produced, ask the doctor or his staff for a copy. Request extra copies of X rays as well (the cost is small). Here are some of the benefits of maintaining your own files:

- If you have a copy of your child's entire medical record, then choosing to leave a given doctor doesn't carry the weight of confrontation or explanation;
- You can seek a second opinion without telling your doctor; this eliminates the hesitation some parents may feel, and your doctor can't be insulted if he or she doesn't know;
- Sometimes, the issue of sexual abuse presents itself years after the abuse began, and the course and pattern of medical issues can become important;
- The fact that doctors and their staffs know each document is being copied and retained by you helps to ensure the highest standard of care.

As with day-care centers, I suggest that once you've chosen a pediatrician, you set forth your expectations in a letter.

Dear Doctor Smith:
Thanks for your time during our recent meeting. Because of your key role in keeping our daughter Kate healthy and safe, we'll be relying upon you to communicate to us early

and clearly any concerns you may have about her health or well-being.

We recognize that some parents desire or perhaps even require a degree of protection from difficult information; we are not among them. We are available to you at any time and will welcome discussion of any topic.

If you ever change your mind in a matter or have second thoughts about something, that won't shake our confidence in you. Rather, we'll welcome your willingness to remain open to every possibility. Your intuition about our child's health and well-being is of interest to us even if you can't cite specific evidence in a given situation.

We'll be giving your name to the Building Blocks Daycare Center, which is caring for our daughter during weekdays.

Some parents may have unreasonable expectations of a pediatrician but we expect only that you meet the highest standards of your profession. Just as we hold you to your duties as a physician, we ask that you hold us to our duties as parents. With all of us working together, our confidence in you will be reearned for many years to come.

[End text as appropriate, i.e., special information, instructions, etc.]

> Sincerely,
> Holly and Ryan Jason

It's unlikely the doctor will be annoyed by your letter, but if so, then you got a great bit of information.

(While on the topic of annoyance, here's an observation directed toward doctors regarding the illegibility of everything you write: Write clearly. If parents choose to seek a second opinion and provide your notes to another physician, they shouldn't have to hire a graphologist to decipher what you've written. And on prescriptions, it's better if both parent and pharmacist can actually read your instructions. One mother told me, "I want the difference between *anally* and *orally* to be very clear. To our kids, it's a very important distinction.")

---

## The Protection Process

1. Detect evidence that sexual abuse has occurred;

2. **Detect evidence that it's likely to occur;**

3. Make careful, slow choices about the people you include in your child's life—and fast choices about the ones you exclude from your child's life;

4. Teach your child about touch, the body, boundaries, communication, assertiveness, and sovereignty over the body.

---

### 2. Detect evidence that it's likely to occur:

Most of the strategies used by predators who are strangers (discussed in Chapter 4) apply again here, except that with sexual abuse we are usually discussing someone a child already knows. It's easier to understand the workings of child sexual abuse by substituting a less objectionable crime, say, fraud. Wisconsin's assistant attorney general, Gregory Posner-Weber, who specializes in prosecuting crimes against children, does this with profound simplicity:

> You're a thief—a con artist. You recently met an elderly widow with a good-sized bank account. Your own financial engine is running on fumes. You decide to take her money.
> So you befriend her. You run small errands for her. You buy

her gifts. You listen to her stories and comfort her when she feels lonely. You put your arm around her and tell her you understand her problems. You spend time with her each day. You tell her she's special. You gain her trust. Her natural suspicion disappears.

Only then does the conversation shift to money. You describe a tremendous investment opportunity. You offer her a chance to share in this special event. If she's curious, you play on her curiosity. You answer her questions and downplay her fears.

And your work pays off. She trusts you. She signs the check.

Three minutes after her bank opens, you're in the wind, cash in hand and ready to target your next victim.

But what if you're a child molester—a predator? What if the object of your desire isn't the widow's bank account, but her six-year-old grandson? What steps will you take to get what you want?

Not much will change. And there, in two hundred words or less, is most of what you need to know about how it works. Just as with the lonely old woman, the child predator targets someone he perceives as vulnerable. And he is perceptive; almost certainly the product of abuse himself, he recognizes the child who feels unloved or unpopular. The attention he pays to the child first buys him access, later trust. Posner-Weber describes the power of the sympathetic ear:

Your parents don't understand or respect you? I do. Other kids make fun of you? I know what that's like—it was the same for me when I was your age. They don't trust you at home? Boy, I know what that's like. But I trust you. I care for you more than anybody else. I love you. I'm here for you.

These brilliant manipulators exploit the needs of their victims. The bored and lonely ten-year-old who leaves his empty home to wander around may find himself lured into the house of the highly attentive and generous neighborhood pedophile.

At some point, the sexual predator introduces secrecy. Any secret will do at first, just to commit the child to a conspiracy with the abuser. "Don't tell your mother about the candy I gave you because she won't like you eating between meals" later evolves into a bigger secret carrying greater consequences: "If your mother knew, she'd hate you." When necessary, secrecy is enforced by threats: "If you tell your mother, I'll kill her" or "I'll kill you."

A parent might fully grasp the analogy of the well-to-do widow and the con artist, could fully understand how predators develop their victims, and yet still not see what's going on. That's because parents aren't the targets. Parents are not along for the leisurely walk toward victimization; thus they must recognize and follow the footprints.

The first footprint is just the mere fact of a child's vulnerability. An unhappy child not getting comfort or support at home will look for it somewhere else. Next is the presence and growing popularity of some adult. Next is the amount of time they spend together, and where they spend it. Is the adult alone with the child by circumstance or by design?

There are footprints right in the house: gifts, phone messages, frequent references by the child ("Mark was once in Mexico"; "Mark didn't do well in school when he was my age"; "Mark says I could make the track team"). Seemingly, there is always a plan in the works for this adult and the child to be together.

When the abuser is a well-liked relative or friend of the family, parents will probably be comfortable with him. After all, if they got the creeps from this guy, he wouldn't be around in the first place. Indeed, because he poses no threat to the parents, their comfort is justified (in terms of their own safety); that's another reason it's so important to keep an open mind. Although they may do terribly hurtful things to a child, abusers don't likely see a sexual encounter as a harm at all, but rather as an expression of affection. They aren't often ogres or frightening people. If they were, most parents wouldn't have granted them access to their child in the first place. And that gets us to number 3 on the list.

# The Protection Process

1.  Detect evidence that sexual abuse has occurred;

2.  Detect evidence that it's likely to occur;

3.  **Make careful, slow choices about the people you in-clude in your child's life—and fast choices about the ones you exclude from your child's life;**

4.  Teach your child about touch, the body, boundaries, com-munication, assertiveness, and sovereignty over the body.

### 3. Make careful, slow choices about the people you include in your child's life—and fast choices about the ones you exclude from your child's life:

Each new person that presents himself in your child's life (and yours) could be the best thing that ever happened—or the worst. He could contribute humor, joy, friendship, even heroism to your family—or he could contribute pain and regret. Parents who appreciate that these are the stakes make more careful choices.

The first step toward making a good choice is so obvious as to be nearly invisible: be sure it's *your* choice, not the choice of the new person, and certainly not the choice of the child. People who select your family and inject themselves into your lives are candidates for more careful scrutiny. People who rush the process of friendship are often in some other process entirely. If they seem overly interested in your child, raise your antenna a bit higher.

Item number 3 encourages slow choices about whom you let in and fast choices about whom you exclude. Here, because we are talking about detecting abuse before it occurs, one needn't know to a certainty that there is a problem in order to take swift action. Your suspicion alone is more than enough justification for preventing time alone with your child. You needn't even totally exclude someone, but can simply change the rules of the relationship: heightened awareness on your part, limited access to your child. There's no punishment involved in this, for the person you are uncomfortable about may have done nothing wrong—but if the signs are there that he might, that's enough.

---

# The Protection Process

1. Detect evidence that sexual abuse has occurred;

2. Detect evidence that it's likely to occur;

3. Make careful, slow choices about the people you include in your child's life—and fast choices about the ones you exclude from your child's life;

4. **Teach your child about touch, the body, boundaries, communication, assertiveness, and sovereignty over the body.**

---

## 4. Teach your child about touch, the body, boundaries, communication, assertiveness, and sovereignty over the body:

Most of the skills necessary for children to protect themselves can be found in the Test of Twelve, but there are a few that relate specifically to sexual abuse:

Children should know . . .

- It's okay to withdraw consent at any time;
- Their body is theirs;
- How to talk about the body;
- How to say No;
- To keep telling if nobody listens and if nobody makes it stop.

Many victimized children feel obligated to let sexual contact escalate or continue because they consented at some point. Withdrawing consent is very difficult for children because to them, it can feel unfair, like taking something back, like failing to keep your word. Such feelings make for easy manipulation. A child who knows that withdrawing consent (or changing one's mind) is permissible can at least consider the option.

What constitutes consent in the first place is usually quite vague. Sexual predators often start with nonsexual touch to desensitize their targets. It might be "accidental" touch, or hugs, pats, strokes, hairbrushing, holding. A child might agree to these touches, might enjoy them, might even request them. This adds shame to the list of reasons a child might not tell parents what's going on. At the top of the list of reasons for not telling, however, is the belief that the information may hurt someone—or hurt everyone.

To pass the Test of Twelve, a child must know that his parents won't be devastated by anything he tells them. The knowledge that parents are strong enough to deal with whatever happens is a gift millions of today's adults didn't grow up with—such that many *still* haven't told their parents about abuse they suffered.

Gregory Posner-Weber says, "The safest child is the child who knows he can bring his problems and concerns to parents and adult caregivers without reproach or retaliation." Of course, even the most receptive and approachable parents will not be told of sexual encounters unless the child has the vocabulary to tell—and many parents have elected not to share that vocabulary with their kids. You could fill a book with the sounds and phrases families have coined to avoid saying these three words: vagina, penis, rectum. The vernacular consists of cute terms like boom-boom, popo, hoosie-doosie (yes, that's a real one), poo-poo, wee-wee, tee-tee, and the ever-versatile pee-pee. Even the least creative people seem to flourish when it comes to finding ways to prevent their young son or daughter from saying vagina.

While cautions such as "Never let anyone touch you on the parts of your body covered by a bathing suit" are popular, parents must also teach children not to touch *someone else* in those same areas. The man who compels a child to perform oral sex on him might not do one single thing the child has ever been warned about. However, if a child is taught that nobody should touch his penis or ask him to touch their penis, it increases the likelihood the child will recognize abuse should it ever occur.

The National Center for Victims of Crime recommends being very specific.

Tell children that no adult or other child should:

- Put their hands down your pants or up your skirt;
- Touch your private parts, even through clothes or pajamas;
- Ask you to touch their private parts, or ask you to remove their clothes;
- Take off your clothes;
- Take pictures of you with your clothes off;
- Take their clothes off in front of you.

One law-enforcement expert supports this approach when he says, "Show me a child that knows nothing about sex, and I'll show you a highly qualified victim." There's another type of expert we can learn from: the convicted child molester. One said, "Parents are partly to blame because they don't tell their children about sexual stuff. I used that to my advantage by teaching the child myself."

Some parents seem to be saying: "We want you to talk about *it*, that if you have any questions about *it* we want you to ask us, that it's not okay if someone does *it*, and that if *it* happens to you, it's not your fault. But what *it* means is so bad that we can't even say the words."

As a way to avoid saying the words, some parents take roundabout approaches, warning, for example, that "there are sick people in the world you have to watch out for." Many kids think of a sick person as someone who is sniffling and coughing. Some parents warn of "bad people" or people who will "hurt" you, but most sexual offenders are not perceived by the family as bad, and most sexual abuse does not hurt, so what are these terms likely to mean to kids?

Cynthia, a good friend of mine who is a teacher, asked her class of seven-year-olds, "What does a tricky person look like?" Answers included: He has a mask; he's dressed all in black; he has some sort of weapon; he has a gun; he is crazy; he is mean; he is grouchy. She then gave a 30-minute presentation using a training program called "Can't Fool Me," which includes enjoyable and well-produced musical numbers to teach kids sovereignty over one's body, how to listen to intuition, how to seek help in public, and how tricky people behave. After doing some worksheets and listening to a song called "Tricky People," the children's answers were far more accurate: He looks like you and me; he looks normal; he looks like a nice person but isn't. (For more information on "Can't Fool Me," see Yello Dyno in Appendix #1.)

Child Lures Ltd., a family-run group, has developed a comprehensive, research-based school program that teaches students how to recognize and avoid the common lures used by sexual predators both known and unknown to the child. Adopted by over one thousand school systems nationwide, the Child Lures School Program employs role playing that combines critical thinking skills with recognizing, trusting, and following instincts. An accompanying Child Lures Family Guide for parents/caregivers allows them to reinforce classroom lessons at home. Observes Child Lures creator, Ken Wooden: "Some parents and educators feel that teaching the dangers of sexual exploitation will frighten youngsters. We have found these reservations to be unfounded. Remember, even very young children know that some things can be dangerous: moving cars, electrical outlets, and so forth. If fear exists, it is nearly always diminished when prevention strategies are provided." (For more information on Child Lures, see Appendix #1.)

Since assertive kids are less likely to be molested, the protection process includes helping children be comfortable with assertiveness. In a study done by the University of Chicago, sexual offenders were asked to describe the type of children they were drawn to. One said, "A look of being vulnerable in some way, not assertive; trusts adults. You can see it in their body language, the way they look with their eyes, the way they hold themselves."

The traits sexual offenders consider ideal in their targets ("quiet, withdrawn, compliant, easier to manipulate, less likely to put up a fight") aren't the traits of children able to pass the Test of Twelve.

Though parents do the important teaching, many of the most beneficial skills are available through IMPACT FOR KIDS. Among other things, students are taught to say (at the very first recognition of inappropriate touch), "Stop or I'll tell." These words imply to the offender that if he stops now, the child won't tell—and that's a good offer. In fact, a graduate of IMPACT FOR KIDS is likely to tell either way. (For more information on IMPACT FOR KIDS and the similar program offered by KIDPOWER, see Appendix #1.)

Might the words "Stop or I'll tell" spoken by a child actually be effective? Absolutely Yes, because those words identify a child who *can* tell.

•    •    •

The experience of Jeff and Jennifer and their son Jason includes all aspects of the predation process but none of the protection process. Virtually everything we've discussed in this chapter is part of their story.

Mark approached Jeff and Jennifer at a Little League game and introduced himself. He was writing an article for the local paper about parents who participate in their kids' activities. He really did work for the paper and he really was doing an article, so he wasn't conning them, not on those points anyway.

When he asked Jeff and Jennifer if they had a son in the game, he already knew they had a son in the game. When he asked for their son's name, he already knew that too. Jeff pointed Jason out, the tallest of the ten-year-olds on the field. During a break, he was happy to introduce the reporter to his son. Mark interviewed Jason for a few minutes and gathered information, but not just for the article.

As Jason ran back onto the field, Mark said to Jennifer: "Look around here; mothers are a rare sight. I think it's great that you do this, and I'm sure it means a lot to your son—I'm sorry, was it Jason?" Jennifer nodded and said she really loved coming to the games but she didn't think Jason felt the same way about having her there. "Last week, driving home from a practice, he was real quiet. Finally, I pulled out of him that he is embarrassed when I cheer."

Jeff said, "Well, she does get a little fanatic about it." And the three friendly adults laughed.

Mark asked if they'd agree to be in his article, and they said sure. They talked a bit about politics (Mark had a lot of inside news from other reporters), a bit about restaurants (Mark got all the restaurant reviews before they came out), current music (Mark occasionally did stories on famous music bands whose tours brought them to Portland).

Jeff and Jennifer liked this guy and they could tell he liked them. Because they'd been in Portland only a few months, and they both worked so much (Jennifer a financial consultant, Jeff an organizer of corporate seminars), they didn't know many people yet, so they welcomed the exchange of phone numbers.

Of course, Mark was the first to make a call. It was a couple of days before his article was to come out. "Interested in an advance copy?" Jeff was, and Mark said he'd bring it by. That would be fun because he'd get to see Jennifer again; he could stop over around five-thirty. Heck, if it's then, Jeff offered, just stay for dinner. Or I could take you guys out, Mark replied. No, Jason's got homework, so just come on over. And thus was a friendship born—or rather, created.

The article was praising to the family, particularly to Jason, who was called a "natural athlete with a future in sports if he wants it." Jason's homework that night was on Brazil, and of course, Mark had been there twice, so he helped the boy.

A week later Mark found some other reason to have contact with the family. He called around four in the afternoon and Jason answered. "Nobody's home," the boy told him. "Well, there's you, buddy. How's it going?" And they talked for a while. Mark offered to take the boy on a tour of a police station, "If your parents agree, of course." Jeff did agree to let his son go, and he told Mark, "You may have noticed that Jason's a bit introverted." Of course, Mark had taken notice of that fact even before they met.

The friendship between Mark and the family grew unbelievably fast—*unbelievably* being the key word. Mark took Jason to interesting things from time to time, but one day, when Mark stopped by and invited the boy to go with him to the scene of a big fire, Jason said he didn't want to. Jeff told his son he had to go, but the boy refused. "We deal with defiance quickly in this house," Jeff told Mark. "Just give me a minute." And that's exactly what it took: A minute later Jason not only agreed to go but he apologized to Mark for "insulting" him.

Fast forward a year to what Jeff called "Jason's unluckiest week." On Monday, the boy broke his leg tripping on some stairs. On Wednesday, he dropped a heavy toolbox on his foot, breaking two toes. The very next night, he bruised his head walking into a sliding glass door he thought was open. It wasn't just an unlucky week. He'd been doing terribly in school for months. Ironically, the boy whom the local newspaper once called a "natural athlete" had lost all interest in sports. It's more accurate to say he'd lost all interest in everything. Each day for months Jason came home from school and went to his room. He'd sleep until he heard his parents getting home, sit quietly through dinner, then go back to bed. Jennifer and Jeff didn't know any of this, but there was a bigger secret they didn't know: Jason hadn't been home alone some of those days after school.

He knew it would devastate his mom if she ever learned what was going on—so he couldn't tell her. Besides, how would he even say it? And as for telling his dad, well, Mark was one of his best friends in Portland. Besides, his dad would hate him if he ever found out. Jason wanted Mark to stop coming over but he'd let it go on so long, he didn't know how to stop it. So it didn't stop until Mark moved to Seattle a year later. It was another seven years before Jason told his parents.

Mark was (and almost certainly still is) one of many sexual predators who are able to gain the full cooperation of their young victims. The teenage girl who needs so badly to hear the words "You are beautiful" may give in and take her clothes off for a video. The young boy who genuinely loves his older cousin may tolerate inappropriate touching, may actually volunteer for it at times. Even kids in these seemingly impossible situations, however, would be less likely to reach that level of vulnerability were they fluent in safety skills.

For some parents, as with Jason's father, the least popular feature of their children is defiance. Yet it is one of the most important for safety. If defiance is always met with discipline and never with discussion, that can handicap a child. The moment the two-year-old defiantly asserts his will for the first time may be cause for celebration, not castigation, for he is building the courage to resist. If your teenage daughter never tests her defiance on you, she may well be unable to use it on a predator.

.    .    .

I certainly don't blame Jeff and Jennifer for the abuse that Jason endured; if they knew what you know, I'm sure they'd have made different choices. Camille Richards made different choices, but she was prepared for parenthood by an unwanted teacher in her youth:

> When I was seven I had a friend, Erica, who, from the time she was six until she turned twelve, was molested and raped by her father. Though I didn't know what was happening, looking back now with the mind of an adult, I see that I did notice important things. For example, one time as Erica's father was saying good-bye to us, he kissed me hard on the lips. I said to him, "Mommy and Daddy kiss on the lips, but kids kiss on the cheek!" and he said, "No, you're confused. Mommy and Daddy kiss on the cheek, and children kiss on the lips, like this." I patiently explained it to him again, and he eventually gave up the discussion. I wish I'd told my parents, but I just thought he'd forgotten where kisses are supposed to go.
>
> At around twelve when I was starting to develop breasts, he made a comment about that to me. I don't recall the words, but I remember the lingering look he gave me and the sick, cringing way it made me feel. I can feel it still. I avoided him from then on. Not long after, Erica had a nervous breakdown and everything came out in the open.

Camille is a parent herself now. She says:

I want to know about any adult in my daughter's life who gets little things wrong like where to kiss, or who needs help doing up clothes, or who offers help doing up hers, or who wants to play touching games. I want to know even if my daughter thinks it's no more than a funny story. I also respect her intuition and her reticence to be friendly with a particular person. If she shows the slightest discomfort with someone, I watch that person like a hawk and he won't get ten seconds alone with her.

I know I cannot guarantee my daughter's absolute safety. But I can guarantee her my vigilance.

Dorothy McGowan is another mother who learned from her personal experiences:

While taking piano lessons at nine years old, I became used to adults putting their arms around me, giving me praise, sitting next to me. After lessons, I'd wait for my father at a local store. The man who worked there also worked on getting me to trust him. By the time I was eleven he was putting his arms around me, squeezing me, asking if I liked "fellas." I felt uncomfortable and I felt guilty for feeling that way. I was ashamed of my dirty mind. One day he moved his hand to what little breast I had. When my father picked me up, I didn't tell him. Instead, I told my mother the minute I got home. She first called the man's wife and then him. She said she wouldn't be telling my father, but if anything ever happened again, she would. She told the man that she would also blow his head off with her shotgun.

Around the same time, I heard of a girl who was molested and was then forced to apologize to her abuser for "causing trouble." She suffered a lot. I know of cases where a kid was molested but it was ignored because the parents didn't want to go to war with an uncle or grandfather. Those kids suffered a lot.

The memories of my own experience are far from devastating,

mostly because I felt empowered and protected; I felt like I mattered. That feeling has assumed a more significant place in my memory than the feeling of fear I felt in the store that day.

It is true that the damage from not being protected is often greater than the damage of sexual assault. Thus, the child who can protect him or herself is not only less attractive to a predator, but will be better able to survive the ordeal in the unlikely event that sexual abuse does occur. Children successfully taught to run, to say "Stop or I'll tell," or to prevent abuse in some other way have learned important lessons from their parents. As you'll see in the next chapter, these aren't lessons they're likely to learn in school.

# CHAPTER TEN

# CHILDREN
# AT SCHOOL

Robert is a computer engineer at a nuclear power plant. Though the stakes are high in his line of work, he is rarely disappointed when he invests his confidence in machines. He readily admits that people don't gain his trust as easily, so when he and his wife sent their son to school, they had to do some letting go. In a letter to me, he explained: "By the time Ellis reached school age, our need to trust someone or something had grown into a giant blob. We had already dragged it to day-care centers and doctors' offices, and we just needed to invest our confidence somewhere, so we dragged it to the school."

Somehow parents get themselves beneath that blob, hoist it onto their shoulders, and with a mix of reluctance and anticipation, heave it at the school, hoping it will stick. It will if they want it to badly enough, and they'll be able to drive away thinking, *Everybody else invests confidence here, why shouldn't we? Schools are highly regulated by government, we were safe in school, no need to worry.* These reassurances can work, but parents may start finding little reasons for uncertainty until it becomes clear that they haven't really invested their confidence at all. They may wonder, *Is it ever actually possible to end doubt?*

The answer is Yes. The way to stop doubt is to find out. Contrary to the belief that learning more will simply give you more to worry about, learning the answers to your questions about the school is the way to get your intuition to stop nagging you. You see, the questions don't go anywhere just because we silence them; they are still there:

- If my son is missing from class, how long will the school administrators wait before notifying me?
- If my daughter gets sick, will they call me immediately?
- What will they do if they can't reach me?
- If my boy is seriously injured, what hospital do they take him to?
- Have they ever had a student bring a gun to school?
- If my little girl wants to call me, will they let her?
- If one of my son's teachers is suspected of sexual abuse, will anybody inform me?

As you seek the answers, I encourage you to stop thinking of the school as an institution. The school is people, period. If they are people you're impressed with, great. If they are people you wouldn't want caring for your child, that's a problem. Not everybody at the school needs to be brilliant, but all need to be in agreement that the welfare of the students is paramount. It's swell if you like your child's teachers, but when it comes to safety, your confidence must be earned by one person above all, the one person who is above all: the principal.

From the principal's office will flow the clear waters of commitment to the safety of children—or will seep the muddy waters of ambiguity, laziness, lack of care, even stupidity. It may be hard to assess a principal because when you were in school, the principal was an authority figure you couldn't question. If you are a parent, the principal is someone you must question.

And let's be clear: The principal is not *your* authority figure. When you visit the principal's office today, you stand on equal ground, eye to eye. If anything, the principal is in your service, is your designate. A couple of years ago, I testified in a case where that designate failed; after reading what follows, you'll be less likely to blindly invest confidence in a school.

Here are the stark facts I was presented with: A seven-year-old boy was sodomized in the school bathroom by another student, whom I'll call Joey. Unlike the sexual predators in the previous chapter, Joey was aided by more than denial on the part of responsible adults: His crime was made easier by astonishing negligence on the part of the school principal.

When the victim and his family sued, the school district (one of the wealthiest in the nation) mounted an impressive defense: They hired an expert willing to testify that perhaps no crime had occurred after all, perhaps the seven-year-old victim wanted the sex. This same expert claimed that even assuming the rape had occurred, it couldn't have been predicted. My side won the case, though that wasn't surprising given one striking fact their expert had chosen to dance around: A month earlier, Joey had been arrested for victimizing *another* boy the same way in the same bathroom! The school had clearly failed on a very easy prediction.

That failure is doubly disturbing when you consider the types of predictions parents rely upon schools to make:

- Will a given visitor seek to harm a child?
- Will a given teacher molest a child?
- Is a given child being abused at home?
- Will a given child bring a gun to school?
- Will a given child act on threats he'd made?

Though it's hard to imagine that a young boy can rape anyone, the school district in Joey's case knew better. They even had a specific written policy entitled "Child-on-Child Sexual Abuse." The existence of that policy makes clear that such things happen, and that raises a predictive question for every principal: Who among the students might sexually abuse another child?

The administrators at Joey's previous school had made the whole matter very simple for the principal: They actually predicted—in writing—that Joey would act out in sexually inappropriate ways, and they sent his records to the school where the rapes ultimately occurred. Here are some of the warning signs Joey wore like a banner: carrying a knife, threatening homicide, threatening and attempting suicide, lighting a building on fire, pouring gasoline on his mother and trying to light a match, displaying fascination with sex and sexual organs, inappropriate sexual conduct toward other children, exposing himself, aggression, violence. As if all these warning signs were not enough, the principal took no effective action even after learning that Joey had sodomized a student. Is this kind of negligence really possible? This and more.

After the first rape accusation, the principal chose not to take obvious steps that might have increased supervision of Joey at the school. He didn't tell the boy's teachers what had happened. Though the school has security guards, the principal didn't tell them either. It gets worse. When one teacher found Joey to be unmanageable, the solution chosen was to send him to a class of younger, smaller boys. By this action, the school provided him a virtual beauty contest of victims, and there he chose the boy who ultimately became my client.

The presence of security guards at a school may add comfort for some parents, but understand that at this school (and at many others), security guards received absolutely no training on any aspect of student safety. They received no written guidelines, no policies on the topic whatsoever. Even if they'd known what their jobs were supposed to be, in this case they weren't told a thing—not "Be extra alert," not

"Keep an eye out," not a thing. When organizations of any kind are pressured to improve security, a typical response is to hire guards. Everyone sighs and feels the matter has been addressed, but if guards are not trained or supervised or properly equipped, if there is no intelligent plan for them to follow, their presence can hurt more than help. That's because, having taken this expensive step, everyone stops looking at other aspects of safety and security.

I've noted the precautions the principal failed to take, but there is one precaution he did take. After Joey was arrested for the first rape, the principal arranged to have him escorted whenever he went to that bathroom. This may sound like a reasonable step until I tell you that the principal had Joey escorted not by a teacher or a security guard, but by another student! I do not imagine many parents would have volunteered their son for the job of escorting a violent criminal, particularly one that even experienced teachers could not handle.

If an adult employee at the school, say for example the janitor, had Joey's background and was arrested for raping a student, would the principal have let him come back to work within a few weeks? I can't answer even this rhetorical question with any certainty. I know only that Joey communicated in the clearest language that he posed a risk to other students, and the principal turned away.

With two rapes under his belt, Joey was finally taken out of school and placed in a treatment facility (where he sexually attacked two people in one day). The investment of abuse and neglect in Joey's own childhood will continue to pay dividends of pain and violence for others, including those he will likely kill one day. As I write this sad but accurate prediction, Joey is only ten years old.

Advising on another case in which a young child was sexually assaulted at school (this time by a nonstudent), I reviewed the school district's policy book. It will not be reassuring to parents to learn that the topic of safety wasn't even raised until page ten, and that reference was about *faculty* safety when breaking up fights. The policy contained three full pages and twenty-one separate items about the protection of keys, but didn't even mention the topic of danger to students until page ninety-one.

It's important to note here that my critical observations are not intended to blame, but rather to educate. While it was easy to make a villain of the principal in the Joey case, my testimony caused me some internal conflict. I had to ask myself what kind of environment could foster that much negligence. Did this principal have to deal with so much awful behavior that even Joey's crime was not a standout? It appears the answer is Yes. School administrators work beneath a precarious glacier of policies, politics, laws, liabilities, complaints, crimes, vindictiveness, and violence. They oversee the most underpaid workforce in America, and put plainly, they cannot possibly accomplish all that we expect them to without the help of parents.

That's one reason I suggest parents become as involved as possible in their child's school, starting with reviewing the school's policy manual. You'll see it was probably written with more influence from lawyers than educators, and probably none from child-safety advocates. It may be a very discouraging read, but your interest alone can help to improve things. Go to the school and ask every obvious question you can think of and see if the answers make you feel better or worse. Ask about the school's background screening process for employees. If they have security personnel, ask to meet them and see how they respond to probing questions.

It is particularly important to ask about the history of crimes at the school. Federal law requires that colleges maintain campus crime statistics and make them available upon request. This law exists so that college students and their parents can evaluate security and safety when selecting a school. There is no similar law requiring grammar schools or high schools to keep such statistics, but there ought to be (particularly given the fact that more students carry guns in high schools than in colleges).

Rather than relying on government, you can make at least as vigorous an inquiry of your child's school as you would of your child's baby-sitter. Appendix #2 has an extensive list of questions that can guide your evaluation of a school. A few examples are:

- Are there policies addressing violence, weapons, drug use, sexual abuse, child-on-child sexual abuse, unauthorized visitors?
- Are background investigations performed on all staff?
- Does the screening process apply to all employees (teachers, janitors, lunchroom staff, security personnel, part-time employees, volunteers, bus drivers, etc.)?
- Can my child call me at any time?
- How does the school address special situations (custody disputes, child kidnapping concerns, etc.)?
- Are acts of violence or criminality at the school documented? Are statistics maintained?
- Are teachers formally notified when a child with a history of serious misconduct is enrolled at the school?
- Will I be informed of teacher misconduct that might have an impact on the safety or well-being of my child?

The school should have a ready answer to every one of these questions; if they don't, the mere fact of your asking (which can be done in writing) will compel them to consider the issues.

•   •   •

Cara Masters is an upbeat, open-hearted woman who has been teaching in public schools for six years. Over that period, she's made reports in fourteen instances where she believed a student had been seriously abused at home. She called the police regarding a boy with a row of burns on the inside of his left arm ("That's the side my dad can reach when he's driving") and had officers refuse to take a report: "Unless he's got a big gash on his head or something, we're not coming out." She worked in inner-city schools where students pass through metal detectors each morning. She has several times heard the distinctive "lock-down" bell that alerts teachers to rush the students to their classrooms and secure the door because someone has entered the school with a gun.

She's made police reports on three of the five occasions that she was threatened by large male students (including the one who visited her classroom when she was alone and said he intended to rape her "the next time I'm horny"). She had one student so high on drugs that the girl slipped out of her chair onto the floor and couldn't be revived until paramedics arrived. She's seen teenagers pretend (perhaps) to be adjusting guns under their coats, and she's had several students afraid to come to school because of gang threats.

Cara has seen a lot and she wants you to know what goes on and what you can do to improve it:

A parent gets a meeting with the principal scheduled around the parent's lunch hour, while a teacher might wait a month for the same audience. Many principals operate on a "don't want to know" basis, and teachers who want to tell may see their meeting with the principal put off indefinitely if the subject is an unpopular one. If a parent makes a complaint or an assertive request, it gets attention. If a teacher makes the same complaint or request, it gets resentment. Parents have the power, though very few use it.

Betsy Rogers has been teaching twenty years longer than Cara:

Chronic troublemakers are sometimes shifted to another school in the same district, a practice that is referred to by those of us who have grown cynical over the years as "the dance of the turkeys." What was our problem becomes the problem of our colleagues across town. Even as we breathe a sigh of relief, we know that tomorrow we'll likely receive one of their turkeys. In such cases, the parents—those people we want to believe are ultimately responsible for their own young—are only mildly inconvenienced. God forbid we should inconvenience the parents of a dangerous and intractable student by trying to prevent that student from causing trouble at our school. I fully recognize that many parents are doing a wonderful job at raising their children—and we teachers send those parents our heartfelt respect and gratitude. At the same time, I see more and more children simply growing up—they are not being raised at all.

I am no psychologist, but I have witnessed over three decades of steady decline in character and work ethic of the students. When I began teaching in the early seventies, a typical class had one or two "bad apples" mixed in with generally decent, hard-working students. These days, however, a typical class not only has more bad apples, but there is a growing population of "swing-voters," a troubling group who can go either way.

I don't share Cara's and Betsy's comments here so you'll be depressed, but rather so you'll be impressed. Imagine someone, particularly someone who describes herself as cynical, finding the personal resources and character to go to work each day and try to teach (and often succeed), try to inspire (and often succeed). Imagine Cara caring enough to make a police report about an abused child knowing the information will likely be unwelcome to the police, enraging to the parent, and unappreciated by the child, knowing nothing might happen, or worse, that the kid may be beaten for the trouble it causes—yet hoping this case is one where the child is actually helped. There's nothing depressing about the heroism teachers show every day.

I mention all this because teachers can be great allies in improving your child's safety at school, but they need the clout of parents—not to mention adequate pay, better training, more staff, a little recognition, and scores of other things that are off my subject. Squarely on my subject, however, is this: Nearly *one million* school kids grades 6 to 12 carried a gun to school last year. When Betsy Rogers started teaching, a statistic like that would have seemed like something from a bad science-fiction story, but it's not fiction. It comes from a survey that's been conducted annually for the last eleven years by PRIDE, the respected drug-prevention program. Almost half of the students who had carried a gun to school did it often (six or more times during the year), and more than half (64 percent) used an illegal drug on a monthly basis.

So that's about 650,000 drug users bringing guns to school, and another 350,000 slightly more responsible students also bringing guns to school. To be certain my report is balanced, what about the millions of students who don't carry guns to school? Well, a 1993 survey conducted for the Harvard School of Public Health found that 59 percent of students said they could get a handgun if they wanted one, 21 percent said they could get one within the hour. More than half of the students surveyed wished their schools would install metal detectors as a solution to the gun problem. Gun advocates also offered a solution: Georgia State Representative Mitchell Kaye announced plans for legislation that would authorize teachers to be armed in class. In Mr. Kaye's crazy arms race, would we someday judge schools by comparing the ratio of armed students to armed teachers?

I know it will be hard for anyone who acknowledges these issues to ever again invest blind confidence in a school—and that's not a bad result because your child's school needs your full-sighted participation. Even if all you do is get the answers to important questions, your confidence won't be blind. It can start with a letter to the principal:

Mr. Charles Harrison
Principal, Green Valley Elementary School

Dear Mr. Harrison:

Our daughter, Kate Jason, is attending Green Valley this year. We recognize that schools face special challenges these days and we want to be certain our expectations are reasonable. If we're off base on any of these items, please let us know:

- We expect the safety of students to be a priority;
- We expect Kate to be allowed to contact us at any time she feels the need;
- We expect the school to inform us of anything that might have an impact on her safety or well-being;
- We expect the school to comply with the policies of the Green Valley School District;
- We expect the school to follow all available "supplemental screening practices" set forth in the *DOJ Guidelines for the Screening of Persons Working with Children*;
- We expect the school to be a weapons-free environment;
- While we authorize you to make decisions on our behalf about educational matters, we do not authorize you to make decisions on our behalf about life-and-death matters;
- We are relying upon you or your designates to notify us of any threats to commit violent acts at the school. Even if Kate is not specifically named, since she could be in the environment of targeted individuals, we want to be informed so we can evaluate the risks. We request that a safety committee of parents be formed, and that the committee be notified of all threats to commit violent acts.
- [other points specific to your child];

Just as we hold you to your duty as principal, so do we ask you to hold us to ours as parents: On this point, please advise us of ways we can help you develop a safer school. Knowing that you face bureaucratic, political, and budgetary challenges, there is surely something we can do to help.

For now, we have a few specific questions:

[from the entire list of questions in Appendix #2, or others].

We're confident that if your office and our family work together, our daughter will have the best possible experience at Green Valley. At the same time, we want to assist you in furthering the well-being of all the students.

Sincerely,<br>Holly and Ryan Jason

The principal won't have ever received a letter like this one, and it can start a dialogue about student safety, particularly if you pursue it. The references to threats and weapons are included in the letter not only because of the famous tragedies at Jonesboro and Springfield. Addressing these things is important for preventing violence far less grandiose than the rare incidents of mass shootings at schools. Those high-profile cases do, however, teach us some lessons about violence (more on this in Chapter 13), and they show us how schools respond to threats. For example, after the Springfield, Oregon, shootings by fifteen-year-old Kip Kinkel, school superintendent Jamon Kent told a news conference: "If we detained every student who said, 'I'm going to kill someone,' we would have a large number of students detained." Though he didn't note that "detaining" a student could take just a minute in some cases (such as with students who are joking), and he didn't specify what he considers a "large number," other principals joined in, saying student threats are so frequent that it's impossible to evaluate them all.

That is not so. It may have been an effective defense from a public relations point of view and it's definitely a smart defense against scrutiny into how schools handle threats, i.e., "Mr. Harrison, you really have no idea how many threats kids make." The fact is, however, schools also have no idea how many threats kids make. Whatever the number, it is a manageable amount.

Here's why I'm so confident: There are individual institutions of society that evaluate literally thousands of threats each year, successfully separating those that require greater scrutiny from those that are mere words. My office helped design threat-assessment systems used for screening threats to the governors of ten states, hundreds of judges, and all members of Congress. Now *these* people know something about getting lots of threats. The same strategies they use could be applied to helping schools evaluate students who threaten. (There's more on this topic in *The Gift of Fear*.)

It would be reasonable if school officials simply said, "We're in way over our heads on this," or "We need more resources and training," or even, "We don't know what to do," but authoritatively telling parents they shouldn't expect improvement does not address the problem.

A parent committee can assist the school in deciding how to respond to a given threat, as well as when to notify other parents. In so doing, the committee can lift a huge burden from the principal. There is precedent for this approach: For example, large corporations receive bomb threats; those with the most effective programs have groups who decide whether to evacuate a building, whether to notify employees, when to bring in the police or fire department. Schoolchildren deserve as much. There is also precedent for bringing members of a community together to help with high-stakes decisions. An obvious one is a jury, but there have also been citizen groups convened by police departments to help solve tough murder cases.

Members of a parent committee can be appointed by the school board or by an elected official. They can be chosen for their levelheadedness, high regard in the community, even for their political connections—it really doesn't matter. The important qualification for each member is having a child who is attending the school. Ideally, the committee would be provided with a liaison officer at the local police department as well as a liaison at the local mental health facility.

Members of the committee can be educated about threats and predictions of violence (I'm glad to help any school with suggested reading material or training methods—see Appendix #4 and Appendix #5). The committee can be convened whenever a case meets some predetermined criteria. That may happen a few times a year, or it may never happen, but parents will get a great deal of comfort knowing they are represented in the process.

What would a parent committee have said if presented with the case of Kip Kinkel, who shot twenty of his schoolmates? Of the facts known to school administrators, there is one that called out pretty clearly the day before the shooting spree: Kip was arrested for having a handgun in his locker at school. A friend had stolen it in a burglary and sold it to Kip (who needed it because his mother had just taken away his own guns). After being suspended and taken to the police station, Kip was charged with two offenses. Then he was released to the custody of his father.

Problem: It was his father who started Kip's collection of guns in the first place, though not in the cliché macho way you might imagine. You see, the Kinkels (both teachers) were not "gun people." Rather, Kip had begged for guns so often that his father finally relented. He felt Kip was going to get a gun one way or another, so why not under parental supervision? This is a bit like saying a teen who wants cocaine is going to get it one way or another, so Dad should just give to him.

A family friend recommended that if Bill Kinkel wanted to get his son a gun, it should be a single-shot rifle. But Bill chose a semi-automatic instead. Later, he surprised Kip with a Glock pistol. Friends of the family said the Kinkels tried to be nurturing with Kip, though one has to wonder what inside the boy was really being nurtured by the gift of guns.

It isn't my preference to criticize parents who can't defend themselves, but in this case I have no choice since Kip killed his father and mother before he went to school and shot twenty teenagers. Anyway, his parents were well defended in the media by their friends. Not knowing what the Kinkels were thinking, we are left only with the facts of what happened—but imagine we could go back to the moment before police released Kip to the custody of his father. Imagine police and the school learned all of what follows from Bill Kinkel, Kip's teachers, and classmates:

- Kip had been building pipe bombs;
- He bragged about cutting up cats and squirrels;
- His parents recognized he was troubled and had taken him to therapy, tried home schooling, and even gave him Ritalin and Prozac;
- His history of lethal behavior included an incident where he threw rocks off a freeway bridge;
- In speech class, Kip gave a presentation on how to build a pipe bomb (complete with illustrations);
- In a literature class, he read from a diary about plans to "kill everyone."

Imagine yourself on that parent committee having just learned these facts about Kip Kinkel. Would you favor releasing him to the custody of someone (his father) who knew this situation intimately, and yet when he went shopping could think of no better surprise for his son than a *second* semiautomatic weapon? If a gun store did the same thing, they'd be liable; if a police department did the same thing with one of their officers, they'd be negligent. I know there are a hundred other factors that contributed to Kip's violence—social, cultural, psychological, genetic—but if his parents hadn't given Kip guns, this would be the sad story of a sad kid. Instead, it's the sad story of hundreds of people damaged by Kip's violence, twenty of them physically, two of them mortally, and all of them permanently.

Bill and Faith Kinkel paid the ultimate price for their involvement, and they leave us knowing that it isn't just violent kids we must protect our children from, but also adults who give up and give in (and give guns), adults who deny, allow, encourage, and facilitate violence. If a parent committee and school officials gathered for ten minutes and learned what you've now learned about Kip Kinkel, would there have been more effective intervention? I imagine the answer is Yes, though some school principals give me reason to hesitate. According to a Department of Justice study, nearly 60 percent recalled incidents involving guns on school grounds, and 45 percent reported at least one student being shot (on or off school grounds), but only 2 *percent considered guns as a serious campus problem*. Parents must convince the remaining 98 percent of principals that guns are a serious campus problem, if only for the fear and anxiety they bring to children.

Be assured that when it comes to safety, you have something to teach your child's school.

# CHAPTER ELEVEN

# PROTECTING OPHELIA

*Men whose acts are at direct variance with their words com-
mand no respect, and what they say has but little weight.*
—SAMUEL SMILES, 1859

Not being the parent of a teenage girl, I've had to ask others to tell me
which milestone caused the most parental anxiety. I'd like to report
that there is some consensus on this question, but there isn't. For
some fathers I spoke with, the hardest milestone was the first time
their teenage daughters slept over at a friend's house. For some mothers, it was their daughter's first date (or seventh or twentieth, depending upon how the mothers felt about the young man involved). For
some parents, it was the first time their daughter drove, or traveled out
of town, or stayed at the library until it closed, or threw a party, or
went to a party, or didn't come home from a party at the time agreed
to, or . . . you get the idea.

Casey, the father of two teenage girls, ages fifteen and seventeen,
gave me his stream-of-consciousness monologue about his daughters:

For every bit of love I feel toward Faye and Hallie, there's a pound of resentment because these girls, doing nothing more than just living their lives, have got me worrying mine away. When they sleep over somewhere, I don't sleep. When Faye goes out with some boy, I don't sleep until after she gets home and the sound of his car engine has disappeared in the distance. I don't really get a good night's sleep until she tells me, "I'm not seeing so-and-so anymore." But there's another so-and-so to take his place and I can't say I've liked any of them, though I *have* said I liked all of them, but I do that because if she ever thinks I hate one of them, that's the one she'll marry. It's great when she gets fed up with some guy and asks me why boys are so awful. I tell her "They just are," and sometimes she says, "I hate boys," and those are the nights I sleep best. I hope she doesn't get married soon, or maybe I just hope she doesn't get married. And when I think of Hallie dating, I have to stop myself. Not ready. Me. I'm not ready. I'm sure she's ready—particularly when I judge by the fifteen-year-old girls I dated when I was a kid. I must *never* think about it that way again.

Why all the worry? Well, this is one time that some of it is justified. Teenagers, especially girls, are the most victimized segment of our population (and at the same time, the least likely to report a crime). In a survey of prison inmates who had committed violence against young people, three quarters of the victims were girls. Why? For starters, they offer less resistance and they pose less risk than adult women. Next, teenage girls are perceived as sexual objects, prohibited perhaps, but sexual nonetheless. The issue is complicated by the fact that teenage girls are themselves exploring the dynamics of male attention and they want to be accepted by men. Some girls mix a feeling of immortality with budding sexuality, seeing fearlessness as a form of sophistication. This coincides with enhanced vulnerability and exposure because teenage girls are at the age to be away from parental supervision, to take a first job, have a first date, experiment with drugs and alcohol.

All these things conspired to make a girl named Kim an ideal target. When she was about ten, her father's friend Denny was a mystery man. He was big and muscular and serious, with his black hair in a crew cut, and his dark eyes always a little sleepy-looking. Kim had never seen him laugh, not even when he drank beer with her father. "Don't be too friendly with Denny," her mother warned whenever he visited. At twelve, Kim wanted more information: "Mom, what's the story with Denny? Dad likes him, and he's a policeman, so why don't you like him?" She didn't get an answer—unless you count, "Just do what I say." When Kim was fourteen, tall and slender with long blond hair, her mother finally decided to tell her the story: Denny had been accused of raping three women; he had supposedly pulled them over for traffic citations, then assaulted them, and gotten away with it. "So watch out for Denny."

Her father's version was different: The three women got together and falsely accused a diligent police officer because he insisted on giving them speeding tickets. Kim's parents periodically argued the merits of the various rumors about Denny, each weighing in with evidence for or against him. Whatever the truth, if he'd done anything wrong it had been years ago, and Kim's mother eventually stopped the warnings. A month after her sixteenth birthday, Kim got her own evidence against Denny.

The family had rented a vacation home in Santa Barbara for the summer, a financial reach that meant prestige for her parents but felt like prison to Kim—until she met Karl and his wife, Rocky. They were the cool couple across the street in the cool house with stained-glass skylights. They were older than Kim's parents, but they acted a lot younger. They cooked on a wood-burning stove, drank lots of wine, always had music playing, plus Karl was funny. He was big like a football player, but laughed like a kid, and he wore a kid's watch that had a moose on its face—the antlers were the hands.

The night it happened, Kim's parents were having a party for some friends and neighbors. Kim went to the garage to get a carton of soft drinks and had just turned the lights out when she heard Denny's voice near her: "Why don't you go upstairs into your bedroom and I'll meet you there in a few minutes." Kim wanted to say "Why don't you drop dead," but she was frozen by the realization that Denny must have done everything he was ever accused of doing. She heard him take a step toward her in the dark and then she felt his breath on her neck. "It'll feel good, I guarantee it—like this." And he stroked the back of Kim's leg.

Suddenly—and blessedly—the garage light came on. Kim looked at the hand on the switch and recognized Karl's funny moose watch. "Leave her alone!"

Denny snorted, then muttered something about as eloquent as a snort, and went back to the party. Karl helped Kim carry the soft drinks into the kitchen, and that was that. When Rocky and Karl were saying good night, Kim mouthed to him: "Thank you." She didn't tell her parents what Denny had done or how Karl had come to the rescue.

The following evening, Denny was spending the night with Kim's parents, and since she intended to avoid him for as long as possible, Kim went over to visit Karl and Rocky. After dinner, she fell asleep on their couch. Rocky telephoned Kim's mother and they agreed to just let her sleep over. Kim liked being with Karl and Rocky, and she slept over there a few more times throughout the summer. She remarked to Karl that she'd miss them when she went back home. He gave her a little hug and said, "You'll get over it."

Karl had a son from his first marriage—Carey—who occasionally slept over in a room above the garage. He was twenty-three and cute and gave Kim still another incentive to spend time at their house. One Saturday when he was there, Kim spent the whole day sunning on the roof and listening to music. In the evening, she and Rocky cooked, and then they all watched a movie. Actually, Kim watched half of it and fell asleep. Again, they put a blanket over her and let her sleep, but after everyone had gone to bed, Kim woke up abruptly. Somebody was on the couch with her, under the blanket, a hand on her mouth, a hand on her thigh. Carey, she thought for an instant, but then she saw something devastating: the watch with the moose on it. And she smelled Karl's wine. And she heard Karl whispering to her. And she couldn't believe it.

When she pushed his hand from her leg, he took his other hand off her mouth and made more progress moving it up her thigh. One hand was groping her breasts, but Kim didn't scream because she knew he'd cover her mouth again. When she resisted him, he whispered, "Okay, shut up! I'll just sleep here next to you," but then after a few minutes, he started again. When she'd get him to stop, he'd fall asleep. If she tried to get up, he'd awaken and start molesting her again. When he became most insistent and aggressive, his hand pushing between her legs, Kim kept repeating: "But you love Rocky, you love her so much," and he stopped for a while.

At one point, Karl must have felt that Kim's voice was too loud, and he covered her mouth again, angrily holding her face so tightly that she couldn't breathe. Part of his hand was literally inside her mouth and the harder she struggled, the harder he held her, so she bit down hard on his hand. Karl was so anesthetized by wine that he barely winced, just moaned and fell asleep again. The watch with the moose read 2:00 when Kim first saw it, and 5:00 when Karl finally went upstairs to bed.

Kim lay there and wept. Even when she heard people getting up in the morning, she stayed on the couch pretending to be asleep. But as she thought about what Karl had done and how she trusted him and how they'd been friends all summer, her teary eyes turned clear and angry. Carey was in the kitchen, and without hesitation, Kim called in to him: "Your father was down here last night trying to rape me.

He got under the covers and wouldn't let me get up, and I begged him to—"

It was Karl who interrupted her—he was also in the kitchen and had heard everything she'd said. "Should we have eggs or pancakes for breakfast?" he called back to her.

Kim really couldn't believe what was happening. This isn't a figure of speech; she actually couldn't believe it. She heard Carey say he was going out, and then heard the back door open and close. She heard Rocky come downstairs. She heard the couple cooking, and then listened as Rocky ate breakfast with the man who'd just molested her. They talked about some syrup that Rocky's mother used to make and laughed about a friend who'd decided to go back to his cheating wife. What happened on the couch during the night did not influence their morning in any way.

After Karl went upstairs, Kim started crying so loud that Rocky came in and asked what was wrong. Kim choked out the whole story, but Rocky kept saying, "No, no, that doesn't sound right. Are you sure?" Reminiscent of her parents prosecuting and defending Denny, Kim searched her memory for compelling bits of evidence—but Rocky was a biased jury.

"Kim, did you scream? You'd have screamed if all that really happened. What you're saying doesn't make sense, Kim, because I'd have heard—"

Rocky interrupted herself as if slapped in the face. Almost too quiet to be heard, she whispered, "That bastard said I seemed nervous last night—he gave me two sleeping pills!"

The now-convinced Rocky ran toward the stairs. Kim called out her closing argument: "Look at his hands, Rocky; I bit him and there'll be a mark."

Kim stood at the bottom of the steps listening as Karl launched his denial. First, he sent out the reconnaissance team: "What are you talking about?" Then the infantry: "She's crazy, that little bitch is crazy!" Finally, he deployed a sniper, a mercenary who fired a single shot deep into Kim's self-worth: "Slut!" he repeated louder and louder. "That slut asked me to lie down with her and I wouldn't! She's a slut, a slut who walks around in her bikini all day. And she's accusing ME! Comes into my house and upsets my wife and then accuses ME!"

They argued for another hour, and though the sounds still reached Kim, most of the words didn't penetrate—there was no room inside her for any more injury. When she heard Rocky sob, "I'm sorry, I should have trusted you," Kim ran outside, down the narrow street, through the unlocked front door of the rented house, past her parents sitting in the kitchen, living the same life they did the day before. She went to her room and fell asleep.

Some hours later Kim awakened to her mother's voice: "That's the last time you're staying over there. You stay up all night, come home and sleep all day." Kim had a second or two in which life seemed normal, a second or two when the incident was not on her mind. But then she could smell Karl's breath again, or thought she could. It really had happened. Karl had held her against her will, molested her, and would have raped her.

As Kim blurted out the details of what had happened, her mother became pale so quickly that it looked like a special effect from a movie. After a long silence, she responded: "Don't tell your father. He'd kill Karl if he knew." Then her mother hugged her hard. It was a hug that said, *Keep this inside.*

Kim believed then—and still does—that her mother's reaction would not have been any different if Karl had fully raped her.

It was ten years before Kim told anyone else what happened, and as important, what had not happened: no police report, no confrontation, no support, no apology, no recognition of reality. It was another ten years before she shook off the shame, the doubts about herself, the subtle belief that she must have done something to compel Karl to act in a way he otherwise never would have, and the belief that she could not protect herself.

By the time she related the story to me, Kim had a daughter of her own. That's when she first came to understand that she had, in fact, protected herself very well. Her strategies with Karl had worked—even her decision not to scream. A scream might well have intensified Karl's use of force, taken him to a full commitment, and in any case, with Karl's son asleep over the garage and Rocky drugged, nobody would have heard it.

Kim had, by her intuitive use of compliance and resistance, saved herself from being raped or injured. As is often the case with victims of sexual abuse, the greatest damage Kim suffered was from the lack of supportive response from her parents, the lack of acknowledgment of what had happened.

Though it didn't end up helping her much, Kim was at least able to tell her mother what had happened. Hundreds of thousands of young women choose to not tell their parents. Recall that one of the items in the Test of Twelve is the need for children to feel comfortable bringing difficult information to their mother or father. That need is every bit as acute for teenage girls, as Charlene described to me in a letter:

I was beaten up and raped by a boyfriend when I was fifteen. Even though I was obviously injured, I told my parents I'd been in a fight at school. I'm from an upper-middle-class family with well-educated parents, but I think if they'd been more forthcoming with me about "what's out there," I would have been able to tell them.

Surprisingly, for some young women who rescue themselves through cleverness or use of force, the experience of victimization can actually be favorable. Prevailing over a predator can leave a woman empowered, more confident, and more competent to meet the challenges of life. I know women who suffered greatly after experiencing a crime of domination or force, and I know others who flourished. The key difference lies in the victim's perception of how she managed the situation.

Over the years, many people have related their stories of victimization to me, often incorrectly anticipating my response: "You're probably going to say what I did was very stupid," or "I'm sure it was the worst thing I could do, but . . ." I make it a practice to praise people for their management of safety challenges. Clearly, whatever they did, they survived adequately to be able to relate the story; they were not killed, they were not destroyed by the experience. Since the belief that she failed to protect herself is one of the greatest harms a victim might suffer, when a victim tells her story and people respond with You-should-have-this or You-should-never-have-that, they are often adding to the victimization.

Never be concerned that a victim of violence or domination didn't learn a lesson—she did. What victims need to recover is the belief that they are competent to protect themselves.

•     •     •

Kim's experience raises a question: How would it be if teenage girls had some initial wariness about every man they encountered? It would be realistic—sad maybe, but realistic. Here's why: Rapes and other sexual crimes are virtually always committed by men, and most rapes and sexual assaults happen to girls under eighteen years of age.

Does this mean a teenage girl should have a "Prove-to-me-that-you-aren't-dangerous" attitude with all new men? No, because dangerous men are the very ones most frequently seeking to "prove" they aren't dangerous. The strategies such men apply are designed to gain your trust. Men who will not harm you needn't persuade you to trust them; they simply act appropriately from the moment you meet them and for as long as you know them. They do not exude forced harmlessness like the drama teacher everyone assumes is gay, or the understanding neighbor who says, "If you ever need to just get away from your parents for a while, consider my place open to you."

Other than by the passage of time, it isn't possible for a man to prove he isn't dangerous, nor is it his responsibility to do so. It is, however, a young woman's responsibility to heed intuitive signals if she gets them, and it is her responsibility to learn and recognize the strategies of persuasion from Chapter 4.

I'm realistic enough to know that teaching teenage girls about safety isn't easy. Warnings of danger haven't become any more compelling than they were when you heard them from your parents. That's partly because there is an appropriate divide between teenagers and their parents; nature wants young adults to tear away for a while and find their own path. Also, while a mother is probably familiar with every important life experience her teenage daughter has had (because she had them herself), their cultural experiences are hugely different. Here are some humorous but true examples:

Your teenage daughter has never feared a nuclear war; to her *The Day After* is a pill, not a movie. She's too young to remember the space shuttle blowing up, she has no idea that hostages were held in Iran, she knows there was a president named Reagan, but doesn't know he was shot, and if she's heard of Robert Kennedy, it's because he's John Kennedy, Jr.'s uncle. The expression "you sound like a broken record" means nothing to her—she's never owned a record player. She doesn't know who shot J.R. or even who he was, and the same for Mork and Mu'ammar Gadhafi. The *Titanic* was found? Until the movie, she didn't know it was lost. She has no idea when or why Jordache jeans were cool, and to her, America, Alabama, and Chicago are places—not music bands. Finally, there's been only one Pope, Jay Leno has always been the host of *The Tonight Show*, popcorn has always been cooked in a microwave, and Michael Jackson has always looked like this.

Indeed, many things in the world have changed, but unfortunately, there are many more that haven't changed, including intimate violence, date rape, rape, and murder. In our violent patriarchy, some mothers and teenage daughters may find that their shared target-status brings them closer together.

Of all the lessons a mother might pass to her daughter, the most valuable can be summed up with just two letters: N–O. Though the word *No* is one of the most potent in our language, it is among the least popular. In part, that's because we grew up associating that word with not getting what we wanted. Most kids hate the word, but as they grow, there is exceptional value from learning to love it. Though perhaps hard to imagine, this single word can play a central role in safety, particularly for young women, and particularly when she gets to dating age.

Teaching teens about this isn't easy because they've learned so much about dating from movies and TV shows. A popular Hollywood formula could be called Boy Wants Girl, Girl Doesn't Want Boy, Boy Persists and Harasses Girl, Boy Gets Girl. Many movies teach young men that if you just stay with it, even if you offend her, even if she says she wants nothing to do with you, even if she's in another relationship, even if you've treated her like trash (and sometimes because you've treated her like trash), you'll get the girl.

Young women will benefit their whole lives from learning that persistence only proves persistence—it does not prove love. *The fact that a romantic pursuer is relentless doesn't mean you are special—it means he is troubled.*

Young women (and all women) benefit from understanding this paradox: Men are nice when they pursue, women are nice when they reject. The most troublesome part of this niceness is the too-popular practice called "letting him down easy." True to what they are taught, rejecting women often say less than they mean. True to what they are taught, men often hear less than what is said. Nowhere is this problem more alarmingly expressed than by the hundreds of thousands of fathers (and mothers), older brothers (and sisters), movies, and television shows that teach most young men that when she says No, that's not what she means. Add to this all the young women taught to "play hard to get" when they don't actually want to be gotten at all. The result is that No can mean many things in this culture. Here's just a small sample:

Maybe
Hmm . . .
Not sure
Not yet
Give me time
Keep trying
I've found my man!

There is one book in which the meaning of No is always clear. It is the dictionary, but since Hollywood writers don't seem to use that book very often, we have to. We have to teach young women that No is a complete sentence. This is not as simple as it may appear. Understand that when a man in our culture says No, it's usually the end of a discussion, but when a woman says No, it's the beginning of a negotiation. This fact brings to mind a popular adage about persuasion: "The sale begins when the customer says No."

What starts as persistence often leads to unwanted pursuit, stalking, even date rape. I've successfully lobbied and testified for stalking laws in several states, but I would trade them all for a high school class that would teach young men how to hear No, and teach young women that it's all right to explicitly reject. If the culture taught (and then allowed) teenage girls to explicitly reject and to explicitly say No, or if more of them took that power early in every relationship, stalking and date-rape cases would decline dramatically.

Looking for Mr. Right has taken on far greater significance than Getting Rid of Mr. Wrong, so young women are not taught how to get out of relationships. That high school class would stress the one rule that applies to all types of unwanted pursuit: *Do not negotiate*. Once a girl has made the decision that she doesn't want a relationship with a particular man, it needs to be said one time, explicitly. Almost any contact after that rejection will be seen as negotiation. If a woman tells a man over and over again that she doesn't want to talk to him, that is talking to him, and every time she does it, she betrays her resolve in the matter. If you tell someone ten times that you don't want to talk to him, you *are* talking to him—nine more times than you wanted to.

When a young woman gets thirty messages from a pursuer, then finally gives in and returns his calls, he learns that the cost of reaching her is leaving thirty messages. For this type of young man, any contact will be seen as progress. Of course, some young women are worried that by not responding, they'll provoke him, so they try letting him down easy. Often, the result is that he believes she is conflicted, uncertain, really likes him but just doesn't know it yet.

When a girl rejects someone who has a crush on her, and she says, "It's just that I don't want to be in a relationship right now," he hears only the words "right now." To him, this means she will want to be in a relationship later. The rejection should be "I don't want to be in a relationship *with you*." Unless it's just that clear, and sometimes even when it is, he doesn't hear it.

If she says, "You're a great guy and you have a lot to offer, but I'm not the one for you; my head's not in the right place these days," he thinks: "She really likes me; it's just that she's confused. I've got to prove to her that she's the one for me."

When a young woman explains her decision not to accept or stay in a relationship, this type of pursuer will challenge each reason she offers. I suggest that teenage girls be taught that they never need to explain why they don't want a relationship, but simply make clear that they have thought it over, that this is their decision, and that they expect the boy to respect it. Why would she explain intimate aspects of her life, plans, and romantic choices to someone with whom she doesn't want a relationship?

The word *rejection* is weighted down with negative connotations; a better word is *decision*, as in "I have made a decision that we won't be having a relationship." This statement offers no reasons and begs no negotiations, but young women in this culture are virtually prohibited from speaking it. They are taught that speaking it clearly and early may lead to unpopularity, banishment, anger, and even violence.

If a teenage boy still pursues after hearing a girl's decision, he is saying, in effect, "I do not accept your decision." If he debates, doubts, negotiates, or attempts to change her mind, her resolve should be strengthened, not challenged. That's because she can be immediately certain that she made the right decision about this person. Obviously, she wouldn't want a relationship with someone who does not hear what she says.

An unwanted pursuer might escalate his behavior to include such things as persistent phone calls and messages, showing up uninvited at her classes or home, following her, and trying to enlist her friends or family in his campaign. If any of these things happens (assuming that she has communicated her decision one time explicitly), it is very important that no further detectable response be given. When a girl communicates again with someone she has explicitly rejected, her actions don't match her words. The boy is able to choose which communications (actions versus words) actually represent the woman's feelings. Not surprisingly, he usually chooses the ones that serve him. Often, such pursuers leave phone messages that ostensibly offer closure, but that are actually crudely concealed efforts to get a response—and remember, he views any response as progress.

MESSAGE: Hi, it's Bryan. Listen, all I'm asking for is a chance to say goodbye; that's all. Just a fast meeting, and then I'm gone.

BEST RESPONSE: No response.

MESSAGE: Listen, it's Bryan. You won't hear from me again after today. I'm calling for the last time. [This line, though spoken often by unwanted pursuers, is rarely true.] It's urgent I speak with you.

BEST RESPONSE: No response.

If a young woman has trouble not responding, she can be reminded of this axiom:

MEN WHO CANNOT LET GO CHOOSE WOMEN
WHO CANNOT SAY NO.

Many unwanted relationships start with a boy's pickup strategies. These haven't changed much in a long time and aren't likely to, but the responses of uninterested girls could certainly include options other than "You're cute but . . ." Somebody recently sent me a list of funny comebacks to popular pickup lines. I'm not necessarily recommending these smart-ass responses, but girls benefit from knowing as many alternatives to compliance as possible:

MAN: Your place or mine?
WOMAN: Both. You go to yours and I'll go to mine.

MAN: What's your sign?
WOMAN: Do Not Enter.

MAN: I know how to please a woman.
WOMAN: Then please leave me alone.

MAN: I'd go to the end of the world for you.
WOMAN: But would you stay there?

MAN: Is this seat empty?
WOMAN: Yes, and this one will be too if you sit down.

However she puts it, every time a young woman says No, she is actually saying Yes to something else: She is saying Yes to herself. One thing's almost for certain: If a teenager is fluent in the use of the word No, she will at some point be called a bitch. That needn't be an insult; bitch can stand for "Boys, I'm Taking Control Here."

.    .    .

The man who will attempt to molest a teenager needs an environment in which that's possible. He needs to get her to a place where there is nobody nearby who will hear her if she resists loudly or calls for help. His other option is to get her in a frame of mind where she *chooses* not to resist loudly and *chooses* not to call for help. Accordingly, there are times and places where wariness is called for, i.e., times of vulnerability. There are times and places where wariness is wasted, i.e., times when teenage girls are not vulnerable. Dangerous men are dangerous only if they can get you somewhere. They are not dangerous on the dance floor, in the restaurant, in the crowded mall. That may be where they meet you, but it's not where they'd try to hurt you.

Do such men actually plot their opportunities? Often, they do, but there is also a type of sexual offender who is on autopilot, operating out of a second nature, an intuitive skill at knowing how to gain control. The good news is that just as he knows when a given environment serves his plans, so can his target intuitively and automatically observe, "I am at a disadvantage here." Since much of what I've said about the nature of men is anything but PC—as in politically correct—I'll borrow the acronym from that tired phrase to characterize the contexts in which young women (and women in general) can recognize their disadvantage: PC will now stand for Privacy and Control.

If a man who intends sexual assault or rape has Privacy and Control, he can victimize someone. If he does not have PC, he is not dangerous, period. Accordingly, just the presence of these two features in a situation can trigger a young woman's heightened awareness and readiness. The presence of Privacy does not mean a man is sinister, but it does mean a girl is vulnerable. At that point, she'll benefit from carefully evaluating how the man got Privacy: Was it by circumstance or by his design?

*Privacy* is defined here as isolation or concealment. A private place is one in which there is little or no chance that a third party will suddenly show up, a place that is out of range of the hearing of people who could assist the young woman. Cars, hotel rooms, apartments, houses, closed businesses, wilderness areas, the auditorium after hours, back corridors at work, a remote parking area—these all can afford Privacy.

The word *Control* defines a relationship between two people, in this case between a victimizer and his target. Control exists when one person is persuaded or compelled to be directed by the other.

Control can exist when a young woman feels persuaded to do what a man wants because she fears being injured if she resists, or because she doesn't want to hurt his feelings, or because she doesn't want him to hurt her reputation, or because she wants to avoid rejection.

Don't think of persuasion as something someone does to us; persuasion is an internal process, not an external one. *We persuade ourselves.* A predator merely manipulates how things seem to us.

Whatever the method, persuasion requires the participation of the target, and human beings are the creatures who most cooperate with their predators. By contrast, the lion has a more difficult predatory challenge than does the man who would rape a teenager. The lion, after all, must walk around in a lion suit; he is burdened by the obviousness of the very assets that give him power (claws, teeth, muscle). Hunting would be easy if the lion could look like a timid kitten when it served him. Man can.

Some men with sinister intent seek control through physical power. Because the target's resistance might be noisy, the power-predator requires more Privacy. He cannot retreat easily because there comes a point where there is no ambiguity about his intent. He commits to likely consequences in ways that most persuasion-predators do not. The power-predator needs more Privacy, more space, more time, more recklessness, and more luck in order to get what he wants. Thus, the power-predator is more rare than the persuasion-predator, but also more likely to do serious injury.

The persuasion-predator gets a target to cooperate and is thus granted much more flexibility when it comes to Privacy. This man can use a room in the girl's home, even if family members are somewhere in the house. For him, Privacy is adequately afforded by a room at work that people don't frequent, even if the business is open. For him, a few empty seats in a theater can offer enough concealment to sexually abuse a teenager. Accordingly, the teenage girl who can be easily persuaded appeals to a far wider group of predators and is more likely to be sexually assaulted than a teenage girl who cannot be easily persuaded.

Note that I've been using the word *target* rather than the word *victim*. That's because being a target need not automatically make one a victim. In fact, it's nearly impossible for a teenage girl to avoid being a target at some point, but it is very possible to avoid becoming a victim. The best way to do that is by recognizing PC at the earliest possible moment, and if things feel uncomfortable (even if it is just the vulnerability itself that feels uncomfortable), taking steps to change the situation.

Of course, teenage girls will often be in private environments with men who have no sinister intent whatsoever. The driving instructor who takes your teenage daughter all over town is granted some PC opportunities, but if he is a good man, no problem. Still, it's appropriate for a teenage girl to recognize the P in PC if several turns take them to some remote area. Ideally, if this occurs, she'd be more alert for the introduction of Control.

Right when a man begins to introduce the P or the C is the defining moment when one can determine—virtually choose—whether to be a target or a victim. A girl can say as the driving instructor's directions take them out of populated areas: "I'd be more comfortable staying in the city," or "Please stay in familiar areas." If the man has sinister intent, this girl has just asserted in the clearest language that she will not be easily persuaded, thus his options for gaining Control are limited to force or fear, and that requirement will exclude the overwhelming majority of predators.

PC is easy to memorize and recall because these concepts are already embedded in the consciousness of human beings, including your teenage daughter. When someone acts in a way that alarms her, she instantly and automatically evaluates PC. She intuitively weighs whether anyone might hear a call for help or whether someone might come along, and she measures what degree of Control the predator might have over her. The key—the trick if you will—is to recognize PC before someone alarms her, even in the absence of obvious sinister intent on the man's part. The impala who finds itself alone with the lion doesn't wait to see how the carnivore will behave. The impala evaluates its options and resources all the while.

Does this mean a teenage girl must be in a constant state of alertness whenever she is in the presence of men? Absolutely not. This is about being alone with a man in a situation in which she is vulnerable. And then, a recognition of PC might be no more than a passing thought that opens the girl to her intuition about this man. If she feels at ease with her boss at the restaurant even though there are no customers around, fine. But being cognizant of PC means she'll sooner recognize the slightest inappropriate comment or unusual behavior, like locking the front door before closing time.

Teenage girls: Memorize PC—Privacy and Control—and when someone has these advantages, be open to signals of that person's intent. That's all, not a fear of every man, just an acceptance of reality.

●　　●　　●

---

## Survival Signals

- Forced Teaming
- Charm and Niceness
- Too Many Details
- Typecasting
- Loan-sharking
- The Unsolicited Promise
- Discounting the Word "No"

---

I wish every young woman in America could have seen these signals as clearly as I did on a flight from Chicago to Los Angeles. I was seated next to a teenage girl who was traveling alone. A man in his forties who'd been watching her from across the aisle took off the headphones he was wearing and said to her with partylike flair, "These things just don't get *loud* enough for me!" He then put his hand out toward her and said, "I'm Billy." Though it may not be immediately apparent, his statement was actually a question, and the young girl responded with exactly the information Billy hoped for: She told him her full name. Then she put out her hand, which he held a little too long. In the conversation that ensued, he didn't directly ask for any information, but he certainly got lots of it.

He said, "I hate landing in a city and not knowing if anybody is meeting me." The girl answered this question by saying that she didn't know how she was getting from the airport to the house where she was staying. Billy asked another question: "Friends can really let you down sometimes." The young girl responded by explaining, "The people I'm staying with [thus, not family] are expecting me on a later flight."

Billy said, "I love the independence of arriving in a city when nobody knows I'm coming." This was the virtual opposite of what he'd said a moment before about hating to arrive and not be met. He added, "But you're probably not that independent." She quickly volunteered that she'd been traveling on her own since she was thirteen.

"You sound like a woman I know from Europe, more like a woman than a teenager," he said as he handed her his drink (Scotch), which the flight attendant had just served him. "You sound like you play by your own rules." I hoped she would decline to take the drink, and she did at first, but he persisted: "Come on, you can do whatever you want," and she took a sip of his drink.

I looked over at Billy, looked at his muscular build, at the old tattoo showing on the top of his wrist, and at his cheap jewelry. I noted that he was drinking alcohol on this morning flight and had no carry-on bag. I looked at his new cowboy boots, new denim pants and leather jacket. I knew he'd recently been in jail. He responded to my knowing look assertively: "How you doin' this morning, pal? Gettin' out of Chicago?" I nodded.

As Billy got up to go to the bathroom, he put one more piece of bait in his trap: Leaning close to the girl, he gave a slow smile and said, "Your eyes are *awesome.*"

In a period of just a few minutes, I had watched Billy use forced teaming (they both had nobody meeting them, he said), too many details (the headphones and the woman he knows from Europe), loansharking (the drink offer), charm (the compliment about the girl's eyes), and typecasting ("You're probably not that independent"). I had also seen him discount the girl's No when she declined the drink.

As Billy walked away down the aisle, I asked the girl if I could talk to her for a moment, and she hesitantly said Yes. It speaks to the power of predatory strategies that she was glad to talk to Billy but a bit wary of the passenger (me) who asked permission to speak with her. "He is going to offer you a ride from the airport," I told her, "and he's not a good guy."

I saw Billy again at baggage claim as he approached the girl. Though I couldn't hear them, the conversation was apparent. She was shaking her head and saying No, and he wasn't accepting it. She held firm, and he finally walked off with an angry gesture, not the "nice" guy he'd been up till then.

There was no movie on that flight, but Billy had let me watch a classic performance of an interview, that, by little more than the context (forty-year-old stranger and teenage girl alone), was high stakes.

●    ●    ●

By the time a girl has reached her teens, she has gone from being an occasional sexual predatory prize to the leading sexual predatory prize. Accordingly, I don't think there's much information she need be protected from. Her understanding of how persuasion strategies work, and her understanding of how targets are selected, is now her armor. Often, merely seeing that armor will incline a predator to choose someone else. We never want him, however, to see the *absence* of armor that is revealed when a teenage girl violates nature's basic safety rules.

The example I see most often is a teenage girl jogging or walking along in public enjoying music through headphones. She has disabled her hearing, the survival sense most likely to warn her about dangerous approaches. To make matters worse, those wires leading up to her ears display her vulnerability for everyone to see. Another example is that while young women wouldn't walk around blindfolded, many do not use the full resources of their sight. A young woman who believes she is being followed might take just a tentative look, hoping to see if someone is visible in her peripheral vision. It is better to turn completely, take in everything, and look squarely at someone who concerns you. This not only gives you information, but it communicates to a pursuer that you are not a tentative, frightened victim-in-waiting. The message for every teenage girl (and woman): You are an animal of nature, fully endowed with hearing, sight, intellect, and dangerous defenses. You are not easy prey, so don't act like you are.

Unfortunately, modern technology has discovered a way to temporarily turn off all of a woman's defenses, and since millions of teenage boys and young men know all about it, teenage girls need to as well. Imagine a pill that costs a couple of dollars, is tasteless and odorless, dissolves completely into a drink, incapacitates for hours whoever ingests it, and then erases the person's memory. Aptly known as the date-rape drug, Rohypnol has a slew of street names: roofies, R2, roofenol, roche, la roche, roachies, and rib. In a typical Rohypnol-rape case a young woman accepts a drink and then feels dizzy and disoriented. To all observers she looks like she's drunk, but the person who dropped a Rohypnol in her glass knows better. Though he seems the gentleman as he walks her outside, he takes her somewhere to rape her. Most victims have little or no memory of what happened, but they later piece together evidence they've had sex with someone.

There are thousands of investigations into Rohypnol rapes each month, which means there are likely thousands more women who never figured out what happened to them, or if they did, chose not to report it. An obvious way to improve what is already epidemic in America (worst in Florida and Texas) is government classification of Rohypnol in the same category as drugs with a high potential for abuse, such as LSD and heroin. Hoffmann-La Roche, the manufacturer of Rohypnol, resists reclassification and notes in their defense that "alcohol is the number one date-rape drug in the country." Okay, so Rohypnol is the number two date-rape drug in the country—but it is still aiding thousands of predators to victimize girls and women.

I consulted with prosecutors on a complex case of a man who drugged a female co-worker on more than one occasion. The young victim was raped several times over a period of months, but recalls little of what occurred. "Someone had sex with my body," she wrote to me. "Even now, months later, a sound I hear or something I see will ring a distant bell in my head. I am suddenly overcome with grief, fear, or horror, and I know that deep down my brain is remembering something horrible that happened to me while I was drugged."

The main defense against Rohypnol rape is knowledge about the drug. Then a young woman can be cautious about accepting drinks and carefully watch that nobody puts anything in her drink.

Nearly all of the hazards teenage girls face can be reduced through teaching, but parents must first un-teach the cultural lesson that girls are not able to defend themselves. The book to read on this point is Ellen Snortland's already classic *Beauty Bites Beast*. "It's not a how-to book," she writes, "but a 'How Come?' book. How come the females of every other species on the planet are fierce, regardless of size, and are the ones who train their offspring, male and female, in defense and hunting?" Snortland says that self-defense training for girls should be as automatic as teaching them to swim, and the best place to get that training is from IMPACT or KIDPOWER (see Appendix #1).

Not surprisingly, teenage girls are at greater risk of rape and other sexual assault than are teenage boys. There is, however, a huge risk that boys and girls face equally: drunk driving. Because it kills thousands of teens each year, I consider drunk driving a form of violence and a car driven by a drunk teenager a weapon. Almost 40 percent of teens, both girls and boys, report that they've either driven after drinking alcohol or ridden with a driver who had been drinking alcohol. This statistic remains fairly constant in grades 9 through 11, but in their senior year, when they ought to be their smartest, teenagers become even more likely to get into a car driven by someone who's been drinking.

Most parents teach teens about the risks of drunk driving, but given that so many teens drink alcohol themselves, effective parental responses have to include more direct forms of supervision.

Ellen, the mother of a sixteen-year-old girl explains her approach:

> I personally meet, look at, talk to, and smell any boy who comes by to pick up our daughter, and then I look at, talk to, and smell him again when he drops her off. If I have what I call "an inkling that he's been drinking," nobody goes anywhere. I also tell his parents. My husband once asked a boy who stunk of beer to hand over the keys to his car. The boy refused and as he was arguing about it, I went out and put my car behind his in the driveway so he couldn't get out. After the kid's dad came over and drove him home my daughter was so embarrassed she didn't talk to me for a week. That's just about how long it was before that same boy drove his car off the side of the road into a drainage canal. There were two other kids with him. One of them, a girl my daughter had known most of her life, drowned.

Suicide is another killer of teenagers, one that has increased dramatically since we were growing up. Perhaps surprisingly, teenage girls are more likely than boys to threaten or plan suicide, and they are more than twice as likely to attempt it. (The boys, however, are seven times more likely to actually commit suicide.) Parents worried that their teenager may be contemplating suicide can look for recognizable warning signs. In addition to outright threats to commit suicide, the American Academy of Child and Adolescent Psychiatry (AACAP) provides the following list of behavioral symptoms that may precede a serious suicide attempt:

- A change in eating and sleeping habits;
- Withdrawal from friends, family, and regular activities;
- Violent actions, rebellious behavior, or running away;
- Drug and alcohol use;
- Unusual neglect of personal appearance;
- Marked personality change;
- Persistent boredom, difficulty concentrating, or a decline in the quality of schoolwork;
- Frequent complaints about physical symptoms, often related to emotions, such as headaches, fatigue, etc.;
- Loss of interest in pleasurable activities;
- Not accepting of praise or rewards.

A teenager thinking of committing suicide may also:

- Give verbal hints with statements such as "I won't be a problem for you much longer," "Nothing matters," or "It's no use";
- Put his or her affairs in order—for example, give away favorite possessions, clean his or her room, throw away important belongings, etc.

When it comes to homicide, girls and boys are at about equal risk until age thirteen. That's when the lives of boys start to become far more precarious. By age seventeen, boys have five times greater risk of being killed than girls, and they understandably yearn for a feeling of safety.

Unfortunately for the rest of us, many try to get that feeling with a gun.

# CHAPTER TWELVE

# TOM SAWYER AND HUCKLEBERRY FINN AND SMITH & WESSON

Elliot Caster was the smallest boy in the seventh grade, a fact made even more noticeable by the presence of Ray, the largest boy in the seventh grade (and eighth and ninth). Ray was a beefy, humorless bully, and the two boys were opposites in other ways as well: Elliot had mirth and was popular for it, Ray had girth and was feared for it; Elliot was sharp, Ray was thick; Elliot was enthusiastic, Ray was bored; Elliot was interested in everything, Ray was interested in bullying Elliot.

Opposites may attract, but not voluntarily, at least as far as Elliot was concerned. He wanted nothing to do with Ray, and even when Ray tripped him or shoved him, Elliot would usually keep moving and say nothing more than: "Cut it out."

Elliot told his parents about the bullying going on at school, and he told them some kids thought Ray might have a gun in his locker. "Did you see the gun?" his father asked him. Elliot shook his head No. "Then it's just a rumor, probably something he bragged about to scare you. Kids brag." Mr. Caster assured his wife, "The only way he'll become a man is if he stands up for himself. They'll fight it out one day and Elliot will grow from it, win or lose." Win or lose? Elliot couldn't win, except maybe with a gun (like the one in his father's bedside drawer).

Oh, how quickly Mr. Caster had forgotten his own experiences as a boy in a class of kids a foot taller than he was. And how easy to sit in the den and sound like a man who knew all about fighting when he'd never had a fight in his life.

Elliot's father told him to just be patient and things would change. Unfortunately, he was right. Things were changing fast, mostly because the chemical factory inside Ray's body was working round the clock to produce its newest formula: testosterone. As the school year progressed, Ray's slaps became punches, his trips became kicks, and Elliot's trepidation became daily fear.

A week after first telling his parents, Elliot again brought up the bullying with his mother, only this time he disclosed the extent of his dread by crying. He showed her a large bruise on his thigh. Ray had pushed him down and punched the same place over and again, saying, "Oh did I already hit you there? I forgot [punch]. I don't think I hit you there yet [punch]."

The lioness inside Mrs. Caster wanted to march over to Bryanston Central District High and punch Ray in the same place over and over again, but she didn't listen to her wild brain. An idea that was a distant second was to meet with the principal and the teacher and have them stop the bullying (more accurately, the violence). As she thought about it logically, she concluded that intervening could make Elliot into a sissy. She wasn't sure exactly how that might happen, or even what "sissy" really meant, but she was certain it was something to avoid. Adolescence is a delicate time, Mrs. Caster reasoned, and she didn't want to embarrass her son by making him appear vulnerable—even though that's precisely what he was. Interestingly, Elliot himself didn't care about the appearances; he just wanted to be safe. He was rapidly boiling down to his essence: a being that had to protect itself.

Elliot overslept on the morning he decided he'd have to kill Ray. Thinking his father had already left for work and hearing his mother in the kitchen, Elliot sneaked into his parents' bedroom. The curtains were closed and the room was dark, but he knew the route to the bedside table from the scores of times he'd shown that gun to friends. Just as he was reaching toward the drawer he heard a groggy voice from the bed: "What are you doing?"

Elliot's fast mind concluded his father must have called in sick to work. "I just wanted to say I hope you feel better." His dad grunted a Thanks, rolled over, and went back to sleep, and Elliot went to school without the gun. Later that day, Mrs. Caster found a small notepad in his room. She glanced at it to see if it was homework he'd forgotten, but what she read made her sit down on her son's bed and cry. *"If Ray Kills Me"* was the title Elliot had written and underlined on the cover. The notepad was his will; a few pages listed his belongings. Beside each entry was the name of the person he wanted the item to go to after he died.

With this powerful statement of Elliot's fear, Mrs. Caster knew she needed to do something, but what? Finally, she found an answer. It wasn't a solution to Elliot's problem, it turned out, but it sure helped relieve her anxiety. Elliot's mother called an expert, a psychologist, and a famous one at that—a radio personality. The long hold on the phone would be worth it, she knew, because that celebrity in a glass booth sixty miles away would surely know more about protecting her son than she did.

"You're on the air, what's your question?"

MRS. CASTER: My son is smaller than the other kids his age and he's being bullied by a much bigger boy. I want to protect him, but—

DR. DONNA: Listen, life is full of bullies and you won't be there to protect him from all of them. He has to learn how to take care of himself.

MRS. CASTER: But should I talk to the school, and—

DR. DONNA: And what? Embarrass your son, make him into the school "momma's boy"?

MRS. CASTER: That's what my husband said.

DR. DONNA: Everybody knows I hate to agree with husbands [laugh], but this time I have to. Boys work these things out. I remember when I was in school, someone would yell "Fight!" and we'd all get in a circle and cheer while they went at it. Eventually, the principal would break it up, and that would be the end of it. The worst thing that could happen is your son gets a black eye.

Or, perhaps, an 85-pound kid being beaten by a 180-pound kid could suffer a fractured rib, the loss of both front teeth, and ten stitches across his top lip. That's precisely what was happening to Elliot that afternoon while Dr. Donna was driving home from the radio studio in her BMW.

Yes, Doctor, life is full of bullies but we don't manage bullies by letting them victimize others. Ideally, we protect the vulnerable and give consequences to aggressors. If you were being threatened or beaten, Dr. Donna, you wouldn't expect people to gather round in a circle and cheer; you'd demand protection. Back when you were in school and the kids got in a joyous circle to watch the weekly fight, they hadn't been raised on violence, and students didn't have to worry about encountering a classmate with a gun. Finally, a conflict between boys with a hundred-pound disparity is not a "fight." It's a beating, and *of course* Mrs. Caster should have protected her child, whatever it took.

But Elliot's protection ultimately came from a stroke of dumb luck: Ray failed to fully close his locker one day and a counselor walking by courteously tried to latch it. She reached inside to rearrange whatever contents were blocking it from closing and she found the handgun Elliot feared was there. Ray was arrested and never returned to that school. It was a more than a year before Elliot told his parents how close he'd come to shooting Ray. To this day, his father doesn't believe it. "Kids brag," he says.

.    .    .

As sad as Elliot's story may be, there are families all over America who'd trade places with the Casters any day; they wish their teenage kids had suffered the injuries Elliot did. That's because their children died of gunshot wounds—another of them just died that way within the last ninety minutes. Some readers who'd understandably like to exclude their own teenage sons from the scary statistics may assume that the victims lived in inner cities or were gang members, or were in some minority, but it doesn't matter: white, African American, urban, suburban, **gunshot wounds are now the leading cause of death for teenage boys in America**.

Can you take comfort if you don't have a gun in your house? Yes, some comfort, but if you've got a son, some of his friends have guns in their homes. Eleven-year-old Omar Soto rode his bike to the home of a friend to ask if he could come out and play. His friend was watching his two younger sisters and was far too responsible to leave them alone, so he invited Omar inside. A potentially boring visit became exciting when Omar's host brought down his father's .357 Magnum. He showed off how he could hold the gun and how he could cock it, but when it came to uncocking it, he was less skilled. It went off, sending a bullet into Omar's head and killing him.

Mark Twain, the great chronicler of boyhood, wrote an essay in 1923 calling guns in the hands of the young "the most deadly and unerring things that have ever been created by man. You don't have to have any sights on the gun, you don't have to take aim, even. No, you just pick out a relative and bang away, and you are sure to get him." Twain speculated that the most effective army in the world could be comprised of young boys who'd found an old gun they presumed to be unloaded—because they never miss. His point has been proved ten thousand times over, recently even by a two-year-old boy who found the family's .357 Magnum and fired into the back of his fourteen-month-old brother.

Another essayist, sixteen-year-old Rachel Boryczewski, wrote:

Just think of all the lives that could have been saved had prevention plans been put into effect sooner. Think of all the lives that can be saved if something is done now.

I don't normally cite the work of sixteen-year-olds, but Rachel earned her credentials a few months ago when she was herself shot to death. (Teenage girls are shot to death far less frequently than boys, but still, ten die that way each week.)

In a sense, the bullets that killed these kids are still moving, still tearing through their families—and those families are important models for the rest of us. That's because if the present statistical curve continues, firearms will soon surpass cars as the leading cause of injury-related deaths for people of all ages. (Cars have become safer while guns have become more dangerous.)

Although I have not expressed a single political thought about guns in this book, some of my comments could be misunderstood as advocacy. so let me be clear:

1. I favor enhanced gun-safety requirements;
2. I oppose allowing children to have unsupervised access to guns.

On the first point, firearms are unique among consumer goods in America in that they are not governed by any federal safety regulations. The Consumer Product Safety Commission, responsible for monitoring injuries from virtually every other product, does not tally gunshot injuries because its founding legislation explicitly excluded firearms from its jurisdiction. By contrast, there are four categories of federal safety regulation covering the manufacture of teddy bears, but none about guns. The gun manufacturing industry is left to regulate itself, which raises an inherent difficulty: While most every business is concerned with delivering its product or service safely, gun manufacturers are studying ways to make their products more lethal. They work to make them more portable, more rapid, and more effective at damaging human tissue.

For some people, restricting gun use in any way—even for toddlers—is the psychological equivalent of government-imposed castration. To respect their sensibilities, I am not herein challenging our so-called right to bear arms (in whose name, by the way, more Americans have died at home than have died at war). And I am not advocating government gun control.

There would be clear benefits for children if we held gun manufacturers to the same product-liability standards we require for every other consumer product. Imagine if caustic drain opener were sold in easy-pour, flip-top, pistol-grip dispensers made attractive to children by the endorsement of celebrities. Drain opener can certainly hurt people, but it isn't made for that purpose. Handguns are made precisely for that purpose, so shouldn't manufacturers be required to build in safety features that have been technologically practical for decades?

Guns could have components that inhibit firing by children, or technologies that allow operation only in the hands of the owner (with a coded ring or wristband, for example, or a built-in combination lock). Since a handgun built today has a shelf life of hundreds of years (far outlasting the consumer that buys it), we'll be living with this manufacturing negligence for a long while. In the meantime, it's easier to shoot most handguns than it is to open a bottle of children's vitamins.

Speaking of tamper-proof containers, the design of billions of bottles of consumer products was changed after the deaths of eight people from poisoned Tylenol—a tragedy completely beyond the control of the manufacturer—while gun-makers knowingly and enthusiastically build products that *kill five hundred Americans each week*, and we don't require a single safety feature.

Gun companies might say their buyers understand and accept the risks of firearms, but that doesn't answer for the forty New Yorkers killed by stray bullets in one year alone, or for all the other people who will become unwilling consumers of ammunition.

Some gun owners explain that they needn't lock their weapons because they don't have children. To them I'd say, other people do have children, of course, and they will visit your home one day. The plumber who answers your weekend emergency will bring along his bored nine-year-old son, and he will find your gun.

The other oft-quoted reason for not locking guns is that they must be ready to fire immediately in an emergency, perhaps in the middle of the night. Imagine being in the deepest sleep and then a split second later finding yourself driving a truck as it careens down a dark highway at seventy miles per hour. That is the condition many gun advocates vigorously insist remain available to them, the ability to sit up in bed and start firing bullets into the dark without pausing to operate a locking device. An Associated Press story described one gun owner who didn't have to sit up in bed; she just reached under her pillow, took her .38 in hand, and thinking it was her asthma medicine, shot herself in the face. As this unfortunate woman proved, we all need a moment to complete the transition between sleeping and waking. Thankfully, most dangerous devices compel us to take that moment: Motor vehicles, chain saws, even power tools require more conscious effort than do revolvers.

Every year there are hundreds of thousands of guns stolen in our country, but with a new handgun manufactured every twelve seconds, we more than make up for the loss. Little wonder that in a typical week about three thousand Americans are shot. Most survive to tell about their ordeal, then those who hear the scary tales rush out . . . and buy guns. There's a lot to think about here, but the point relevant to child safety is that those stolen guns would be worthless and harmless if a locking system or owner-recognition technology made them inoperable.

In the meantime, if you own a gun, you can do something for children that the manufacturers have decided not to do: Lock the gun, not just the cabinet or the closet or the drawer, but the gun itself. Doing so is the opposite of government gun control; it is personal gun control. This paragraph is a survival signal for some child because that is who will likely find the gun an adult felt certain was too high to reach or too hard to fire.

(Just as I have suggested letters to doctors, day care, and schools as a way to avoid misunderstanding and establish expectations, there's a letter about safety that can be sent to gun manufacturers. See Appendix #3.)

The second item about which I am expressing an opinion involves children having access to guns. I hold the seemingly uncontroversial view that teenage boys with handguns are more dangerous than teenage boys without handguns. We don't let kids drive, buy alcohol or cigarettes, vote, or get married, but many parents provide them access to guns. Almost a decade ago, the *Journal of the American Medical Association* reported that 1.2 million elementary-school-aged latchkey kids had access to guns in the home. Given that 20,000 guns enter the stream of commerce each day, that figure is even worse today.

All these sad facts about the most armed nation in history boil down to this: The danger posed by guns must be considered in your home—and when your kids visit or sleep over at someone else's home.

The larger solutions to the firearms-injury epidemic aside, each family can educate their kids about guns. Teens need the information even more than adults do. After all, it is they and not we who live in a social world populated by young men full of testosterone, young men raised on violence, young men competing for status and identity, young men able to get a gun if they want to.

At least sixteen states have tried to force parents to take responsibility by enacting laws that impose criminal penalties on the gun owner if a child harms someone with an unsecured gun. An American Medical Association study indicates that states with CAP laws ("Child Access Prevention" laws) saw dramatic drops in unintentional firearms deaths of children. Florida was the first to pass a CAP law, and accidental shootings declined there by 50 percent in the first year. Laws, of course, aren't the ultimate solution to child safety—parents are.

(Most CAP laws do not impose criminal liability if guns are kept locked. See Appendix #3 for a sample statute.)

Where has law enforcement been on the issue of firearms safety? Chief Peter Herley, the visionary president of the California Police Chiefs Association, tells the truth: "For far too long, the law enforcement community has stood silent, permitting other voices to speak for us. We have focused too much on firearms violence being a crime problem rather than a social crisis that threatens us all—particularly the young."

•    •    •

Having likely though unintentionally offended some gun advocates, let me say some praising things about firearms. It's easy for me to do, in part because the male brain is wired to like guns. That fact may be of interest to any woman who's ever been perplexed by the love affair we men have with these loud and dangerous metal objects.

It all starts with a bundle of nerves, called the corpus callosum, that connects the right and left hemispheres of the brain. It is larger in females than in males and accordingly, women enjoy more cross-talk between the left and right brain. That dialogue brings many benefits; for example, women have greater reading skills, they excel at empathy and at understanding facial expressions. Men, oblivious to many left-brain matters, are more focused on right-brain matters—such as spatial relationships. In *The Wonder of Boys*, Michael Gurian explains that we're drawn to a sport like football because it "fills in the large spaces and challenges the male brain to hone its skill at moving objects through space."

Well, nothing moves objects through space as impressively as a gun moves a bullet. But even more impressive than that, the gun brought a feature to hunting that would appeal to any creature: the utter safety of distance. The gun became our lowest-risk hunting tool. With it, we could kill one bear while simultaneously scaring off others. We could take on the most dangerous animal, defeat any defense system, while leaving the hunter free of personal risk. With gun in hand, man finally declared absolute victory in the evolutionary battle of the species.

Having beaten down every other creature on earth, the gun next transformed lethal conflict between humans, particularly if one's adversary didn't also have one. All other weapons required that we get closer, and the more proximity, the more risk. Animals always risk injury when they attack, so they must carefully evaluate each adversary: Is he larger? Stronger? With the gun, none of that matters. The scrawniest male can prevail over the mightiest, in effect distorting one of nature's ranking systems. There's a reason the gun is called "the great equalizer."

Because of guns, we can kill anything while enjoying absolute personal safety. Little wonder we love them—shot from the porch at some tin cans or shot from an aircraft carrier at some Iraqis—no matter, we love guns.

So while you may be able to keep your son Jimmy from owning

one, if you try to talk him out of wanting one, you are up against a pretty strong argument: *You mean I shouldn't want a device that grants me power and identity, makes me feel dangerous and safe at the same time, instantly makes me the dominant male, and connects me to my evolutionary essence? Come on, Mom, get real!*

And when Jimmy enters his teens, a million cells swimming in testosterone will stir mysterious male cravings that call out: "Dominate!"—because that's how you get the good chicks. So are we curious about guns? Curiosity doesn't touch it—we are enraptured. On the news, on TV, on a shelf in the attic, at a movie, at a toy store, at a friend's house, in a magazine, in the bedside drawer—try to keep it from us.

The gun industry doesn't need the NRA to promote guns to boys—it's already done.

Some boys go through a gun phase we could call a brief fling; others marry the gun for life. Whichever your son ultimately does, he'll need to have a clear understanding of your policies about firearms, as well as the consequences of violating those policies. That means parents have to make some decisions:

1. Do we want to have a gun in the house?
2. If so, where do we want to keep it?
3. How do we want to store it?
4. How do we want to secure it?
5. Do we want it to be a secret from the kids?
6. Do we want to teach our kids how to use a gun?
7. Do we want to give our son a gun of his own?

Some of these are parenting issues (which I've committed to avoid) but others are safety issues (which I've committed to explore). I've already discussed the need to keep guns locked; that's an easy one. The question of whether to keep the location of a gun secret from a child is also easy: You may elect to treat it as a secret, but never, ever rely upon the belief that a child cannot find a gun in the house. Even a denier will have trouble finding some meaning hidden between the words *never* and *ever*.

The toughest issue is whether or not to have a gun in the house at all. Since my perspective is solely the safety of your children, it's easy to conclude that for most families, having a gun in the house increases risk. That isn't just the conclusion of this one expert, but also of the National Center for Victims of Crime, the National Crime Prevention Council, the American Medical Association, the U.S. Department of Justice, the Department of Health and Human Services, the National Center for Health Statistics, and most relevant to our topic, the American Academy of Pediatrics.

No exploration of your child's safety can be complete without taking a clear-eyed look down the barrel of these statistics:

- Every day, about seventy-five American children are shot; most survive—fifteen do not.
- The majority of fatal accidents involving a firearm occur in the home.
- Gunshot wounds are the single most common cause of death for women in the home, accounting for nearly half of all homicides and 42 percent of suicides.
- An adolescent is twice as likely to commit suicide if a gun is kept in the home.
- A gun is not likely to be a key element in protection from an intruder, and is far more likely to harm a family member.

(For a more comprehensive look at the role of guns in home protection, see Defensive Gun Use in Appendix #3.)

Not surprisingly, a gun store sales pitch avoids the gloomy information above and focuses instead on the fear of crime: "You don't want to become another statistic" (even though having a gun is far more likely to get you *on* a list of statistics than keep you off). The guy across the sales counter will forgo any reference to the risk of suicide in favor of the reassurance that "with all these shots, you'll be ready for anything that comes through your front door." Sure, just put this $350-thing in the bedside drawer and you'll never have to take any other home-safety precaution.

Since I mentioned sales, it's interesting that our country knows more about why someone buys a particular brand of shaving lotion than about why he buys a gun. Among the few things we do know is that the most reliable predictor for purchasing a gun is having had a gun in one's childhood home. (Eighty percent of all current gun owners were raised by parents who owned guns.) Accordingly, when you decide to have a gun in your home, you are probably also deciding that your children will have one in theirs and that your grandchildren will live with it.

Considering that so many parents make that choice, it's no wonder the rate of firearms deaths for the young in America is twelve times higher than in all the other industrialized countries *combined*.

Protecting teenage boys from violence and keeping them from guns amounts to almost the same thing. Thankfully, you have the right to not bear arms; you can choose to make your home a weapons-free environment. That still leaves a world of guns outside, of course, but here again there's something parents can do: Protect children from the most likely delivery system of violence. In other words, keep them from dangerous friends.

# CHAPTER THIRTEEN

# FRIENDS
# AS ENEMIES

Raymond Belknap couldn't have known when he met James Vance
that the friendship would end so badly. And those gathered at Saint
Augustine's on Christmas Eve couldn't have fathomed why two
eighteen-year-old boys would stand in the shadow of their church and
each shoot himself in the mouth with a sawed-off shotgun.

Young people commit suicide with guns all the time (every six
hours, in fact), but this was no regular suicide. Still, as with all such
tragedies, loved ones are forced to take a hard look at everything in
their lives. They begin an awful and usually unrewarding search
for responsibility. Some blame themselves and some blame others:
the kids their children spent time with, the other parent, the jilting
girlfriend—someone will invariably be doused with the family's
shame and rage and guilt.

Parents might blame the person who sold their child drugs or provided the gun, but James Vance's mother went much further from
home. She blamed a heavy-metal rock band called Judas Priest, and

she blamed the mom-and-pop record store that sold their records. She insisted the proprietors should have predicted that the album *Stained Class* would compel her son to enter into a suicide pact with his friend Ray. She felt the store should have warned the boys about the lethality of that album, and Ray's mother joined in the lawsuit.

When I was asked to testify in the case on behalf of the owners of the record store, I anticipated an interesting study into the media's impact on violence. I did not expect it to be the only case of my career I would later wish I hadn't taken. I had volunteered for many unpleasant explorations and performed with fairly unhesitating professionalism, but when the time came, I did not want to go into that churchyard, I did not want to feel the quiet depression and grief of Ray's mother, nor challenge Mrs. Vance's strong denial. I did not want to study the autopsy reports, or see the photos, or think about the suicides by people in my own life.

But I did it all, and James Vance ended up as my unlikely guide into the lives and experiences of many similar young Americans. From him, I learned how they feel about drugs, alcohol, television, ambition, intimacy, violence, and death. He would help me answer the questions of so many parents: What are the warning signs that a child (ours or someone else's) might be prone to violence? How can I spot dangerous friends of my children? Much of what James taught me applies to gang violence, but it also helps explain the sometimes more frightening behavior of middle-class young men whose brutality takes everyone by surprise.

James Vance was obsessed with Judas Priest, attracted to the sinister and violent nature of their music and public persona. As he watched his friend Ray shoot himself in the head, the sheer gruesomeness of it did not impress him. Like most young Americans, he had been getting comfortable with graphic violence for a long while; images of gory skulls were fairly mundane to him.

Standing in the churchyard looking at Ray's body, he momentarily considered breaking the suicide pact they'd made. But then he figured if he didn't shoot himself, he'd get blamed for Ray's death anyway, so he reached down into the blood, picked up the shotgun, put it in his mouth, and pulled the trigger. But James Vance did not die.

In his less than enthusiastic positioning of that shotgun in his mouth, he failed to kill himself but succeeded at creating an unsettling irony: He became as frightening to behold as anything that ever appeared on the cover of a Judas Priest album. In his hesitation to murder himself, James shot off the bottom of his face. His chin, jaw, tongue, and teeth were all gone, blown around that churchyard. I cannot describe how he looked, but I also cannot forget it. I've seen my share of alarming autopsy photos, of people so injured that death was the only possible result, people so injured that death was certainly a relief, but something about James Vance living in a body damaged more than enough to be dead was profoundly disturbing.

Even jaded lawyers who thought they'd seen it all were shaken when he arrived at depositions, a towel wrapped around his neck to catch saliva that ran freely from where the bottom of his face had been. Since there is little aftermath in a movie or video game, most teens never have to confront what guns do. But James had to confront it: His appearance had become a metaphor for what had been going on inside him. Like so many teenagers, he had wanted to be menacing and frightening. He had aspired to the specialness he thought violence could bring him, and he got there . . . completely.

Aided by his mother (who helped interpret his unusual speech during the days he was questioned), James told lawyers about his case, and also about his time. I listened carefully. I learned that when he and Ray discussed doing something big and bad, it wasn't necessarily suicide. They had considered going on a shooting spree at a nearby shopping center. It was the violence they wanted, not the end of life. Unlike thousands of teens who commit suicide, they were not despondent that night—they were wild. High on drugs and alcohol, their music of choice blaring, they destroyed everything in Ray's room, then jumped out the window with the shotgun and ran through the streets toward the church.

The lawsuit claimed that listening to heavy-metal music made them do it. The question of whether it would have happened otherwise is, perhaps, a reasonable one, but I'd have chosen to look a little closer to home. For the case, however, I asked researchers in my office to study tragedies that were supposedly associated with music albums. They found many, like the young man who mailed a final letter to a distant recording star he "loved," and then committed suicide. They came across an article with a headline that at first seemed relevant: MAN KILLED WHILE LISTENING TO HEAVY-METAL MUSIC. The victim, it turned out, was walking along listening to Ozzy Osbourne songs on headphones when he was struck by a train. On the news clipping, a dark-humored associate of mine had written the words "killed by heavy metal, literally." Well, the heavy metal in trains surely has resulted in many more deaths than the heavy metal in music.

You see, the group Judas Priest did not create James Vance—in a sense, he created them. When asked about a particular lyric, "They bathed him and clothed him and fed him by hand," James recited it as: "They bathed him and clothed him and fed him *a* hand." He had done more than just react to the songs; he had actually rewritten them, taken a lyric about someone being cared for and turned it into something about cannibalism.

Even his admiration was expressed in violent terms. James said he was so enamored of the band that he would do anything for them, "kill many people or shoot the president through the head." He told lawyers that if the band had said "Let's see who can kill the most people," he would have gone out and done something terrible. In fact, the band said no such thing, and he did something terrible anyway.

Preparing for my testimony, I started a list of the pre-incident indicators (PINS) that might precede teen violence. It was sad work for me because James and Ray were long past being helped; I hope the warning signs will be of value to other families now:

### Alcohol and drug use

Unlike music, alcohol and drugs are proven and intended to affect the perceptions and behavior of all people who ingest them. James Vance put it simply when he described an acquaintance who was violent and self-destructive. Asked if that individual had a drug problem, he replied, "Yes, that goes hand in hand." He also stated, "An alcoholic is a very violent individual, and when you drink excessively, you become violent, and that has been my life experience." (I wonder with whom he gained that experience.)

### Fascination with weapons and violence

This was a central part of James's personality (but not Ray's). James wanted to become a gunsmith and excelled at games involving guns. As part of what he called his "training to be a mercenary," he often pretended to be in gunfights. "There would be two cops and one criminal. The criminal would be behind you and would have to flush you out, you know, how cops check a house out. Ninety-nine percent of the time I always got both of the cops."

About his less violent friend Ray, he said: "I would usually get him because, you know, just watching TV, you learn. TV is a really good teacher." James said he watched the news and saw "a lot of violence and killing and fighting go on." He summarized all this succinctly: "*Violence excited me.*"

### Addiction to media products

James spent more time consuming media products than he spent on any other activity in his waking life. In a recent cover story on guns, *Time* magazine noted that "Academics who study such things widely agree that exposure to media violence correlates with aggression, callousness, and appetite for violence." Add gory video games and Web sites to the equation and it's clear that kids now have, as writer Sisela Bok observes, "depictions of violence never available to children and young people in the past."

Further, it isn't only the behavior this consumption promotes that is significant; it's the behavior it prevents—most notably human interaction.

### Obsession

James referred to the members of the band Judas Priest as "metal gods." He said they were his bible and that he was "the defender of the Judas Priest faith." Of his relationship with these people he'd never met, he said, "It was like a marriage—intimacy that developed over a period of time, and it was until death do us part." Thus, he had a closer "relationship" with these strangers than with anyone actually in his life.

### Seeking status and worth through violence

James said he felt "ignored for twenty years." Like many other teens, he became "unignorable" with the pull of a trigger. Young people whose upbringing did not invest them with a feeling of self-worth will do almost anything to become significant. James interpreted his favorite song ("Hero's End") to mean that one has to die to be recognized, and he apparently felt that his life hadn't made him worthy of attention—so maybe his death would.

### Aimlessness

If you were to take away James's obsession with Judas Priest, you would have another young man with goals and ambitions that changed day to day, with unrealistic expectations of the world, and without the perseverance or self-discipline to reach his goals. At various times, James planned to write a book, be a gunsmith, be a member of a band, even be a postal worker, but in the end he is most remembered for just a few seconds in his life—a few seconds of barbarism in a churchyard.

When asked if anything other than the lyrics might have caused the shootings, James responded, "A bad relationship? The stars being right? The tide being out?" Though he was being sarcastic, any of these is probably as reasonable as blaming the lyrics in an album, for once he excluded family life and parenting from the inquiry, he might as well have cited anything. By pointing his trigger finger at a rock band, James washed away all of the scrutiny that might reasonably have been focused on himself, his family, or even his society.

Though the court eventually decided that the proprietors of the record store couldn't have predicted the shootings, James Vance did not get to finish his search for someone to blame. He died, finally, from that single shotgun blast to the head, though the complications took a long time to kill him, longer than anyone could have expected. I never got to ask James about his early years and never learned about the childhood that had been so effectively eclipsed by his mother's lawsuit.

•    •    •

After months on that case, it was clear to me that Ray would not have acted so violently on his own; his best friend James had become his worst enemy—and that's not so rare. The key that unlocks a boy's destructiveness is often held by another boy. While it's a characteristic of the species that males can be particularly aggressive, aggression needn't evolve into violence. Michael Gurian points out that "Violence is not hard-wired into boys. Aggression is hard-wired. Violence is taught."

Mustn't it be then that nonviolence can also be taught? It can, indeed, and most effectively by fathers. Unfortunately, fathers are undervalued in America—virtually to the point of being an oppressed minority. That poses a problem for everyone, since the absence of a father in a boy's life is one of the predictors of future violence. David Blankenhorn, author of *Fatherless America*, notes that 80 percent of the young men in juvenile detention facilities were raised without fully participating fathers. While I've directed much of this book toward mothers, it is fathers who can most favorably influence a boy's behavior.

Without fathers (or other men in the paternal role, such as stepfathers, grandfathers, mentors), too many boys learn from the media or from each other what scholars call "protest masculinity," characterized by toughness and the use of force. That is not the only way to be a man, of course, but it's the only way they know.

The absence of adult males upsets the natural order in our species and in others. For example, game wardens in South Africa recently had to kill several teenage male elephants that had uncharacteristically become violent. These young elephants behaved like a contemporary street gang—and perhaps for the same reason: There were no adult males in their lives. To solve the problem, park officials imported adult male elephants from outside the area. Almost immediately, the remaining juveniles stopped misbehaving. Testosterone ungoverned by experience is dangerous, and older males temper the craving for dominance—merely by being dominant themselves.

In addition to curbing the worst natural tendencies of young males, fathers also contribute in the same ways as mothers: with kindness and care. Among animals, the most heroic example is the emperor penguin. After his mate lays a single egg, she goes off to sea to regain her strength. The father cares for the egg, balancing it on his foot. He joins other males huddled on the ice doing the same thing. Given the freezing winds and perpetual night, you might think some of these penguin fathers would abandon their young, but they don't. They stay, all the while balancing the delicate eggs on their feet—for two long, cold months.

Some men, of course, choose to abandon their children, but between divorce, court decisions, and outright discrimination, many are pushed away from their sons, leaving impressionable boys in search of role models. That's when a friend like James is most dangerous to a boy like Ray.

The 1998 case of two boys in Jonesboro, Arkansas, who shot fifteen people at their school also seems to involve one boy inciting another. Eleven-year-old Drew Golden and thirteen-year-old Mitch Johnson had little in common before they became famous killers. For example, Santa gave Drew a shotgun when he was six, but Mitch was never allowed to have a gun. Drew was taught to hunt as a tot and later perfected his reflexes with violent video games, but Mitch's family wouldn't pay for video games. Drew wore military fatigues; Mitch wore choir robes as he sang in a Baptist church. Drew talked about "taking over the school"; Mitch got A's in several subjects and made the basketball, football, and baseball teams. When they wanted guns, they went to Drew's house because guns were banned at Mitch's house. (To his credit, Drew's father had a gun vault the boys couldn't open; to his discredit, the boys were still able to find three handguns that had been left unsecured. They got seven more guns from the home of Drew's grandfather.)

Both these boys had problems, to be sure, but based on what you know, does it seem likely Mitch Johnson would have gone on a shooting rampage without Drew's influence? These stories show the importance of coming to know the boys around your sons. A Temple University study found that half of America's parents said they didn't know their children's friends. Be in the other half so you're able to intervene if one of them is like James Vance or Drew Golden.

Those two boys made it clear they might end up violent, but there are more insidious routes to the same destination, as I learned myself from a classmate in high school.

Jeffrey had straight black hair and a very soft-looking face with red cheeks. He walked stiffly, moved awkwardly, rarely spoke, and kept to himself—or would have if we'd let him. He was mercilessly picked on by many of his classmates, most effectively by me and by an athletic, handsome student named Mick. Jeffrey wouldn't defend himself, never really fought back, and took abuse as if he were born for the job. In gym class, Mick and I would have an hour's access to Jeffrey and we'd pepper him with whatever ridicule and verbal abuse we could come up with. Eventually most of the class joined in the taunt, greeting Jeffrey each day with jeers of "Queer, fag, wimp." If he responded, that would just encourage more abuse, and if he didn't respond, Mick would shove him or hit him. When this happened, his passive face turned even redder than usual, but he never reached the point of pushing Mick back.

This went on for months, with Jeffrey eventually adding a new wrinkle to his passivity: He started grinning when he was mistreated. I intuitively knew it was time to stop picking on Jeffrey and I dropped out of the group of boys that competitively thought up new insults and names for him. I wasn't willing to go so far as to become his friend, but I did exchange a couple of awkward civilities with him. Around this time, I slipped on some steps at home and broke my leg. In a cast for six weeks, I was relegated to just sit during gym class and watch the other kids interact. It was a good lesson for me, looking into the group from outside, seeing our classmates as Jeffrey did.

Over those weeks, I saw a lot: There was a stack of white towels near the showers, but one was sort of pink. "Jeffrey, here's your towel," somebody called out. He just grinned. A group of boys pulled his shirt away from him and tossed it around, yelling, "Fag rag!" Jeffrey just grinned. One day, someone brought a woman's bathing cap to school; it was light blue, decorated with plastic flowers. Some boys held Jeffrey down and forced it onto his head. He just grinned. In the school weight room, though some exercises took two people, each boy one after another refused to pair up with Jeffrey. He just grinned.

The day everybody stopped picking on him, we were in that weight room. Two boys were searching for a steel rod that was part of a set used to hold up a heavy weight bar. I hobbled around on my cast trying to find the missing rod. Even after everyone else gave up the search, I was, for some reason, intent on finding that rod. Mick was at a far corner of the room doing rapid sit-ups with his head at the bottom of an inclined slant-board, but something wasn't right, something I saw out of the corner of my eye. I heard myself yell out, "JEFFREY!" He was standing above the slant-board, the missing steel rod held high over his head in both hands. He might have heard me, but he wasn't at all distracted. The steel rod was already on its way down into Mick's face, where the collision turned the handsome into the gruesome. Having injured Mick severely, Jeffrey calmly put the rod down and just stood there, the grin on his red face.

Both boys were taken away, Mick by ambulance to be seen weeks later with a much-changed appearance, and Jeffrey by police, never to be seen by us again.

These days, a boy like Jeffrey might be diagnosed with some form of autism. Though not typically violent, autistic children are unable to easily distinguish sincerity from deceit, are deficient in empathy, and have poor self-control. Since autistic children's response to teasing can be way out of proportion, some act out violently. These kids need special help, and above all they need protection from the abuse of peers and siblings. (Autistic disorders occasionally contribute to violence, but it needn't necessarily occur. This is explained in a moving and eloquent essay by Dr. Mary Arneson in Appendix #6.)

Almost thirty years have passed since Mick received the consequences for taunting a boy who was secretly seething. Move that story to current times and you have Kip Kinkel attacking kids at his school for much the same reason. When Kip filled out an application for Internet service, he listed his profession as "student surfing the

Web for info on how to build bombs." He made threats, bragged about killing animals, and gave a speech at school on how to build a bomb—all that bravado to cover the hurt and shame of being teased by classmates.

Author William Pollack says boys have an "exquisite sensitivity to shame." In *Real Boys: Rescuing Our Sons from the Myths of Boyhood* (a book for everyone with a son), Pollack explains that many try to thwart shame and dishonor by going on the offensive. America has no shortage of cases to affirm that concept. For example, sixteen-year-old Luke Woodham shot nine students at his Pearl, Mississippi, high school, two of whom died (including his girlfriend, who had broken up with him). Motive: Fellow students were picking on him.

Another sixteen-year-old boy, Evan Ramsey, told friends he planned to bring a gun to school and shoot some people. He kept his word on February 19, 1997, when he killed the principal. He also shot three students, one of whom died. Motive: The boy he killed had been picking on him. Nearly all boys who commit terrible violence at school were teased or felt rejected.

School shootings are rare, but because so many details are known about the boys who commit them, these cases provide valuable insight into teen violence. Dr. James McGee is a widely recognized forensic psychologist who has participated in my firm's workshops on assessing and managing threats. He has extensively studied boys who committed these terrible acts. Working with Dr. Caren DeBernardo, he found that in cases where all the facts are known, 100 percent of the boys were Caucasian, 100 percent lived in rural communities, 100 percent were social outcasts, 100 percent verbalized threats before the incidents, and 100 percent had demonstrated an interest in violence (movies, TV, music).

Though I don't believe media products on their own cause boys to be violent, they clearly become a part of the process. Seventeen-year-old Gary Pennington shot and killed his teacher in front of classmates at his Grayson, Kentucky, high school. Prior to the incident, he had presented a book report on Stephen King's novel, *Rage*, about a student who shoots his teacher in front of the class. Fourteen-year-old Barry Loukaitais walked into his algebra class and killed the teacher, then shot three students, two of whom died. Prior to the incident he told a friend it would be "pretty cool" to go on a killing spree like in the movie *Natural Born Killers*. In West Paducah, Kentucky, a fourteen-year-old named Michael Carneal shot eight students (three died). He had talked about *The Basketball Diaries*, a film in which the lead character opens fire on his classmates with a shotgun.

Interestingly, boys at risk of committing terrible violence don't necessarily have a history of getting into trouble. Of those studied by McGee and DeBernardo, only 12 percent had a record of serious offenses. This means that if several pre-incident indicators are present in a given boy, one's concern should not be turned into denial just because someone says, "Oh, he's never been in trouble."

Guns happened to be the weapon of choice for most of the boys discussed in this chapter, and indeed guns bring permanence to hostility that might otherwise be transitory, but guns are not the main issue here. Rather, it is that we can spot the inclination toward violence in those around our teenage boys. The predictive signals evident prior to major acts of violence by schoolboys are similar to those of adults who perform multiple shootings in the workplace. (School administrators can find more information on this in Appendix #5.) Here is a list of the PINS:

- Alcohol and drug abuse;
- Addiction to media products;
- Aimlessness;
- Fascination with weapons and violence;
- Experience with guns;
- Access to guns;
- Sullen, Angry, Depressed (SAD);

- Seeking status and worth through violence;
- Threats (of violence or suicide);
- Chronic anger;
- Rejection/humiliation;
- Media provocation.

Most of these PINS are self-explanatory but I want to add a couple of brief elaborations: Note that alcohol and drug abuse are at the top of the list; one recent study shows that an astonishing 75 percent of homicides by young people occur when they are high or drunk. Next, the term SAD is used by my firm's behavioral scientists for easy identification of sullenness, anger, and depression, (the symptoms of which include changes in weight, irritability, suicidal references, hopelessness, and loss of interest in previously enjoyable activities).

The PIN called Media Provocation evolved because widely publicized major acts of violence often stimulate people who identify with the perpetrators and the attention they received. Because these cases tend to cluster, violence is more likely during the period following a widely reported incident. (Two weeks after Michael Carneal shot classmates at his school, another boy, Joseph "Colt" Todd, did the same thing at his. Four weeks after Drew Golden and Mitch Johnson shot students at their school, a boy named Andrew Wurst did so at his, and four weeks later, Kip Kinkel did so at his.) Proximity to major acts of violence understandably increases media coverage (i.e., the incidents become local news stories as well as national). It is remarkable that seven of the twelve cases in the McGee/DeBernardo study occurred within a 350-mile radius of each other.

Daniel Goleman's book *Emotional Intelligence* adds further insight. He describes seven key abilities human beings need to effectively manage life: the ability to motivate ourselves, to persist against frustration, to delay gratification, to regulate moods, to hope, to empathize, and to control impulse. Many of those who commit extreme acts of violence never learned these skills, and if you know a young person who lacks them all, it's an important pre-incident indicator, and he needs help.

Just like adult men, young men in our culture are discouraged from showing emotion. Violent boys are frequently expressing what William Pollack calls "the only 'acceptable' male emotion—anger." Indeed, chronic anger is an important predictor of violence. It simmers beneath most of the pre-incident behaviors we've explored in this chapter, raising an obvious question: How did these boys get so angry? Most of them got that way at home.

# CHAPTER FOURTEEN

# ALL IN THE FAMILY

*Life's miseries fall disproportionately on children.*
—FRANK SULLOWAY, *BORN TO REBEL*

By the time I was eleven, I'd seen a lot of fights, some on the television, some in our living room. On TV, the stars walked away unhurt: no bruises, no cuts, no regrets, no resentment, no humiliation. When my mother fought with my father, and later with my stepfathers, and when she hit my sister and me, it was nothing like what I saw on TV. At our home, violence lasted longer, resolved less, and didn't seem to advance our story any. Nobody won anything, no justice was served, no hero emerged.

I won't tell you about this with the perspective or judgment of an adult, but rather as it was when I was a boy—as if this were a late entry in my diary.

Watching those fights on TV, I wondered what it looked like when my mother hit me. It certainly wouldn't seem like a fight because she didn't hit me in an organized way with each blow landing, and then the next. And she didn't beat me like I imagined some fathers whipped their sons with belts: one, two, three, four—just a chore of discipline to get through. The fathers of my imagination were not emotionally involved, but my mother was.

At the worst times, she was like a wildcat catching and mauling some prey, all over me, wildly striking, punching, biting, dragging, twisting, and scratching. Not that one got to choose favorites, but I would take anything over the scratching. My mother kept her fingernails long and strong, and she'd dig them into my arms, pushing the skin back, leaving four identical wounds in an even row.

When my mother was depressed, she longed for energy, for change, for a lifting of that deadness. For her, it seems violence was a way to get energized, to get her blood moving. In a very real sense, my mother used the energy of us kids to run her body at those times. Like someone getting up and running around to get refreshed, she could draw fuel from our fear and tension, and though I know it sounds bizarre, she got *exercise* by attacking us.

After an attack, which could include several hours of beating and yelling, we would be drained. Brutality from the very same person a child relies upon for love is like a series of roundhouse punches to one's optimism. For each measure of energy a violent adult draws from the melee, the same measure of energy is sucked out of the child.

Though children are naturally full of hope and enthusiasm, those who are abused can take on the worldview of the hopeless adults around them. At the worst times, I felt detached from my enthusiasm for life, and in a sense detached from myself. Though I always seemed optimistic to others (and even to myself), I can see hopelessness in one or two pictures of Chrysti and me as kids. Sometimes I see those same eyes in a child today.

Just as my mother needed more sleeping pills, more heroin, more drama, so did I come to need ever-bigger events to get my attention. I did not want violence, of course, but since I knew it was coming anyway, I anticipated it. Eventually, I was anxious in the calm times. For me back then, no upcoming event or activity, no birthday or holiday, could possibly compete with the anticipation of violence and madness. If I came home from school and Chrysti said, "Let me tell you what happened today," it was not going to be that we'd won the lottery. It was going to be that our mother was in the hospital, or had been arrested, or was missing, or dead. It was going to be something that threatened what little order we had.

Life back then was lived in the place between fear and violence. In that anxiety, almost anything is a relief, and this leads to a classic codependence between abuser and abused. Abusers use their victims to change how they feel, and victims come to rely on abusers to deliver relief from the waiting. Violence was the relief, but even when it stopped, I couldn't let my guard down. That's because when it seemed over, it wasn't always over. Sometimes my mother would come find me and start again, though differently. Since she would have already used up much of her energy, she would now use a less aerobic method.

She'd make me stand in front of her while she slapped my face. I knew the routine, though practice didn't make perfect. I'd have to stand with my arms at my sides and look at her. As she pulled her arm back for a wide swing to slap me, I'd have to be sure I didn't flinch. I also had to avoid looking pathetic or tragic, because that would make her angrier. I had to show no reaction; she could thus strike me without having to see that she was hurting a person, hurting me.

Afterward, I'd walk down the long hall of our apartment, my ears ringing, the side of my head hot from the blows, the various cuts and scratches stinging. By the time I reached my room, I'd have stopped crying. I never cried for myself anyway, but rather so my mother could see she was getting somewhere. For me, it was a way to communicate, not a way to express emotion. To cry when I was alone would be to acknowledge that something had happened, and my primary defense was to deny the past, even the past just seconds behind me. Back then, I lived only in the future.

As a ten- and eleven-year-old boy, I never really gave any of this much thought, aside from the practical. After an incident, I'd check my face and arms in the mirror to see if there was anything to interfere with going to school the next morning. I became an expert at knowing which injuries would fade and which would have to be explained away at school. Other than lying about how I got a bruise or mark, I never talked about it afterward. Some of it I never told to anyone, until now, to you.

Since you know only the violent side of my mother, you could easily hate her—but I do not. My memory includes her humor, her love of literature and art, her intellect, and her kindness. These attributes don't negate the violence or the cruelty, of course, but they do make her actions doubly confounding. Violent parents can be as complex as any parents—as good at their best, perhaps worse at their worst. Though much tested when I was a boy, I loved my mother as much as you likely loved yours—it's in our cells to do so. And in the end, no matter what they may have done, we who do not have them miss our mothers.

Abuse teaches children to deny, minimize, suppress, and compartmentalize. People with backgrounds similar to mine (and there are many more than you might think) know that it's far easier to bury the past than to conjure it now—and I am no different. I take no pleasure in recalling and refeeling hard times, but I do it because these memories connect me to the children who will—this very day—experience what I did and worse. *Children need adults to remember.*

I could have forgotten it all—at least in the conscious sense—but my work brought me into close contact with people who'd been brutalized as children and gave it back to society tenfold. They learned that when it comes to violence, it is better to give than to receive—and most of them taught that same lesson to their own children.

●   ●   ●

As I explore the practical steps for protecting children from family violence, I begin with this premise: The hands that hold this book do not also beat a child. It would make no sense for a parent to study how to keep a child safe from the violence of the world at large, only to deliver a more destructive violence at home.

I am starting with the starkest example: violence against infants. To beat and torture a baby is to attack the very idea of offspring and it must emanate from the most acute self-hatred. This is not like parents frustrated by a baby that won't stop crying. That at least is an experience we can all relate to on some level, but you'll find it hard to believe you are even in the same species as the parents whose cases I'm about to cite.

Some parents do exactly this, of course, but I am not addressing them here—I am studying them here. Though we may judge such parents harshly, the real benefit will come from fully understanding violence against children, recognizing that it's one of the things people do, accepting that it's a feature of our species. Though it is hard to imagine this violence has a purpose in nature, it occurs too frequently to be dismissed as an aberration. In any event, such dismissal is often a protection against having to look at something directly, which we're about to do.

As you read on, your inclination will be to recoil from such an unwelcome dose of reality. I understand this, for even having experienced what I did as a boy, and even with all the experiences in my work, I too am inclined to first visit denial when this topic presents itself. If I get the intuition that some adult I know might be abusing his child, I too will first think, *Bob would never harm his daughter.* Getting past that nearly automatic denial is possible only after we've humanized—not excused—child abuse. It will not be easy to look at, but your doing so will make you more able to save a child from abuse—and it's likely that life will call on you to do that one day.

Violence toward children almost always takes place in secret, but Dr. David Southall, a pediatrics professor at Keele University in England, exposed the secret forever. Before his work, we could only imagine how brutal a parent might be, but he has made it clear with videotapes that show the beating and torture of infants and toddlers.

How can such macabre tapes exist? Southall got permission to film parents visiting children who were hospitalized after suspected incidents of abuse. Nurses were able to monitor the visits through hidden cameras and intervene if necessary. Southall's project filmed thirty-nine children. In all but six of the cases, the cameras caught a parent slapping, kicking, torturing, trying to suffocate, or otherwise harming a child.

Let that number—thirty-three out of thirty-nine—remove any belief that serious abusers have merely a singular, momentary loss of control; parents who abuse almost always abuse again. As you'll see, I'm not talking about a raised voice or rough handling or other things most parents have done and then regretted. I am talking about a six-week-old baby boy taken to the hospital after three episodes of near-suffocation. On his father's first visit, he told the infant he intended to cut off his limbs. Such threats may have little meaning to a six-week-old baby, but on the second visit, his father switched to the universal language of pain: He woke the infant by twisting the baby's ear and flicking his eyelids. Minutes after that, the father obstructed the baby's nasal breathing, stopping only when a nurse entered. Next, he put his hands over the struggling infant's mouth, and stopped when he heard a noise outside the room.

The following day the father put his finger into the infant's throat, and by the sixth day, he tried an outright suffocation, pressing his hand firmly over the nose and mouth of his baby. You might wonder how caring professionals could watch these events and not intervene at the earliest possible moment. I assure you, they were profoundly disturbed by what they watched, but they knew how weak the system can be when it comes to child abuse. A father like this might not be stopped by anything less than the most graphic evidence. And this father was stopped: When informed of the videotape, he admitted abusing his son, which was, of course, obvious. But he also admitted to killing another child, a stepson whose death had been wrongly classified as sudden infant death syndrome.

In another instance, a young mother with a history of drug abuse was observed while visiting her eighteen-month-old baby girl. The child had been in and out of the hospital since birth with episodes of near-suffocation and cardiac arrest. Each nurse that entered the room saw the mother comforting her child, but the camera saw something else: throwing toys at the child's head, hitting, kicking the child in the stomach, and, eventually, forcing a pillow over the baby's head. After nurses intervened, the mother was arrested. The child was placed with a foster family.

Another of the thirty-nine cases involved a three-month-old girl who was hospitalized after several episodes of near-suffocation. Before the videotaping even began, nurses found this baby choking and gray after being alone with her mother just briefly. The videotape shows the nineteen-year-old mother slapping, shaking, and cursing at the baby, while also demanding that the baby kiss her. At one point in the film, the mother intentionally bends her child's arm backward at the elbow. When the baby screams, the mother calls for a nurse and then explains that the baby's arm was caught in one of the toys attached to the cot.

Unfortunately, the mother was then alone with the infant for just thirty seconds more. The video shows her again bending the tiny arm backward, but this time it broke. The mother was arrested and the baby and her seventeen-month-old sister (also a victim of abuse, of course) were eventually adopted.

You wouldn't learn much more if I told you the other thirty stories—only a few details would change. What makes these particular stories unique is that the abused children were saved from continued abuse. Most are not. Thus, children who are treated this way and survive are raised with torture and violence, sometimes escalating, sometimes decreasing, but always a factor in their lives. (Autism makes some children extremely difficult and tests the patience of parents way beyond the norm. Many of these parents fail the test and resort to violence. See Appendix #6 for more information on autism.) There are a million confirmed cases of child abuse each year in America, but nobody knows for sure how many millions more are unknown—except to the sad participants and their silent witnesses.

• • •

It is easier to have contempt for abusive parents—to dismiss them as monsters—than to ask this hard question about human beings: Does violence toward children serve a purpose in nature? Unquestionably it does with other species. For example, there are circumstances in which abandoning or killing a newborn increases the likelihood of survival for other offspring. Mothers required to choose have more incentive to invest in an older child than in a younger one. That's because older children have already survived the hardest times and, being closest to maturity, they are more likely to carry out their genetic mission.

In some species, and occasionally in ours, newborns deemed unlikely to survive are abandoned or killed outright (basically the same thing). Why, nature seems to ask, take precious resources away from the rest of the family for a newborn that's going to die anyway? Applying the merciless logic of survival, earlier is better than later.

Since much human behavior was field-tested by our primate cousins, the apes and monkeys, it's striking that they do not kill their biological offspring and we do. Few people have studied primates with so superb an insight as Harvard University's Richard Wrangham, co-author of *Demonic Males*, the definitive work on the origins of male violence. "An ape mother," Wrangham explains, "doesn't have a new baby until the current one is weaned, so she may not face the tough choices about the survival of competing offspring that humans do."

Indeed, given the number of children a human mother might be expected to care for at once, we've evolved to accept and seek social support, and that offspring born to mothers without it are less likely to survive. The odds get even worse if mothers don't have enough food and are overburdened by the demands of older offspring. Newborns in such situations have received the least parental investment throughout human history. It's likely that all these factors apply frequently in modern America.

Imagine a woman married to a violent man who frequently beats her and her older children. She is imprisoned in his home. Since her whole life is a secret kept from neighbors and family, she gets little help. Is she likely to fully invest in a new baby? Or imagine a teenage single mother living in the dangerous inner city: Already raising two kids without enough food or resources, and without social support (that's help from the rest of us), is she likely to fully invest in a new baby?

Wrangham explores the killing of offspring: "With most animals, negligence would be enough to do the job, as it were, so it's hard to see why violence would be necessary. It may be needed in humans, however, for human-specific reasons, e.g., to be quick enough to avoid witnesses, or perhaps to overcome an emotional bond that all indications say isn't going to be productive."

Wrangham describes ape mothers "so amazingly attached to offspring that if their babies die, they'll carry the corpse for days, even weeks." Surely, this degree of dedication exists in human mothers, so it must be all the more confusing when a woman finds herself feeling resentment and even hostility toward her own baby. After all, isn't she supposed to feel love and kindness? It may be that the bonding most parents experience doesn't occur if there is an inability to adequately parent, whether it's because of hardship, peril, drug addiction, or just plain unfitness. Do some mothers in these circumstances neglect and abuse their babies? Of course they do. Do some discard or even kill their babies? Of course they do.

What could appear to be acts of cruel choice might sometimes be acts of biology. Nature does nothing to stop such killing, and may even encourage it. But was it this way in ancient times as well? Researchers seeking to interpret behavior from archaeological samples found that juvenile skeletons lacked the injuries associated with long-term abuse. This suggests that lethal violence against children is more a modern phenomenon than a basic feature of our species. That's good news, because it means we can do something about it.

Since millions of mothers meet extraordinary challenges with heroism and kindness toward their children, I certainly intend no generosity toward those who are abusive. I haven't explored the evolutionary issues to excuse horrible brutality, but rather to acknowledge that nature is ruthless. And so is society itself, for even though our nation could easily feed, care for, and protect every child, and could offer social support to mothers in need, we don't. Why not? That's best answered by a brief look at the history of our social policies.

Child abuse has been around a long time, but it's only recently been considered a social problem. In 1874, some people trying to stop the abuse of a young girl named Mary Ellen Wilson turned to the Society for the Prevention of Cruelty to Animals because there was nowhere else to go. From Mary Ellen's case emerged the first Society for the Prevention of Cruelty to Children. Because they removed children from their homes and placed them in child-care facilities, such organizations fell out of favor fairly quickly, and many disappeared entirely. Isn't it telling that the SPCA has long outlived the SPCC?

It wasn't until 1962, with the publication of Dr. C. Henry Kempe's article "The Battered Child Syndrome," that child abuse as a social issue was officially reborn. *The Saturday Evening Post* said Kempe's report of injuries done to children "read like a case book of a concentration-camp doctor." The nation was shocked and within a few years, every state in America passed laws designed to protect children. In *Making an Issue of Child Abuse*, Barbara Nelson's solid study of the topic, she explains why this legislation was so attractive: It didn't cost any money and it offered politicians "the opportunity to be 'on the side of angels' by protecting children."

Soon enough, however, the angels changed sides. Protective custody procedures again stirred a great controversy that continues today: Either government has a duty to protect our most vulnerable citizens, or it has no business ever interfering with the sanctity of the family—we can't have it both ways. Though most people agree that severely abused children should not remain with their tormentors, courts around the country have always been reluctant to take children from biological parents—even in the most outrageous cases, like that of Latrena Pixley.

Pixley admitted in court that she'd given away her first child, hadn't seen her second in more than five years, and had killed her third. Despite being in custody for that murder, a judge granted Pixley custody of her fourth child. In a similar case last year, a judge in New York reunited a five-year-old boy with his mother even though she had killed her other son. In Virginia, a woman was allowed to retain custody of her eight-month-old daughter despite being charged with fracturing the infant's skull. This past Mother's Day, that same baby was stabbed to death. Who do you suppose has been charged with the murder?

Favorably, President Clinton has signed the Adoption and Safe Families Act, which puts more emphasis on the safety of children and less on keeping dangerous families intact. Still, the fact remains that biological connection—the very bond that compels most parents to protect their children—is frequently a license to harm them.

Another aspect of biological connection, or more accurately, the lack of it, brings me to the toughest issue in this book: stepfathers. Put simply, violent and abusive stepfathers are one hundred times more likely to kill a child than are biological fathers. Children are also at higher risk of sexual abuse by a stepfather, and since teenage girls in particular tend to underreport victimization, the task of ensuring safety falls to the biological mother and other adults who might detect abuse.

Given that a male in any species is highly motivated to promote his genetic legacy (and only his), violence in step-relationships is predictable. Among many animals, males routinely kill offspring that are not theirs. Richard Wrangham explains: "The issue is confused with humans because society expects a stepfather to accept a parental role with his spouse's children, even though evolutionarily he is a rival to the previous father."

An amazing example from the animal world occurs in mice: When a pregnant female meets a new male, she loses her fetuses. Nature's idea is that since this potential mate would kill the newborns anyway, it's better to lose them in pregnancy and get on with production of babies more likely to survive.

To bring the theoretical to the practical, a single mother's selection of a new husband or boyfriend is highly relevant to the safety and well-being of her children. If she does not protect them from an abusive partner, there may be little to inhibit escalated violence or sexual abuse. I called this the toughest issue in the book because some readers will have to acknowledge to themselves right here that they've had reason for this concern in their own lives. That realization can come early, or as it did for Theresa Ritzert, too late.

Theresa's son Sean wanted to be an artist and go to work for Disney, but the guy his mom married was of tougher stock. John Ritzert had played football in school, became a bricklayer, and passionately loved hunting. Theresa and John had two kids together and the family made a home in Jasper, Indiana, a town so safe that there hadn't been a murder there in nearly 150 years.

Even though Theresa didn't know John would eventually change that statistic, there came a time that she wanted him to move out, shotgun and all. But just days after the divorce became final, John was back—uninvited—and he brought his shotgun. It was 5:00 A.M. as he walked around to the side of the house and cut the phone wires.

When Theresa heard him break in, she tried to call the police; finding the line dead, she ran to a neighbor's house to try again. She heard the shotgun go off as her son Sean was killed. He was twelve. Her ex-husband also killed his own two children and then himself.

There are more step-relationships now than at any time in world history, and accordingly, more children are at risk. This means that parents must seek to know and evaluate the new spouses of their ex-wives and ex-husbands. I acknowledge without hesitation that millions of stepfathers are exceptional parents to their wives' children. As just one example, I am forever grateful to my own stepfather Arthur Shurlock for the stability and kindness he brought into our otherwise chaotic family. We remain friends today, even though it's been thirty years since he and my mother were divorced.

Whether by husbands or boyfriends, intimate violence is the most predictable serious crime in America. It is directly relevant to protecting children because 75 percent of the homes where there is spousal violence also have violence toward the children. With a woman killed by a spouse or boyfriend every two hours in America, there was no shortage of cases for my office to study in developing this list of warning signs:

1. *The woman has intuitive feelings that she is at risk.*

2. At the inception of the relationship, the man accelerated the pace, prematurely placing on the agenda such things as commitment, living together, and marriage.

3. He resolves conflict with intimidation, bullying, and violence.

4. He is verbally abusive.

5. He uses threats and intimidation as instruments of control or abuse. This includes threats to harm physically, to defame, to embarrass, to restrict freedom, to disclose secrets, to cut off support, to abandon, and to commit suicide.

6. He breaks or strikes things in anger. He uses symbolic violence (tearing a wedding photo, marring a face in a photo, etc.).

7. He has battered in prior relationships.

8. He uses alcohol or drugs with adverse effects (memory loss, hostility, cruelty).

9. He cites alcohol or drugs as an excuse or explanation for hostile or violent conduct ("That was the booze talking, not me; I got so drunk I was crazy").

10. His history includes police encounters for behavioral offenses (threats, stalking, assault, battery).

11. There has been more than one incident of violent behavior (including vandalism, breaking things, throwing things).

12. He uses money to control the activities, purchases, and behavior of his wife/partner.

13. He becomes jealous of anyone or anything that takes her time away from the relationship; he keeps her on a "tight leash," requires her to account for her time.

14. He refuses to accept rejection.

15. He expects the relationship to go on forever, perhaps using phrases like "together for life"; "always"; "no matter what."

16. He projects extreme emotions onto others (hate, love, jealousy, commitment) even when there is no evidence that would lead a reasonable person to perceive them.

17. He minimizes incidents of abuse.

18. He spends a disproportionate amount of time talking about his wife/partner and derives much of his identity from being her husband, lover, etc.

19. He tries to enlist his wife's friends or relatives in a campaign to keep or recover the relationship.

20. He has inappropriately surveilled or followed his wife/partner.

21. He believes others are out to get him. He believes that those around his wife/partner dislike him and encourage her to leave.

22. He resists change and is described as inflexible, unwilling to compromise.

23. He identifies with or compares himself to violent people in films, news stories, fiction, or history. He characterizes the violence of others as justified.

24. He suffers mood swings or is sullen, angry, or depressed.

25. He consistently blames others for problems of his own making; he refuses to take responsibility for the results of his actions.

26. He refers to weapons as instruments of power, control, or revenge.

27. Weapons are a substantial part of his persona; he has a gun or he talks about, jokes about, reads about, or collects weapons.

28. He uses "male privilege" as a justification for his conduct (treats her like a servant, makes all the big decisions, acts like the "master of the house").

29. He experienced or witnessed violence as a child.

30. His wife/partner fears he will injure or kill her or her children. She has discussed this with others or has made plans to be carried out in the event of her death (e.g., designating someone to care for children).

*If a stepfather, add . . .*
31. He is jealous of his wife's son(s), or jealous of his wife's relationship with her son(s).

32. He is combative, competitive, demeaning, abusive, or violent toward his wife's son(s).

Though only some readers will see these features in their own families, all of us can see them in some family that touches our lives—or our children's lives. If you know a woman with children whose relationship with her husband or boyfriend has many of the features on this list, you can help prevent escalated violence, and possibly murder. Literally. Refer the woman to a battered women's shelter, if for nothing else than to speak to someone who knows about what she is facing, in her life and in herself. Refer the man to a battered women's shelter; they will be able to suggest programs for him. When there is violence, report it to the police.

This list can say to women who are in these situations that they must get out. It can say to police officers who might not arrest that they must arrest, to doctors who might not notify that they must notify. It can say to prosecutors that they must file charges. It can say to neighbors who might ignore violence that they must not. It can say to anyone whose children are occasionally in a violent home that they should not be. (I write more extensively on understanding and escaping domestic violence in *The Gift of Fear*.)

People in America have been so reluctant to intervene on behalf of abused women; hopefully, more will learn that it's usually children they'd be helping most.

Children in violent homes are hurt in another, more insidious way: Many of the ten million American children who witness violence between their parents this year will model the behavior they see. Thus, as a mother accepts the blows, so likely will her daughter, and as a father delivers the blows, so likely will his son. Though not speaking about violence, Clarence Kelland said, "My father did not tell me how to live. He lived, and let me watch him do it." No father on earth proved the effectiveness of this teaching method more decisively than a man name L. D. Hudson.

Hudson and his wife Otelia lived in Flint, Michigan. Because they shared eleven children, some who knew them were doubtless surprised when Otelia filed for divorce, but she wanted out. A judge not only granted her the divorce, but awarded her custody of the kids as well. One cold evening in the winter of 1965, as Otelia prepared dinner for eight of the children, Hudson walked into the house with a shotgun. His sons and daughters watched him shoot their mother to death as she lay screaming on the kitchen floor. Hudson surrendered to police and confessed to the killing, but a judge later reduced the charge to second-degree murder. Why did a killing that seemed so clearly premeditated get the lesser charge? Because one of Hudson's boys testified that as he tried to get the shotgun away from his father, it had gone off accidentally. L. D. Hudson went to prison, but it wasn't over.

Twenty years later, the sins of the father were visited on the son. Marlow Hudson, by then thirty-seven, fired four shots into his girl-friend's back, killing her. He was convicted of first-degree murder and sent to prison—but it still wasn't over.

Last year, Marlow's younger brother, Larry, continued the family tradition. His wife Sheila had decided to get a divorce (like his mother had), so he killed her (like his father had). After shooting her in the driveway of their Flint home, he dragged her body into the garage. He then fixed breakfast for the kids and went to work as usual. Sheila's sister called the police because she felt something wasn't right; they forced open the garage and found the body. Larry Hudson has now been sentenced to life in prison.

L. D. Hudson said at his trial that he didn't mean to shoot his wife. Marlow Hudson had said he was "caught off guard and panicked." Larry Hudson says he "just snapped." Larry was a fourteen-year-old boy when he saw that terrible scene in the kitchen and a forty-six-year-old man when he delivered the same lesson to his own children. It may not be over yet.

•    •    •

The warning signs of family violence are usually seen by plenty of people, but acknowledged by few. Like with the Los Angeles man accused of killing his wife, three of his children, and three other family members. Neighbors told TV reporters, "He always seemed normal." Another said, "I can't imagine that a father would kill his own children." Well, if you cannot imagine it, you also cannot predict it or prevent it.

When will we have seen this story often enough to realize that when several members of a family have been killed, it was almost certainly done by another member of that family? In this case, the man whose neighbors couldn't imagine was responsible for the murders had already tried to kill his wife three other times, and had been arrested twice on domestic violence charges. Sounds predictable to me.

When terrible family violence occurs, disbelief is the most common reaction, even though this is the most common violence. Another reaction that's popular after a parent kills a child is praise for that very same parent. There is always somebody on the TV news saying what a nice person the murderer was.

Here's what a neighbor said about Mary Hinkleman, an Indiana mother who'd just shot her two daughters to death: "She was very good to her children. She loved them. She gave them whatever she could give them." But there was one thing Mary refused to give them: a visit with their father. During the rough divorce from her husband Carl, Mary fought hard for sole custody. She mostly got her way because Carl moved out of the state. After not having a single overnight visit with his daughters in three years, Carl petitioned the court to let the girls visit him over the summer.

Mary was agitated as she testified at the court hearing, her lawyer later describing her as "high strung" but "rational." The next day, even though the court hadn't yet ruled on the visitation issue, Mary made the decision herself: She killed her two daughters, her live-in sister, and then herself.

Carl's brother told reporters: "I don't think this was anything anybody could have seen coming." It's understandable that we want to believe human violence is unpredictable because as long as it remains a mystery, we have no duty to consider it or anticipate it. We need feel no responsibility for failing to read signals if there are none to read. We can tell ourselves that violence against children just happens without warning, but in service of this comfortable myth, children suffer.

That neighbor who so praised Mary Hinkleman's parenting of her daughters also said, "She was very protective of them." Protective? If this degree of denial can exist just hours after a parent has killed two children, imagine the ease with which people can deny abuse that is less lethal. Some of Mary's other neighbors said they "almost wished the killings had been done by an intruder" rather than by a mother. Of course they wish that; intruders are people we don't know. We don't have to face any hard questions when intruders kill, so they are the preferred enemy. Unfortunately for our comfort, they are not the most likely enemy.

Hundreds of cases like Mary Hinkleman's are why I said at the start of the book that the solution to violence in America is acceptance of reality. You now know enough about human beings to believe these things happen. All by itself, that makes you more able than most to see the warning signs, and that ability makes you a better neighbor to some child.

•    •    •

Most kids who are not rescued from family violence just take it—in secret, indefinitely. As they grow older, some run away, but this usually trades familiar risks (those of the family) for unfamiliar risks (those on the streets). Paul Mones, a lawyer and author who has dedicated his life to the protection of children, explains in *When a Child Kills* that the majority of runaways in America leave their families to escape abuse or to call attention to it. But some of those who stay at home, Mones says, "lay family secrets bare with the report of a gun."

It's no surprise that some kids kill their abusive fathers or stepfathers. You will, however, be surprised at how young they can be. A boy I'll call Robbie shot and killed his father after watching his mother being beaten. The drunk father had left a gun on the table and though Robbie confessed to the killing, few people initially believed that he could have done it. That's because he was only three years old. After gunpowder tests confirmed him as the killer, he explained to authorities: "I killed him. Now he's dead. If he would have hit my mother again, I would have shot him again."

Children who kill their parents are far more rare in human nature than parents who kill their children. These young people are usually found to have been beaten, degraded, sodomized, tied up, or tortured in other ways. Mones tells of one sixteen-year-old, Mike, whom prosecutors described as "just one of those violent, rebellious, degenerate teenagers who are coldhearted killers." But there was much more to the story than that. Mike had been beaten by his father from kindergarten on. Though he was an athletic and coordinated boy, he was constantly injured by "falling off his bike," "tripping," or "cutting himself." During the trial, he was asked to strip to a bathing suit so the jury could see the scars his father had given him over the years.

The abuse ended abruptly one night. Mike had returned home late and his father was waiting for him with a pistol. "You got two choices," he explained to the boy. "You kill me or I kill you." The ultimatum had been offered before, but this time Mike's father actually held the gun out to him, and this time Mike took it and shot his father in the head.

Another young boy who killed a parent told Mones that living in prison is better than living with the abuse at home. He described himself as "locked up but free."

Some people believe that children who kill shouldn't have been so docile during their abuse; they should at least have reported the abuse before it reached the point that murder seemed their only way out. Proponents of these ideas may have forgotten that adult victims of rape or hijacking are often as docile as children, and we don't later blame them for failing to do something.

We cannot expect abused kids to defend themselves; they are raised to believe that the treatment they get is the treatment they deserve. We cannot expect abused kids to report abuse they suffer at home—they are raised not to. When I was a boy, I was vigilant to conceal what was going on because I feared that my sisters and I would be taken away from my mother. In this concealment, I was but the youngest conspirator among a cadre of family members and neighbors who knew. Perhaps if I could act like nothing happened last night, then maybe nothing happened; maybe the crying the neighbors heard, the yelling and the striking—maybe it all didn't happen.

And even if someone had tried, you could no more have talked me into leaving my family back then than I could talk you into leaving yours right now. For most people abused as children, the secret is so well guarded they keep it for a lifetime. That means the duty is ours: family members, teachers, doctors, neighbors, and most challenging, friends. To intervene when a friend is abusive to a child is an act of great kindness to the entire family—even to the friend, who may someday thank you. The popular slogan about drunk driving could be amended to "Friends don't let friends abuse kids."

Intervention can work because though many crimes strike without conscience, violence by parents strikes with conscience. Accordingly, reviving conscience can protect children. I am reminded of Keith, an alcoholic and drug addict who beat his wife and daughter. He grew past his addictions and his violence because a child forced him to see himself; a child revived his conscience. In Keith's words:

> I know what it's like to stand in my kitchen at six-thirty in the morning taking a hit off a bottle of vodka, and I look down the hallway at that little nine-year-old girl. She's looking at me and I'm looking at her, and she didn't run down that hallway and grab me around the leg and say, "Daddy, come play with me today." She didn't even say, "Daddy, please don't beat me and Mommy." I took a hit off that drink, and when I looked back, she was gone. All she wanted to know was which direction I was going so she could go the other way.

The presence of children—the joy and energy of children—is threatening to those who hate life. Most of all, though, the love of children is threatening to those who do not love themselves. Keith eloquently describes his moment of realization about himself and his daughter:

> She is in there like an animal, like a wounded animal, in there with her hair on her face and her chin on her chest and she hides in there. And I run into that bedroom at two or three o'clock in the morning and I put my ear near her mouth to listen. She's got a busted lip and a black eye and I had broken her arm—she had it tied up around her neck—and I put my head down there next to her mouth and I listen to see if she's breathing 'cause it's just a matter of time till I kill her. I've got to kill her. You know why I've got to kill her? She loves me.

•   •   •

Obviously, we cannot always intervene in ways that force parents to stop abusing children, and we cannot touch all abusive parents in ways that help them stop the violence themselves—as Keith did before it was too late. What we can always do, however, is stop or prevent violence in our own families. We can always be alert to signs of violence in any family our kids spend time with. Protecting our own children comes first, of course. To do more, to help children not our own, is a luxury many feel they can't afford. In fact, however, since some of the children now being mistreated will grow up angry and violent, and our kids will live in the same society with them, we cannot afford to do less.

In the most literal sense, anyone abusing *any* child might as well be abusing yours.

# CHAPTER FIFTEEN

# PROTECTING THE VILLAGE

*Continuing society's present attitude toward children is like keeping the patient alive but not healing him—when we have the ability to heal him.*

—SCOTT GORDON, CHAIRPERSON
DOMESTIC VIOLENCE COUNCIL

To care about children, to invest time in protecting them as you have done, is to believe there is a future. Parents today are writing much of that future, writing the history of the next generation, and just as the sins of the father (and the mother) are visited on the children, so are acts of parental kindness. Your love outlives you—literally—and moves on through your children.

Given life's hectic pace, parents who ask the extra question, who take the time to meet their children's friends, who invest the energy to occasionally insist their reluctant kids compromise for safety, have much to be proud of. They won't always be popular with other parents, to be sure, or with the school, or with their own kids, but that's precisely why it can take so much character to listen to intuition.

Some of the human behavior described in this book has been difficult to read about, I know, but having done it, you are in a unique minority among parents. Fourteen chapters ago, I asked if ignorance about violence could possibly be an effective approach to enhancing the safety of children. You've now answered the question. You've walked to the ledge of a parent's greatest fears, looked over, and backed away better prepared for the rest of the mountain climb. It's as if you took an oath that you'd be willing to see, willing to know, and willing to act. Able as you are to recognize man's darker features, you can now more easily see what Abraham Lincoln called "the better angels of our nature." When you have enough faith in those angels to set aside unwarranted fears and worries, when you accept prudent risks, when you let your kids grow, it's an act of both kindness and courage. You are, as Anne Cassidy encourages, "parenting by heart."

Your resolution to learn about violence is an expression of so much love for your own children that you likely have enough in your heart for children not your own. Thus, having explored solutions to violence for your family, we come to the larger family, the social family. Victimization will doubtless continue to increase until *that* family takes an entirely different view of children, not as temporary visitors who will someday grow into citizens, but as full-fledged, fully contributing, fully entitled members of our society, just as they are right now.

Children are often seen as burdens, just hapless victims of their circumstance, but that view is inaccurate. They are, in fact, the primary child-care providers in America: Siblings caring for siblings and children caring for themselves represent an important part of our economy. They also care for the elderly (and inspire the elderly), cook meals, take cigarettes out of the hands of sleeping parents, share their laughter and creativity, and give to society much more than they take.

Halfheartedly acknowledging that not all families are safe places for children to live, each community has a child-welfare agency, but it's usually perceived as just another apathetic and expensive bureaucracy. But what about the people in these systems? Child-welfare workers are expected to be capable advocates for children, yet they're portrayed in the popular media as intrusive, meddling, unfair, and heartless. The people who take one's kids away are villains. The people who fail to take someone else's kids away are incompetent. They are reviled either way.

The truth is that child-welfare workers are more frequently heroes than villains. They volunteer to see things every day that would crease your heart. Though despised by the abusive parents they catch and the abused kids they try to rescue, they persevere. Family members can practice tough love by cutting off that drug-using daughter or ne'er-do-well brother, and then hope their kids will fare okay, but the social worker must charge into the pain and drama relatives want nothing to do with. Imagine how you might feel driving away from a home where there was enough evidence to make you certain a child was being abused, but not enough evidence to do anything about it.

Shirley doesn't have to imagine a thing because she saw it all during her career as a child-welfare worker. That's the career she chose after being profoundly affected in her early teens when a neighborhood boy was beaten to death by his stepfather. Twenty years later, at thirty-four (and with a child of her own), she was trying to save other people's children. One case—her last—teaches less about neglectful parents than about communities so put off by the reality of child abuse that they refuse to participate constructively.

One of Shirley's investigations brought her to an upscale apartment-duplex with an impressive carved stone entry. An anonymous caller had reported that a five-year-old named Elias was being left alone for days at a time. Shirley observed the stack of newspapers outside the door and the delivery-attempt notice from Federal Express. She'd been there twice before but never found anyone at home. This time, 7:00 P.M. on a hot summer night, she just kept ringing the bell. After ten full minutes of no response, she walked around the back of the building to see what she could learn.

There on the back porch, she found Elias—her evidence of neglect—a skinny boy stroking a skinny cat. He told her he'd accidentally locked himself outside a few hours ago: "I was supposed to stay in my room. My mom said she'd be back on Friday and it's Friday, isn't it?" He explained that his mother had been gone for several days, but quickly added that he was big enough to take care of himself. Shirley sat down on the porch with him and asked what he'd been eating. "I've got lots of food, all different kinds of cereal."

Shirley had heard enough to take the boy into protective care, but just as she made that decision, an unlucky coincidence occurred: Elias's mother returned, entered through the front door, and came out the back door calling for her son. Obviously overjoyed, the boy ran toward her with open arms.

The predictably unpleasant conversation ensued after Shirley identified herself, for there is nobody less welcome than the visitor whose job it is to question your competence as a parent. Elias's mother claimed she'd been home the whole time, told Shirley it was none of her business anyway, then abruptly cut off the discussion and took her son into the house. Shirley rushed around to the front door. The papers and delivery notice she'd seen just a few minutes before were gone. Intent on completing her assessment, she rang the bell, and after a few minutes Elias's mother came to the door, holding Elias by the arm.

She said, "Tell the woman that I was home all day." So Elias did. Shirley was surprised to hear a man's voice from inside the apartment, but she wasn't surprised when he called out his curt support of the woman's story: "She's been here all day, the kid was confused. Have a nice evening." The door closed. Knowing that she was being lied to, Shirley nonetheless had to leave Elias there and hope to find something later on that would stick.

Driving home, Shirley felt she had failed Elias. True, she'd put lots of her own time into the case, true she'd visited three times, and true she wasn't giving up, but Elias's face nonetheless began to blend with those of a hundred other kids she'd been unable to help. Some had been injured, some had been killed, some had grown into teens who killed others. After ten years, the failures were looming larger for Shirley than the uncertain and unappreciated successes—and she was tired. It wasn't the being yelled at or being run out of people's homes or having her cases rejected by prosecutors or even the anger of the kids she tried to help. It wasn't the sadness and hopelessness of so many children she'd seen imprisoned in violence and neglect. It was less explainable than all that: It was as if her heart simply couldn't contain any more pain.

The next day, she discussed the case with her supervisor; having no other reports regarding Elias's mother, they knew they'd need to catch the boy alone again in order to take action. The following Saturday morning, Shirley left her own son with his grandmother and visited the apartment again. No answer at the door. A few hours later, she stopped at the apartment again. Still no answer, and no way of knowing if Elias was inside. Shirley knocked on the next door in the entry hall to see if the neighbor could contribute any information. The man who answered the door said of Elias's mother, "She's a good parent; that's for sure. Always quiets the boy down when he's too loud. I'm sure he's with her now, I mean, she wouldn't leave him alone."

If Elias was no longer being left alone, and if that improvement came about because of her visits, Shirley thought, that would be plenty of consolation for having opened the case. But early Monday morning, the case closed itself. Shirley was getting dressed for work, when she heard the news on the television in the next room: A young boy had died in a fire the previous night. She doesn't recall rushing to the TV; but somehow she found herself staring at the screen. Against every resistance she could muster, she recognized the carved stone entry of the apartment building behind the news reporter. Shirley was so deeply cut by the image of that half-burned building that she couldn't even cry.

The next day, arson investigators told her that the fire was likely an accident caused by a faulty stove, but there was more to the story: Evidence indicated the boy had been locked in his room from the outside. They were never able to prove that, though.

When the local newspaper learned (from an anonymous caller) that the Department of Child Welfare had known the boy was being neglected, Shirley became the subject of public scorn. Community leaders were quoted in the papers calling her incompetent and lazy. The neighbor she had talked to appeared on the TV news saying, "I told that social worker she'd better come back." One commentator who didn't care enough to even learn the correct name of the agency called the tragedy "another example of fumbling by the Child Services Bureau." Shirley left her job about three weeks later, mostly by her own choice.

When Elias's mother was tried for felony child neglect, she claimed to have hired a baby-sitter to stay with Elias that night. "The sitter must have left my boy alone," she sobbed on the stand. The same man who'd been at the apartment when Shirley was there supported the story. Unable to identify the phantom sitter, Elias's mother claimed the woman must have been a criminal who gave a false name, an invisible fiend to join the ranks of psychotic nannies and murderous au pairs. "It could have happened to any parent, to any of us," the defense attorney said in his closing argument. The jury's not-guilty verdict caused no community outcry; the public had already found someone to blame in Shirley. And nothing much changed.

But things will change if more people make reports when they suspect a child is being abused or neglected. *No crime can flourish in view of millions of attentive eyes.* I thought about that not long ago when I visited the small apartment building on Cardiff Avenue in West Los Angeles where the worst events of my childhood occurred.

When I was a boy I never wanted anyone to make any report, of course, but as an adult, I reluctantly acknowledge that's what would have been best. Someone like Shirley, informed by an anonymous neighbor who could have washed his hands of the matter once the phone was hung up, might have visited our apartment on one of those days when reality would have been undeniable. I don't have a clear picture of what might have happened then, though it's unlikely it would have been worse than what did happen.

Walking along Cardiff Avenue, I could hear pieces of conversations from inside people's apartments. I know the noisy madness from our apartment awakened neighbors on many nights, and it's hard to imagine how it was so easily set aside each morning. But I've got the least business being surprised about that; after all, I set it aside each morning too.

·  ·  ·

I never met a child-welfare worker when I was a boy, but I met lots of police officers. They too are protectors of children, and society acknowledges them in many ways. We give them tickets to ball games and awards for heroism, we make television shows about their work and our kids greet them warmly on the street, but at the same time, child-welfare workers go unnoticed unless they fail. What could you do to connect with and encourage child-welfare workers in your community? In addition to your own ideas, some answers are available from the National Children's Advocacy Center (see Appendix #1).

Appropriate support of child-welfare agencies (in the form of both funding and personal encouragement) is important to children, of course, but also to our own safety. That's because the issues child-welfare workers address happen to be the widely established risk factors for future criminality: poverty, child abuse and neglect, drug addiction in a parent, drug or alcohol abuse by the child, and single-parent childhood. Combined with other social programs, child-welfare agencies offer us protection from violent crime that is more effective and less expensive than our local police department. Why? Because it's easier to deal with children at risk of becoming criminals than it is to deal with adults who already are criminals.

That truth became clear to Los Angeles Deputy District Attorney Scott Gordon as he pioneered new strategies for prosecuting child abusers. He says, "For every dollar we invest in kids in their young years, we save a thousand dollars in their teen years. It's a better investment than any Internet stock."

Speaking generally, mothers protect children, fathers protect territory, and all adults protect the village. For our national village, that means embracing the simplest social equation: Reducing child abuse reduces crime. A federal research project selected 1,600 children who had been abused or neglected and followed them for nearly twenty years. As of two years ago, fully half of them had been arrested for some crime. Young people are telling us in the most urgent language—crime and violence—that things aren't going well, but few Americans are really listening.

The good news is that children who are at risk of growing up violent can often be helped more easily than most people realize. In her emotionally evocative books (including *The Drama of the Gifted Child* and *The Untouched Key*), psychiatrist and child advocate Alice Miller makes clear that if mistreated children have effective human contact, some recognition of their worth and value, some "witness" to their experience, this can make an extraordinary difference.

I have learned that the kindness of a teacher, a coach, a policeman, a neighbor, the parent of a friend, is never wasted. These moments are likely to pass with neither the child nor the adult fully knowing the significance of the contribution. No ceremony attaches to the moment that a child sees his own worth reflected in the eyes of an encouraging adult. Though nothing apparent marks the occasion, inside the child a new view of self can take hold.

Not just a person deserving of neglect or violence, not just a person who is a burden to the sad adults in his life, not just a child who fails to solve his family's problems, who fails to rescue them from madness or addiction or poverty or unhappiness. No, this child might be someone else, someone whose appearance before this one adult revealed specialness and lovability and value.

A child's value might be revealed through appreciation of his or her artistic talent, physical ability, humor, courage, patience, curiosity, scholarly skills, creativity, resourcefulness, responsibility, energy, or any of the many attributes that children bring us in such abundance.

It might literally be a matter of a few hours with a person whose kindness reconnects the child to an earlier experience of self, a self that was loved and valued and encouraged. I can say from experience that it doesn't take much. As a boy, I needed most of all to know that the violence and the madness was not my fault. The people who gave me that knowledge gave me the great gift of my life.

As an adult, I learned it again from a man named Richard Berendzen. He is the much-recognized astronomer who became president of American University. The violence and sexual abuse he experienced as a child (told in his powerful book *Come Here*) is not what you'd expect to read about the childhood of a university president. When criminals have awful childhoods, we're not surprised, but because Berendzen is at the top of our society, his story is not as easy to ignore. It says that successful, contributing people may come from violent places. He taught me that my adversity was my university.

You and I can give that same gift to abused children, children who are not, contrary to popular belief, destined to become violent adults. If we show them that they are the residents of their homes and not the architects, then where they are needn't limit where they might go.

All of this applies to girls as well as boys, of course, with one important difference: When troubled boys get into their teens, the community begins to recoil from them and fear them, often with good reason. Though overall crime rates have dropped in recent years, violent crimes by boys and young men have dramatically increased. We know that generosity toward at-risk boys when they are young is more effective than punishment when they are criminals, and yet our number one social program for young men is, illogically enough, building prisons.

To put our situation in perspective, I studied countries that are doing worse for their children than we are. Most of those countries have a far better excuse: They are at war. In Sarajevo, for example, almost one child in four has been wounded. A UNICEF survey found that more than half of the children in Bosnia have been shot at by snipers, and 66 percent have been in a situation where they thought they were about to die.

In Iraq, though politicians say we are at war with the leadership, it is children who make up the casualty lists. At the start of our boycott and war, a few hundred children under five were killed each month by respiratory infections, malnutrition, and diarrheal illnesses. The shameful number is now more than 5,000—*per month*.

Over the last decade, about two million children have been killed in armed conflicts around the world, more than double that number have been disabled, and more than twelve million made homeless. Our challenges must be considered manageable by comparison—and they are.

Americans protect children brilliantly when they are very young (we have one of the lowest infant mortality rates in the world) and then dismally when they are teens and young adults. Indeed, it takes a village to protect a child, but that's tough to accomplish when the village itself is not a safe place, as with our inner cities. While journalists are half a world away covering some buildup of troops, an unreported civil war is raging here, fought by angry American boys. We have drive-by shootings instead of snipers, and drug addiction instead of starvation and disease, but it's war nonetheless, with all the predictable fear, suffering, and bitterness. Quite unlike almost every other conflict in the world, however, this one is not being negotiated.

America has surrendered. Big as we are, we just take the casualties as if we can afford them. We abandon many of these inner-city boys, then arm them, and eventually either imprison or bury them.

There are plenty of things we could do instead, including increasing access to constructive activities for at-risk boys. Those offered by reputable organizations such as Boys Clubs, Little League, Pop Warner Football, American Youth Soccer, the YMCA, and others allow boys to engage in less-than-lethal competitions that can absorb hostile energies. But these important alternatives to violence are not always available to the boys who need them most. To play basketball at night, for example, boys need a place, a ball, a basket, lighting, and an adult patron. These are far from insurmountable challenges—except for one sad fact: Most of us are afraid of these boys. Never convinced that anyone else would protect them, they are reduced to their most basic selves, like threatened creatures determined to stay safe. They are strong, agile, clever, and dangerous—with the emotional makeup of boys. They are warriors with terrible judgment, unconcerned about consequences, lacking impulse control—of course we're afraid of them.

And that's all the more reason for each of us to be part of the truce. We can volunteer at a shelter, a school, a park. We can spend time with the very children and teenagers we would fear on a dark street, for if we do, there will be fewer of them to fear.

# CHAPTER SIXTEEN

# PROTECTING THE GIFT

Having explored violence in these pages from the standpoint of the species, the family, institutions such as schools and day care, the nation at large, and even the world, I want to go back to where we started, to an individual mother. Unlike Holly, the mother in the following story was not the lone protector, for her children joined her army, contributing their intuition and power to defeating a predator.

Betty Baird Kregor recalls that morning being like most: Her husband had left for work, her two older children for school. After an early lunch, she decided to take one-and-a-half-year-old Paige and three-year-old Mollie for a walk. She got them into their double stroller and headed down the long driveway of their Kentucky farm. It was a beautiful afternoon, the kind of hot day where you take it slow and take it all in, and Betty noticed everything: the sound of her daughters laughing, the sunlight raining through the trees, the family's two golden retrievers chewing on a huge branch that had fallen from a tree. Betty probably noticed something else too: a red truck that passed by slowly and pulled into a neighbor's property. She has no conscious memory of seeing that truck, but as she told me later, "Thank God for the unconscious part of my brain." The man in the truck, we now know, was watching her.

About an hour later, Betty returned from her walk. It was time for the girls to nap, but Betty got the impulse to let them play on the swings for a moment—that's another thing she was later grateful for: "If I'd taken the girls inside the house, I'd have been where my attacker wanted me." Thus, Paige and Mollie were on the swings when the noisy red truck came up the driveway. Before even seeing the driver, Betty was full of fear—though she wondered why: "In ten years of living in this house, I've had literally hundreds of people pull up the drive and wasn't ever before afraid of anyone." But fear was working for her, getting her ready.

She quickly gathered the girls and watched the slender young man with red-blond hair step out of the truck. He glanced at her but didn't approach at first, stopping instead to wordlessly stroke the Kregors' two golden retrievers. He wanted to be certain they'd be friendly long enough to let him get into the house. Betty's daughters were rarely apprehensive about anyone, but as the man walked toward them, they were afraid, and they clung to their mother. The man said he wanted to discuss his lawn care service, though Betty noticed there wasn't any lawn care equipment in the back of his truck. She took in all the small details: the Confederate flag on his license plate, the red rust above one of the wheels, the wavy hair showing under the brim of his baseball cap. And she took in a big detail: For someone supposedly trying to sell a service, he talked about everything but lawn care.

He discussed boarding horses, and then brought up the barn at the back of the Kregors' property, telling Betty he knew someone who would rent it. "When he asked if I could show it to him, my heart rate skyrocketed. I said I'd pass his name and number to my husband, and he asked if I'd go inside to get some paper to write it down. It was as if he could hear my heart pounding, because he somehow knew I was afraid and quickly said he had a paper and pen in his truck."

The man then did something brilliant: He apologized for scaring Betty, which instantly put her at ease. In fact, she felt embarrassed for fearing him. As capable predators know, riding that roller coaster between dread and relief lessens the power of fear. But when he came closer to give her the piece of paper with his name and number (both later proved fake), the fear was back. "I lifted the baby up onto my left hip and pulled Mollie to my side. I told the man it was time for him to leave, but instead of leaving, he kneeled down to talk to Mollie. She squeezed my hand tightly as this stranger smiled at her and asked her questions even though I had just asked him to go. We backed up one step and he took one step forward. I froze, but then he nicely said goodbye and walked toward his truck."

The roller coaster of her feelings leveled out and her panic stopped. "I distinctly remember thinking about how paranoid I'd been, telling myself there was no reason to be afraid." In fact, it turned out, there was. As Betty carried Paige toward the house, Mollie uncharacteristically sped away, ran ahead twenty yards and opened the heavy security door leading into the kitchen. Since her little girl had never before been able to open that door, Betty thought, "How in the world did she do that?"

At that same moment, the man who'd been so brilliant at manipulating Betty to ignore her fear made a reckless mistake: He attacked a mother holding her baby.

Rushing up behind her, he put one hand over her nose and mouth, grabbing at her chest and throat with the other. Betty was stunned, but held on to her baby girl: "Falling to the ground, I went stiff, imagining for a moment being killed with my daughters. I was motionless as he hit me in the head and dragged us toward the house. I remember being paralyzed, not fighting back or doing a thing.

Though I seemed incapable of even making a sound, my baby let out a shrieking, animal-like scream I will never forget."

That call to action entered through Betty's ears and came out through her fists. "The power was awesome. I immediately started to punch, kick, spit, growl, gouge, and bite my way through that man."

Though holding her baby, Betty fought with one side of her body. She bit down hard on the man's hand and slammed him against the brick wall of the house. Her knee colliding with his groin eloquently communicated the consequences of his attack. Needing no more persuasion to go somewhere else, he limped toward the haven of his dirty old truck—but Betty wasn't ready to see him go just yet. Still holding her baby girl in one arm, she ran after him, pausing without thinking to pick something up. It was the huge branch she'd noticed the dogs chewing on earlier.

Betty doesn't recall what she was yelling as she pursued her enemy, but a neighbor later reported to police that it was something along the lines of, "You've picked the wrong house! I will hunt you down and eat your heart when I find you." Whatever the exact words, the man hustled to shut the door and get his truck started. Unable to hit him directly, Betty went after his truck, knocking out one headlight, destroying the turn signal and the fender, and leaving a collection of other damage before he could drive off.

You've heard the expression, *I could take you with one arm tied behind my back*. Well, Betty Kregor had just proved it, beating up a man (and a truck) with one arm.

As the noisy truck careened down the road, Betty realized she had a bloody nose, some cuts, some scratches—and most pressing, a criminal to catch. But before calling the police or going to the hospital, she sat both girls down. "I told them what had happened and that Mommy beat up the bad man and will always protect them. Even as I said these words, I knew it was my two small girls who had helped protect me. They were certain he was a 'bad man' before I was.

What's most interesting is why Mollie ran inside when she did. Did her intuition get her out of the situation while I was wasting time criticizing myself for being afraid? Then when the attack happened, I was paralyzed and unable to speak, but my baby could scream. I was thinking too much—my girls weren't."

Betty Kregor is a successful golf pro, well known in Kentucky. She used her access to the media to publicize the incident, and sure enough, investigators received an anonymous tip directing them to a suspect. Lucky for him, the police found David Morris Bryant before Betty did. Bryant matched the description and composite Betty had given, and his truck bore the souvenir marks of his visit. Police compared the parts Betty had knocked off the vehicle, and had more than enough evidence to charge the twenty-one-year-old with several crimes. He has since been found guilty and is now serving a seven-year sentence.

If Betty could fight so well while holding her child, then she could have done at least as well without her child—or even before she became a mother. If she could have done it before she became a mother, then your teenage daughter can do it. We don't want another generation of girls raised to believe they can't protect themselves, waiting until motherhood to deploy the defenses nature gave them. By the same token, we don't want another generation of boys raised to believe they can be safe only if they dominate. We must teach children that our primary defense weapons are the mind and the heart. Human beings didn't get the sharpest claws or strongest jaws or fastest legs. We got the biggest brains—and the best parents to show us how to use them.

·    ·    ·

Though children can teach us a thing or two about honoring intuition, as Betty's daughters did, the most important lessons we learn from kids are about love. I heard many stories from caring parents in the past two years, but one epitomizes the gift we seek to protect. It is about a father who had scolded his four-year-old daughter on Christmas Eve because she had opened a double pack of gold wrapping paper without permission. He was angry that she'd wasted a whole roll decorating one small box.

The following morning, when the little girl mustered the courage to present the gift-wrapped box to her father, he was embarrassed by his earlier overreaction. His anger flared again, however, when he found that the box was empty. "Don't you know," he yelled at her, "that when you give someone a present, there's supposed to be something inside?" The little girl looked up at him, tears already filling her eyes, and said, "It's not empty, Daddy. I blew kisses into the box. All for you, Daddy."

The father was crushed. He put his arms around his daughter and asked her to forgive him. For years, he kept that gold box by his bed, and whenever he was discouraged, he would take out an imaginary kiss and remember the love of the child who had put it there.

In a very real sense, children give every parent a gold container filled with unconditional love. In return, we can protect children, knowing that love grows best in safe places.

Bestselling author Gavin de Becker is America's
leading expert on predicting violent behavior.
Advising such clients as the C.I.A. and the United States
Supreme Court, this three-time presidential appointee has
changed the way the United States government protects
its highest officials. He is a senior fellow at UCLA's
School of Public Policy and Social Research.

# ACKNOWLEDGMENTS

Working on this book over the last two years, I've asked lots of people for lots of help. Those whose patience I tried the most get the small reward of being named here first. Susan Kamil, my friend and heroically dedicated editor, and Kathy Robbins, my friend and dedicated agent, will doubtless welcome the novelty of not speaking with me every day. Carole Baron, Leslie Schnur, Roberto de Vicq de Cumptich, Mary Fischer, Mark Pensavalle, Brian Mulligan, Susan Schwartz, and Johanna Tani: I am grateful to each of you.

My chief researcher Dayna Michaelsen can find anything, whether it's a fact lost by an absentminded scholar or—more frequently— a stack of papers misplaced by an absentminded author. Dayna, you did your job with grace and good humor, and it is a pleasure to work with you. Dennis Kirvin, the administrative director of my office, says, "It's already been done" about things I didn't even know I'd thought of yet. Thank you, Dennis, for your remarkable effectiveness and for handling the thousands of details that are part of our work together.

To Cynthia Bain (and all the students in your classes), Eve Somer Gerber, Anna McDonnell, Donna Ebsen, Colleen Friend, and Linda Mills: Each of you gave me insight, humor, and encouragement. Thank you.

To Oprah Winfrey: Thanks for the encouragement you've given me, and far more significantly, for your remarkable contribution to children. It's bigger than anyone (including you) can ever calculate.

To Barbara Nelson, Dean of UCLA's School of Public Policy and Social Research. You may think you appointed me as a Senior Fellow, but what you really did was make me a college student for the first time. Thank you.

Thanks to Special Agents Eugene Rugala and Wayne Lord of the FBI for sharing some of your wisdom, and to all those at the FBI Academy who welcomed me and encouraged this work.

Thanks to Richard Wrangham and John Monahan for your important contributions to man's understanding of man's violence.

Thanks to Cathy Nahirny of the National Center for Missing and Exploited Children, to Ann Pleshette Murphy of *Parents* magazine, to Ken Wooden, to Chief Peter Herley, to Jeff Jacobs, and to Jan Wagner— for helping so many children who may be targets, but need not become victims.

Thanks to Susan Herman, the visionary executive director of the National Center for Victims of Crime, and Reveta Bowers, the heroine of the Center for Early Education.

Thanks to the first members of my advisory board of parents: Robyn Stevens, Donna and Dusty Ebsen, Kate Day, Julia Flaherty, Stephen and Juliane Glantz, Shelley Godfree, Phyllis Klein, Mary Wehbi, the Nishinaga family, Kim Kelly, Joanna Moran, and Stacy Wittingham.

A special thanks to Jenny Cashman, for courage and caring.

To the threat assessment experts who've attended my firm's Advanced Training courses at the UCLA Conference Center: If there's wisdom in this book, much of it came from you. To David and Rita Boyd: Thanks for sharing some of what you've (unavoidably) learned through parenting fourteen children.

There are three people I think of gratefully whenever I write: Bill Phillips, the editor of *The Gift of Fear* and my first real writing teacher; Erika Holzer, who gently tells me the truth about my manuscripts; and Ted Calhoun, who less gently tells me the truth about my manuscripts.

Whenever I think about selling books I am grateful to have as my teachers the world's leading experts, Sandi Mendelson and Judy Hillsinger.

To Richard Berendzen: Writing on difficult topics is an uphill hike made much easier by the trail you cut. Thank you.

Thanks to Bernice Abrams and Tom Sirkel of the L.A. County Sheriff's Department, to Haley Mortison to Nannette Bricker-Barrett and Kathy Wessels of the San Bernardino County Library, to Dr. Michael Durfee, Dr. Mary Arneson, Libby Boyles, Steve Raizes, Chris Young, Kerry Kollmar, Charlene L., Dorothy McGowan, Loren and Clark Blowers, Deanne Tilton, Talmage Cooley, Kelly Biren, Christi Metropole, Gregory Dern (and your students at the John Adams Middle School), and Dr. Beatriz Foster.

A special thanks to the dedicated, creative, and always dependable professionals at Gavin de Becker, Incorporated. Michael LaFever, my firm's president and senior partner, carries the heaviest load and makes it look light. He and I are aided by Michelle Taylor, Robert Martin, David Batza, Jeff Marquart, Michael W. Kolb, Geoff Towle, Hank Rivera, Ed Myers, David Falconer, Rob Nightengale, Charles Cogswell, Michael Varga, Ellen Song, Ryan Martin, Stacy Barnhart, Sandy Abowitz, Raquel Matsubayashi, Amy Prenovitz, and fifty others whose role in our work is nonpublic.

Thanks to my dear friends in Fiji, adults and kids, who showed me that children can be raised without fear.

And thanks to the much-loved friends who not only gave me support and encouragement but tolerated a one-topic social companion for two years: Shaun and Susan, Carrie, Garry, Michelle, Ed and Rachelle (you're going to need this book soon!), Brooke, Nancy and Andrew, Jeff, Kevin and Linda, Tania and Eric, Jaime, Jim, Jennifer, Tom and Rita, Jennifer, Harry and Judith, Nina and Jerry, Laura, Scott and Lisa, Tom and Lynne, Lisa and Eric, Kevin and Ruth Anne, Alice and Peter, Becky and Tony, Tom and Romi, Victoria and Harry, Lesley Ann, Cortney, and Olivia.

Much love to my godchildren, Claudia Rose and Juliet and Hunter, and to the other extraordinary children in my life: Dustin and Sydney, Jake and Caitlin, Baron and Geronimo, Billie, Owen and Drew, Joey, Charlie and Louie, Matthew, John, Maxson and Jasper, Annabel, Lily, Chester and Truman.

And thanks to Geena, who proved to me that it's never too late to have a happy childhood.

Finally, my love to Melissa—thanks for choosing me as a father in your life.

# HELP-GIVING RESOURCES

## IMPACT:

IMPACT Personal Safety conducts many types of safety programs, including courses in basic self-defense for women, men, and children and school-based programs at grammar school, high school, and college levels. Basic self-defense courses teach practical, full-contact self-defense using fully padded instructors who pose as assailants. All courses teach practical physical and verbal skills to avoid confrontation and realistic ways to make victimization less likely. Courses available in most major American cities.

IMPACT FOR KIDS courses are hands-on workshops taught by experts in child safety in an emotionally and physically safe environment. Children are encouraged and taught to recognize potential danger and are offered solutions to the types of interactions they are likely to encounter, such as bullying, peer pressure, and inappropriate adult behavior. Techniques include setting boundaries, accessing adult help, and getting to safety. Scenarios include situations with peers and adults, both strangers and people they know.

You can contact IMPACT using their national toll-free number, 800-345-5425. You can also visit their Web site at *www.prepareinc.com*.

## Child Lures:

Child Lures Ltd. offers its comprehensive Child Lures Community Plan, consisting of Child Lures School Program, Family Guide (available in English and Spanish), Community Awareness and Prevention Seminar and Television News Inserts/PSAs. For more information visit *www.childlures.org*, write Child Lures, 5166 Shelburne Road, Shelburne, VT 05482, or email *lures@together.net*.

## Yello Dyno:

Yello Dyno is dedicated to preventing the abduction and abuse of children through the use of unique confidence-building programs. The musically based educational system helps children remember vital personal safety information. Because of the method of learning, children are likely to recall appropriate action steps when in danger. If you wish to reinforce or build safe and confident children, please call or write:

Yello Dyno
203 Barsana Avenue
Austin, TX 78737
*www.yellodyno.com*

Schools, preschools, and community organizations, call 512-288-2882. Parents call 888-954-5437 or email: *jan@yellodyno.com*.

## Big Brothers/Big Sisters of America:

Call 215-567-7000 for a number in your area and details on how these exceptional mentoring programs work.

## ALANON Family Goups:

ALANON helps families affected by alcoholism and addiction. Special groups for children and teens are available in most areas. ALANON is reached through directory assistance or a local office of Alcoholics Anonymous. Or call 888-4AL-ANON. Internet Web page: *www.al-anon.alateen.org*.

## National Children's Advocacy Center:

The number to reach this organization in Huntsville, Alabama, is 256-533-0531.

## CIVITAS Initiative:

CIVITAS Initiative is a nonprofit organization whose mission is to provide parents, frontline professionals, and policymakers with better ways to protect, educate, nurture, and enrich children. CIVITAS Initiative partners with public and private institutions to create and distribute innovative products and services that will result in more child-sensitive processes, programs, and policies. If you are interested in investing in the optimal development of children, please write or call:

CIVITAS Initiative
1327 West Washington, Suite 3D
Chicago, IL 60607
312-226-6700
*www.civitas.org*

## National Domestic Violence Hotline:

800-799-SAFE. This hotline provides information, support, and referral to battered women's shelters in your area.

## The National Center for Victims of Crime:

Call 800-FYI-CALL (TTY 800-211-7996) for comprehensive information and referrals to more than 10,000 victim assistance programs throughout the nation. Each caller can receive up to five INFOLINK bulletins on 70 different crime-victim-related and legislative topics free of charge, as well as referrals to local service providers. Descriptions of the National Center's services and all INFOLINK bulletins are available on-line at *www.ncvc.org*.

## Parenting Packs:

Parenting Packs
P.O. Box 7580
Santa Monica, CA 90406-7580
310-395-5292
*www.parentpacks.com*

## The National Center for Missing and Exploited Children:

The National Center for Missing and Exploited Children (NCMEC) spearheads national efforts to locate and recover missing children and raises public awareness about ways to prevent child abduction, molestation, and sexual exploitation. A private, nonprofit organization established in 1984, NCMEC operates under a congressional mandate and works in conjuction with the U.S. Department of Justice's Office of Juvenile Justice and Delinquency Prevention.

National Center for Missing and Exploited Children
2101 Wilson Boulevard, Suite 550
Arlington, VA 22201-3077
703-235-3900
www.missingkids.com

24-hour Hotline: 800-THE-LOST

*www.ncmec.org*

## YMCA/YWCA:

YMCA of the USA
101 North Wacker Drive
Chicago, IL 60606
800-872-9622
*www.ymca.net*

YWCA of the USA
Empire State Building, Suite 310
350 Fifth Avenue
New York, NY 10118
212-273-7800
*www.ywca.org*

## American Youth Soccer Organization:

AYSO National Support Center
12501 South Isis Avenue
Hawthorne, CA 90250
800-872-2976
*www.soccer.org*

## Little League Baseball:

Little League Baseball International Headquarters
P.O. Box 3485
Williamsport, PA 17701
717-326-1921
*www.littleleague.org*

## Victory Over Violence:

The official advisory board to the Domestic Violence Council, an organization of people from the entertainment industry, business, and government dedicated to increasing public awareness about domestic violence, and providing direct support to families fleeing from violence. Co-chaired by Victoria Principal and Gavin de Becker, VOV funds or coordinates nursing care for women and children at shelters, art therapy for children, cosmetic surgery programs for women disfigured by domestic violence injuries, and children's play areas at district attorneys' offices so women can give crime reports without being overheard by their young children. We welcome your help, financial or otherwise.

*Victory Over Violence Board*

| VOV *Chairpersons* | Roseann Donnelley | Stephanie Klopfleisch |
| --- | --- | --- |
|  | Betty Fisher | Marlee Matlin |
| Victoria Principal | Carrie Fisher | Jerry McGee |
| Gavin de Becker | Mark Fleischer | Rosie O'Donnell |
|  | Richard Fleischer | Michelle Pfeiffer |
| VOV *Advisory Board* | Jeff Goldblum | Meg Ryan |
| Ed Begley, Jr. | Dr. Harry Glassman | Anita Santiago |
| Lisa Campanaro | Jennifer Grey | Caroline Thompson |
| Laura Dern | David E. Kelley | Lesley Ann Warren |

*Domestic Violence Council*

| Scott M. Gordon | Linda Ikeda-Vogel | Linda Lange |
| --- | --- | --- |

# The Autism Society of America:

The Autism Society of America
4910 Woodmont Avenue, Suite 300
Bethesda, MD 20814-3015
800-3AUTISM
*www.autism-society.org*

# Kidpower:

Self-defense and empowerment training for children
Call 800-467-6997, email: *safety@kidpower.org*, or visit their Web site: *www.fullpower.org*

# QUESTIONS FOR YOUR CHILD'S SCHOOL

- Do you have a policy manual or teacher's handbook? May I have a copy or review it here?
- Is the safety of students the first item addressed in the policy or handbook? If not, why not?
- Is the safety of students addressed at all?
- Are there policies addressing violence, weapons, drug use, sexual abuse, child-on-child sexual abuse, unauthorized visitors?
- Are background investigations performed on all staff?
- What areas are reviewed during these background inquiries?
- Who gathers the information?
- Who in the administration reviews the information and determines the suitability for employment?
- What are the criteria for disqualifying an applicant?
- Does the screening process apply to all employees (teachers, janitors, lunchroom staff, security personnel, part-time employees, bus drivers, etc.)?

• Is there a nurse on site at all times while children are present (including before and after school)?

• What is the nurse's education or training?

• Can my child call me at any time?

• May I visit my child at any time?

• What is your policy for when to contact parents?

• What are the parent notification procedures?

• What are the student pickup procedures?

• How is it determined that someone other than I can pick up my child?

• How does the school address special situations (custody disputes, child kidnapping concerns, etc.)?

• Are older children separated from younger children during recess, lunch, rest-room breaks, etc.?

• Are acts of violence or criminality at the school documented? Are statistics maintained?

• May I review the statistics?

• What violence or criminality has occurred at the school during the last three years?

• Is there a regular briefing of teachers and administrators to discuss safety and security issues?

• Are teachers formally notified when a child with a history of serious misconduct is introduced to their class?

• What is the student-to-teacher ratio in class? During recess? During meals?

• How are students supervised during visits to the rest room?

• Will I be informed of teacher misconduct that might have an impact on the safety or well-being of my child?

• Are there security personnel on the premises?

• Are security personnel provided with written policies and guidelines?

• Is student safety the first issue addressed in the security policy and guidelines material? If not, why not?

• Is there a special background investigation conducted on security personnel, and what does it encompass?

• Is there any control over who can enter the grounds?

• If there is an emergency in a classroom, how does the teacher summon help?

• If there is an emergency on the playground, how does the teacher summon help?

• What are the policies and procedures covering emergencies (fire, civil unrest, earthquake, violent intruder, etc.)?

• How often are emergency drills performed?

• What procedures are followed when a child is injured?

• What hospital would my child be transported to in the event of a serious injury?

• Can I designate a different hospital? A specific family doctor?

• What police station responds to the school?

• Who is the school's liaison at the police department?

# GUNS

Just as parents can send letters to schools, day-care centers, and doctors in order to state expectations and avoid misunderstandings, they can send the following letter to gun manufacturers:

Dear Gun Manufacturer:

We are writing to inform you that your products as presently manufactured interfere with our obligation to protect our daughter by placing her and our entire family at unnecessary risk. We do not accept the risks posed by your failure to meet the standard of safety met by nearly every other manufacturer of consumer products.

Notwithstanding any implied consent you may feel you have with purchasers of your firearms, we do not sign on to any agreement with your firm. We are relying upon you to undertake effective design upgrades and modifications in order to reduce the predictable and clearly established risks to anyone within range of your firearms.

We hold you entirely accountable for your failure to build in sufficiently effective locking and child-safety features that would clearly reduce deaths. Please acknowledge your understanding of our position.

Sincerely yours,

Mailing addresses of major gun manufacturers:

Beretta U.S.A Corp.
17601 Beretta Drive
Accokeek, MD 20607

Heckler & Koch, Inc.
21480 Pacific Boulevard
Sterling, VA 20166-8903

Browning
One Browning Place
Morgan, UT 84050-9325

Smith & Wesson
Customer Service Department
2100 Roosevelt Avenue
Springfield, MA 01104

Colt's Manufacturing Co., Inc.
P.O. Box 1868
Hartford, CT 06144-1868

Springfield Armory
Springfield Inc.
420 West Main Street
Geneseo, IL 61254

Glock, Inc.
6000 Highlands Parkway
Smyrna, GA 30082

Sturm, Ruger, & Company
Lacey Place
Southport, CT 06490

If you write such a letter to a gun manufacturer please feel free to copy Gavin de Becker at 11684 Ventura Blvd, Suite 440/Studio City, CA 91604.

# Defensive Gun Use

In Chapter 12, I noted that a gun is not likely to be a key element in protection from an intruder. Some gun advocates contest this, usually citing much-publicized estimates that guns are used to foil crime as many as 2.5 million times a year. These defensive gun uses (called DGUs) have been comprehensively studied in the recent National Survey on Private Ownership and Use of Firearms, sponsored by the Department of Justice and conducted by the Police Foundation. Survey respondents were asked to describe incidents in which they reportedly used a gun to scare off a trespasser or fend off an assault. Such reports are, by their nature, difficult to evaluate for several reasons: It is not possible to know what might have happened in the absence of a gun; it is not possible in all cases to know the intent of the person supposedly scared off; the incidents are not investigated by police, so there is no questioning of participants or witnesses, and there is no evidence gathered. Finally, many of these reports have been exaggerated by respondents.

For example, almost half of respondents claimed they had used a gun to fend off crime *more than once* in the preceding 12 months; one woman reported 52 such incidents! Many claimed to have shot an intruder, but if all those accounts were accurate, armed citizens would have wounded or killed 130,000 criminals—a figure completely out of line with what we know about the number of gunshot cases. For another example, since only a small fraction of rape victims use guns in self-defense, it does not make sense that the reports of women claiming to have defended themselves with a gun exceeds the number of rapes that occur in America.

Let's take a look at a typical report of a defensive gun use, this one by a 38-year-old man:

> I heard noises downstairs that sounded like somebody walking around. I got my gun and went to the top of the stairs and called out: "I'll blow your goddamned head off if you don't get out of here." Whoever was there ran away.

It is not possible to conclude that there was an intruder in the house, nor that the gun made a decisive difference. In fact, we could ask this man why he needed a gun to go to the top of stairs and call out his warning. (He might say, "Well, I sure wouldn't do it without a gun!" and indeed many people do things with guns they wouldn't do without guns.)

Another type of DGU report from a 32-year-old man:

I was stopped at a stop sign on a deserted boulevard at around three o'clock in the morning. My car window was down. Even though the streets were empty, a man suddenly appeared and walked up to the car window. I aimed my gun at him and he ran off.

Calling this a defensive gun use requires that we are certain the man approaching the car intended to commit a crime. It may well be that the frightened pedestrian was the actual victim. Also, the driver who brandished his gun had another piece of technology available to him: the gas pedal—he could have simply driven off.

Because of the difficulty of fairly evaluating situations like these, researchers developed criteria to weed out those that didn't appear genuine. They excluded reports in which the respondent did not actually see a perpetrator or could not identify the particular crime that was reportedly foiled. They also excluded any but the most recent incident in the cases of respondents who reported more than one DGU. Even using these more restrictive criteria, the claims of respondents still indicate that millions of attempted assaults, thefts, and break-ins were foiled by armed citizens in the last 12 months. The problem? *That would mean guns are used far more frequently to defend against perpetrators than to perpetrate crime.* If that were true, crime would be a risky business indeed.

All in all, the Department of Justice/Police Foundation study concluded that an "estimate of millions of DGUs each year greatly exaggerates the true number."

## Child Access Prevention Laws

In an effort to reduce the number of children injured and killed in accidental shootings, some states have enacted laws to hold adults responsible when children use an unsecured gun to harm themselves or someone else. Child Access Prevention (CAP) laws impose criminal penalties when adults are negligent in storing their firearms. California's Penal Code §12035 can serve as a model:

A person commits the crime of "criminal storage of a firearm of the first degree" if he or she keeps any loaded firearm within any premise which is under his or her custody or control and he or she knows or reasonably should know that a child is likely to gain access to the firearm without the permission of the child's parent or legal guardian and the child obtains access to the firearm and thereby causes death or great bodily injury to himself, herself, or any other person.

A person commits the crime of "criminal storage of a firearm of the second degree" if he or she keeps any loaded firearm within any premise which is under his or her custody or control and he or she knows or reasonably should know that a child is likely to gain access to the firearm without the permission of the child's parent or legal guardian and the child obtains access to the firearm and thereby causes injury, other than great bodily injury, to himself, herself, or any other person, or exhibits the firearm either in a public place [or in violation of existing gun laws: Drawing, exhibiting, or using a firearm or deadly weapon].

California's Child Access Prevention law does not apply when:

- The firearm is kept in a locked container or in a location which a reasonable person would believe to be secure.
- The firearm is equipped with a locking device.
- The child obtains, or obtains and discharges, the firearm in a lawful act of self-defense or defense of another person, or persons.
- The child obtains the firearm as a result of an illegal entry to any premises by any person.
- The person who keeps a loaded firearm on any premises which are under his or her custody or control has no reasonable expectation, based on objective facts and circumstances, that a child is likely to be present on the premises.

A person convicted of first degree criminal storage of a firearm in California may receive a sentence of up to three years in a state prison, be required to pay a fine of up to $10,000, or both. For criminal storage of a firearm in the second degree, the penalty is up to one year in a county jail, a fine of up to $1,000, or both.

# PAX

PAX is a nonpartisan, not-for-profit organization whose mission is to create a powerful national movement against gun violence. Through innovative media and communications initiatives, PAX intends to amplify the gun violence issue, empower individual action, and unify the grass-roots movement, leading ultimately to a passionate and informed demand for fundamental change. They can be reached at:

PAX
25 East Tenth Street
Suite 4-B
New York, NY 10003
212-254-5300
*www.paxusa.org*

# GAVIN DE BECKER, INCORPORATED

The seventy-person firm provides consultation and support to universities, schools, public figures, government agencies, corporations, and others who face high-stakes predictions of violence.

The Threat Assessment and Management Department (TAM) evaluates and assesses inappropriate, alarming, and threatening communications. The firm provides expert-witness consultation and testimony on court cases that involve stalking, threats, and the foreseeability or prevention of violence. It also develops artificial intuition systems, which currently include:

• MOSAIC-2: Used by government agencies to evaluate inappropriate communications to public officials.

• MOSAIC-3: Used to evaluate threats to judges and prosecutors.

• MOSAIC-5: Used by universities, corporations, government agencies, and other large organizations for evaluation of angry current or former employees who might pose a hazard to others in the workplace.

• MOSAIC-20: Used by police and prosecutorial agencies to determine which domestic violence situations are most likely to escalate.

• MOSAIC-50: Used to evaluate which child abuse cases are most likely to escalate.

(Note: MOSAIC-2 and -3 are available to government agencies only.)

Gavin de Becker, Incorporated, provides advanced training on the assessment of threats, high-stakes predictions, case management, and the prediction of violent behavior to police departments, prosecutors, child-protection professionals, state and federal agencies, corporations, schools, and universities. One-, two-, and three-day courses are taught at Boulder Creek, the firm's 18-acre training facility just outside Los Angeles. On-site, specialized training is also available.

Gavin de Becker, Incorporated
11684 Ventura Blvd., Suite 440
Studio City, CA 91604
Fax: 818-506-0426
Email: *infoline@gdbinc.com*

Additional information on high-stakes predictions involving child abusers, violent spouses, stalkers, and angry employees is available at the firm's Web site: *www.gdbinc.com.*

MOSAIC-2000 was designed to help schools evaluate situations that might escalate to violence. Though MOSAIC systems have been used for years by universities, MOSAIC-2000 is the first system developed for high schools. A 57-member advisory board of principals, threat assessment experts, psychologists, school superintendents, and others guided the project. See *www.mosaic2000.com* for more information.

# PREDICTING VIOLENT BEHAVIOR

As noted in Chapters 10 and 13, schools and universities are frequently required to evaluate and manage situations involving students who threaten or might attempt multiple shootings at school. In terms of predictions, the major acts of violence by schoolboys that we see in the news are similar to those involving violent employees in the workplace. *Understanding & Preventing Workplace Violence* is a series of videotapes that provides advanced training for universities, schools, government agencies, and large corporations. The program includes interviews with perpetrators and victims of major acts of violence. Co-written by Dr. Park Dietz and Gavin de Becker (both of whom are extensively interviewed), it received the Mercury Video Awards Gold Medal for best training tape. Narrated by Efrem Zimbalist, Jr., and produced by Emmy-nominated filmmaker Gregory Orr, the program covers such topics as predicting violent behavior, the warning signs of violence, the legal issues, screening, and separating from violently inclined people.

Originally sold for $1,750 (with proceeds benefiting the National Victims Center), the eight-part, four-hour series can be purchased for $875 through *www.gdbinc.com*, or by writing to:

Video Distribution
3727 West Magnolia Boulevard, Suite 162
Burbank, CA 91510-7711

# AUTISM AND ASPERGER'S SYNDROME

Some children who act out violently do so because of autism. Children with classical autism, those who have mental retardation and disordered socialization, are virtually incapable of committing crimes and are unlikely to be blamed for their actions. That is not true of kids with Asperger's syndrome, or high-functioning autism, and the mildly autistic personality traits seen in some so-called "geeks" and "nerds."

Below, Dr. Mary Arneson shares some of what she has learned from the most personal experiences with autism.

• • •

When I was a girl, I might have been diagnosed as mildly autistic by today's standards, but as far as my family was concerned, I was normal.

From my own experiences, and the things I saw happen to my classmates and relatives, I have a picture of an autistic childhood. It is a world of people who act friendly and then turn out to be enemies. School is a place where people do mean things all the time, for no reason. The things that matter most, or are the source of most comfort, are objects of ridicule. For example, the autistic child dresses to please himself. In my case, the problem was that girls simply did not wear roomy shoes, and I simply did not wear shoes that hurt. Even tennis shoes had pointed toes, so I chose boys' tennis shoes. My school shoes were "old lady" shoes. Other kids could have ignored this, but they didn't. What I remember, instead, is a girl phoning me and saying that she really admired the shoes I wore and asking where she could get some. Unsuspecting, I told her, not realizing that my believing anybody could admire those shoes was the funniest thing she and the other girls listening on the line could imagine. It seems like a small thing in retrospect, but that little story repeats itself over and over with autistic kids. They have narrow, focused interests. A normal kid pretends to be interested, gets the autistic kid to talk about his cherished topic, then laughs about it all over the school.

Many autistic kids have unusual gaits. They may count their steps or walk unusually straight. Normal kids imitate them in the halls and on the playgrounds. Autistic boys are awkward around girls and don't know what they are expected to do. Normal boys—and girls—lead them astray by telling them that particular girls want to be kissed, or are in love with them, or would like to get a valentine from them. I thought I was going to be strangled by a severely autistic boy who had been told I was his girlfriend and objected when I tried to run from him.

In junior high, I was studious, unfashionable, and very proper. I didn't know the significance of the number 69, and I don't know whether the boys who wrote it on my papers did either, but they did not seem to ever tire of making sexual remarks to me and seeing whether they could make me uncomfortable. Recently, one of them came up to me at a thirtieth high school reunion and apologized.

These things seem so normal, and so trivial, that it is hard to see the cumulative effect of them on a child who does not know how to defend against them. Many autistic kids never learn to recognize deception; they learn only that people will deceive them. Others have to struggle to memorize the clues that normal kids can read instinctively. They remain easy to fool, and normal kids feel compelled to play tricks on them every day. The autistic kids get into trouble, get laughed at, get hurt—and the normal kids roll on the floor laughing.

It is hard for a normal person with a normal childhood, who may well have done these things to autistic kids, to realize what it is like to be teased without being able to tell—and without being able to learn—when someone was just fooling. I was just nerdy rather than severely autistic, and perhaps because I had my family as a refuge, I didn't end up hating the world. If an autistic person does hate society, however, I understand it.

Autistic children are at special risk. Not only do these children lack some of the internal "wiring" that ordinarily controls social behavior, they bring out the cruelty in other children. Adults, even their own parents, often find them unlikable. Most autistic people are shy and peaceful. Their obsessive, focused interests distract them from worldly concerns, and they often fail to notice that they are being teased and harassed. When they do feel aggrieved, though, their tendency to be obsessive, their lack of perspective, shortage of normal coping skills, and social isolation can make them unusually dangerous. Autistic features sometimes occur together with explosive rages in children whose brains don't inhibit rage properly. This is a deadly combination that requires expert treatment.

Thanks to Dustin Hoffman and the film *Rain Man*, many people are familiar with autism. It's easier than it used to be to explain its core defect of "mindblindness." Normal people "read" each other's minds from gazes and gestures. If they didn't, city traffic would be impossible. Unspoken messages fly back and forth even when we try to suppress them. Imagine being unconscious of a flirtatious glance, recognizing only its angle and duration. Imagine confusing an indifferent look with a meaningful glare or not knowing who was being scowled at. Mindblindness dims or darkens that "inner eye." It occurs, to varying degrees, in classical autism, in Asperger's syndrome (high-functioning autism), in some cases of Tourette's syndrome, and after some head injuries and brain infections.

## Society's Reaction to "Mindblindness"

People with mindblindness aren't naturally vicious. They are often too absorbed in their own interests to notice or understand teasing, taunting, and cruelty. But when they do turn against society, they are less predictable than ordinary criminals and less likely to be constrained by the social norms that keep even some criminals from going too far.

Lives depend on making sure that children with autistic features are treated compassionately by their peers and parents. They need special help to integrate into society. Mostly because of ignorance, our society shuns or mistreats them, encourages their parents to abuse them, teaches them violence, and makes it easy for them to kill.

How do ordinary people react to autistic children? I recall a letter in an advice column written by a father who was troubled about a strange 12-year-old neighborhood boy who played with the man's small children. He noted that he rarely saw the boy with kids his own age. The boy had once pushed a smaller kid off some steps, and he had hit another. The boy had been warned to ring the bell before assuming it was all right to play with toys in the family's front yard, but he persisted in visiting without permission. The boy was later seen peering in the windows, which really spooked the letter-writer's wife.

## The Autistic Experience

Here's what the boy might have said were he able:

> I live in this place with my mom. Sometimes my dad is there. I like my mom. She doesn't say, "Look me in the eyes when you talk." She doesn't yell at me and say, "You're a stupid kid." I like to play with kids, but they say, "Go away, you moron." The yard at my friends' house has lots of toys. They are my friends because they don't say mean things to me. Their dad is mean, though. My mom says, "You have to share your toys," but he says, "You have to ask to play here." He says to ask even if nobody is using the toys. I have to ring the doorbell. I don't like to ring the doorbell and just wait, so I look to see if anybody is home. Now he says I can't look. If I don't look, how can I know who is home?

This child didn't choose to play with younger kids. It's just that boys his own age shun him. Perhaps their parents called his mother and told her to keep him away. Perhaps they got him into so much trouble that he learned to stay away. Each time a worried parent chases this child off, he moves closer to people and groups who will welcome him because they know how to use his loneliness and gullibility to their advantage and to society's disadvantage.

## Helping Concerned People Be Helpful

What if the worried father had written:

> There's an autistic boy in my neighborhood who is bright and tries to be friendly, but I don't know how to help him without getting more entangled than I'd like. The kids his own age don't play with him, so he tries to make friends with my youngsters, and I worry about that. He uses the toys in our yard without

asking and intrudes when he isn't expected or welcome. His mother obviously has autism, too, which makes it hard for me to talk to her. How can I be helpful without putting myself and my family in an uncomfortable position, or even in danger?

There are ways to reach out to autistic children and reduce rather than increase the chances that they will ever become dangerous.

The rules for communicating with autistic people are different. Touching and eye contact frighten, distract, or confuse them. They aren't being cold or evasive; they're just trying to keep their sensory input manageable. The language they understand best is written language, or a spoken version of it. Any conversation that depends on gestures, facial expressions, or subtle hints is going to be lost on them. They do better with letters. They like email. Phone conversations are easier for them than face-to-face conversations.

Autistic people, especially autistic children, aren't insulted if someone explains a social rule. It's okay to explain that you need time for yourself. Avoid using the old standard "How would you like it if someone . . ." When you can't imagine someone else's point of view, being asked to do so doesn't provide any insight.

When a particular approach doesn't work with an autistic person, turning up the volume will just make it worse. It's like yelling at foreigners to make them understand English. Back off and try something different, or just back off.

It's tough to adapt to the social needs of an autistic person, but it can be rewarding. They can be touchingly naïve and straightforward. They seldom lie (even when lying is socially expected and accepted). They are incapable of complex deceptions. They can be creative, inventive, devoted, and brilliant. Hans Asperger, who described the syndrome that is sometimes called high-functioning autism, wrote that their narrowly focused interests drive them to accomplishments that are impossible for normal people. Unless mistreated or misled, they try very hard to follow society's rules. With most autistic people, society has to work hard to make monsters of them.

The very least that society should do is to protect these children from other children. Nobody would let a normal child send a blind kid out into busy traffic, but society tolerates similar abuse of mindblind children.

Normal kids routinely mislead autistic kids or use them to commit misdeeds like saying a bad word in class or writing on walls. Kids give them fake love letters from someone who doesn't even know them, or direct them into the wrong bathroom. The autistic kids get into trouble and lose their faith in society. At worst, they develop an implacable hatred for people. When they misbehave, schools put them into classrooms with incorrigible junior criminals.

But we don't stop there. Our society assaults autistic children with violent lyrics. We present violence as normal in movies and television. We make access to guns easy and provide gun training in video arcades. Autistic children who could grow up to be harmless eccentrics in a kinder, gentler nation are groomed for violent crime here.

## Rage Disorder

Shy, quiet autistic children are hard enough to raise well, but unfortunately, some mindblind children pose nearly impossible challenges to parents and society. Congenital hypersensitivity to touch or noise (common in autistic children) interferes with the parents' ability to comfort them and damages or destroys their bond. Conflicts arise and escalate into uncontrollable behavior. Some autistic children have mini-seizures of unfocused rage. Parents facing these challenges need sympathy and support but usually get criticism and condemnation instead.

A six-year-old curses his mother and bloodies her nose in a store. If she stays calm (which is what she needs to do), bystanders urge her to give the kid a good whipping. If she blows up, they call Child Protection. She needs respite care, but she fears that peculiar or violent behavior from the child will get him excluded and the family subjected to investigation. If she seeks help for violent behavior in a young child, she is lucky to be judged merely incompetent rather than criminal.

When children are defiant, insulting, violent, and emotionally distant, it isn't surprising that some parents turn abusive, but this creates the most difficult circumstance for finding help. There is little to prevent a spiral of violence that will eventually end in death. Usually, it is the children who die, but when the children do the killing, they don't always stop with their parents.

## Effective Intervention

Autistic children with rage disorder need early intervention consisting of medication, behavioral intervention, and avoidance of triggering events.

Finding the right doctor can be challenging, as dozens of quacks offer quick fixes to worried parents. Anticonvulsants, stimulants, sedatives, even antihypertensives each sometimes control rages. Combinations of medications may be needed. Treating mild childhood allergies can reduce rages that are triggered by physical discomfort.

Everyone knows that children should be rewarded for good behavior and punished for bad behavior. With autistic children, you don't necessarily know what is a reward and what is a punishment. Furthermore, the child may not be able to make the connection between the behavior and the consequence. In other cases, the "behavior" may not be a conscious action at all, but rather a mini-seizure, or a tic, or an unconscious movement. Punishing these is about as effective as punishing a sneeze, with the same predictable effect: The child gets mad. Autistic kids are often punished for things they thought were good behavior. Sometimes they are told not to do one thing and are surprised to be punished for doing something similar. It takes experience and patience to teach an autistic child good behavior.

Violent autistic children require structured environments that eliminate the triggers for their outbursts. Home schooling worked for Thomas Edison, whose childhood behavior strongly suggests high-functioning autism. If the normal children in schools, and especially on school buses, can't be controlled, it may be best to keep the autistic child out of that environment. Separate, quiet classrooms and even separate schools reduce the stresses that provoke violence. Television, video games, music, the Internet, and reading material must be controlled.

Hunting is a very dangerous sport for families with autistic children, and guns are best kept out of the household altogether. Even kitchen knives, power tools, household chemicals, and normally harmless objects may have to be kept out of sight. Parents must recognize when the violence is beyond their control, and society must support them in finding safe living arrangements for children who can't stay at home.

## There Is Hope

Families of children with autism and autistic features can reach other families through the Internet and local support groups. It is wonderful to watch older autistic kids glow when younger ones look up to them. When autistic kids can get together and support each other, they gain a sense of control over their lives. Schools and camps are finding ways to teach and support autistic kids. Informed teachers no longer tolerate the playground activities of past generations, in which boys would urge autistic classmates to kiss girls, assuring them that the girls wanted to be kissed (I watched one classmate go through this "training" in the 1950s, then heard adolescent girls laughing in the 1960s over the fake love letters they had written to him under another girl's name. He died, and I have always felt that these "jokes" were partly responsible.)

My own autistic kids have rage disorder and are headed for productive lives after a childhood that wouldn't have inspired anybody to be optimistic. They never spent a full year in school until the past two or three years. My son punched, bit, tripped, stabbed, and strangled me. He was kicked out of so many schools, summer schools, after-school programs, and activities that I have long since lost track. He spent a year in a residential program where he had one-on-one staffing. His sister usually wasn't kicked out of more than one school or camp a year, and she didn't actually try to kill people, so her education has been easier. We have used every technique and resource I have mentioned. After years of hard work, our daughter found success in a school program that combines gifted and talented classes with special education support services, and she is headed for college.

My son's program combines small classes with work opportunity. In his case, he can spend more time with engineers than with high school kids. Not everybody would regard this as great socialization, but he does. He aspires to a career in engineering.

They have both gone from being potentially dangerous to being good citizens.

As mentors for some younger children, we see how much easier it can be when resources are available early. The school programs that we had to search or fight for are now being offered to parents of preschoolers in our area. Health insurers have finally recognized Asperger's syndrome as a diagnosis. Newspapers and magazines report on neurobehavioral disorders. Advice columns that used to just tell worried parents to keep their kids away from weird neighbors now suggest counseling. Many younger autistic children are experiencing less trouble, and I think they will find it easier to integrate into society.

These opportunities need to be available nationwide and to be publicized so that every family can find needed help. The public must recognize that people don't all think alike. Children who are handicapped by mindblindness must be protected from torment and exploitation. When that happens, the world will be safer for both normal and autistic people.

Dr. Mary Arneson
May 1999

•   •   •   •

THE AUTISM SOCIETY OF AMERICA
4910 Woodmont Avenue, Suite 300
Bethesda, MD 20814-3015
800-3AUTISM
*www.autism-society.org*

# APPENDIX SEVEN

# THE INTERNET

Tens of thousands of kids have Web sites containing personal information that makes them easy to locate. Many sites include photographs and text that make them ideal fodder for pedophiles. Seemingly innocent photos of teenage friends in bikinis or in pajamas might not be so innocent to a pedophile.

If you allow your kids to have a Web site, apply this rule:

Don't include anything in a Web site that you would
not be willing to post on the bulletin board of every
supermarket in every city in America.

# RECOMMENDED READING

Becker, Ernest. *The Denial of Death.* New York: Free Press, 1985.

Berendzen, Richard and Laura Palmer. *Come Here: A Man Overcomes the Tragic Aftermath of Childhood Sexual Abuse.* New York: Random House, 1993.

Blankenhorn, David. *Fatherless America: Confronting Our Most Urgent Social Problem.* New York: Basic, 1995.

Branden, Nathaniel. *Honoring the Self: The Psychology of Confidence and Respect.* New York: Bantam, 1985.

Cassidy, Anne. *Parents Who Think Too Much: Why We Do It, How to Stop It.* New York: Dell, 1998.

Chaiet, Donna and Francine Russell. *The Safe Zone: A Kid's Guide to Personal Safety.* New York: Beech Tree, 1998.

Clinton, Hillary Rodham. *It Takes a Village: And Other Lessons Children Teach Us.* New York: Simon and Schuster, 1996.

Dutton, Donald and Susan K. Golant. *The Batterer: A Psychological Profile.* New York: Basic, 1995.

Freeman, Lory and Carol Deach (Illustrator). *It's My Body.* Seattle, WA: Parenting Press, 1984.

Goleman, Daniel. *Emotional Intelligence: Why It Can Matter More Than IQ.* New York: Bantam, 1995.

Lamott, Anne. *Operating Instructions: A Journal of My Son's First Year.* New York: Fawcett Books, 1994.

Larson, Erik. *Lethal Passage: The Story of a Gun.* New York: Crown, 1994.

Miller, Alice. *Banished Knowledge: Facing Childhood Injury.* New York: Doubleday, 1990.

Miller, Alice. *The Drama of the Gifted Child: The Search for the True Self.* New York: Basic, 1994.

Miller, Alice. *Thou Shalt Not Be Aware: Society's Betrayal of the Child.* New York: NAL-Dutton, 1991.

Miller, Alice. *The Untouched Key: Tracing Childhood Trauma in Creativity and Destructiveness.* New York: Doubleday, 1990.

Monahan, John. *Predicting Violent Behavior: An Assessment of Clinical Techniques.* Beverly Hills, CA: Sage, 1981.

Mones, Paul. *When a Child Kills.* New York: Pocket, 1992.

Pipher, Mary. *Reviving Ophelia: Saving the Selves of Adolescent Girls.* New York: Ballantine, 1995.

Pollack, William. *Real Boys: Rescuing Our Sons from the Myths of Boyhood*. New York: Random House, 1998.

Siegler, Ava L. *What Should I Tell the Kids?: A Parent's Guide to Real Problems in the Real World*. New York: Plume, 1993.

Snortland, Ellen. *Beauty Bites Beast: Awakening the Warrior Within Women and Girls*. Pasadena, CA: Trilogy Books, 1996.

Sulloway, Frank J. *Born to Rebel*. New York: David McKay, 1996.

Wagner, Jan. *Raising Safe Kids in an Unsafe World: 30 Simple Ways to Prevent Your Child from Being Lost, Abducted, or Abused*. New York: Avon, 1996.

Wooden, Kenneth. *Child Lures: What Every Parent and Child Should Know About Preventing Sexual Abuse and Abduction*. Arlington, TX: The Summit Publishing Group, 1995.

Wrangham, Richard and Dale Peterson. *Demonic Males: Apes and the Origins of Human Violence*. Boston: Houghton Mifflin, 1996.

# INDEX

Abbott, Denny, 48
Abductions of infants, 49–50
Accountability, 110
ACE (Access, Cover, Escape), 77
Action, as antidote to worry, 58
Adam Walsh Child Resource Center, 48
Adoption and Safe Families Act, 257
Age, of baby-sitters, 117–118
Aimlessness, 237–238, 244
Air safety, 13, 55
ALANON, 293
Alcohol use, 236, 244, 245
    questioning-baby sitters about, 113
Allport, Susan, 132
Alone in public, 91–102 (see also Lost children)
    calling home, 96
    teaching risk without excessive fear, 98–99
    Test of Twelve and, 92–94, 101
    walking to school, 20, 96–97, 101–102
American Academy of Child and Adolescent Psychiatry (AACAP), 216
American Academy of Pediatrics, 156, 230
American Medical Association, 227, 230
American Youth Soccer Organization, 279, 295
Anger
    chronic, 245, 246
    rude responses and, 75
Animal world, 130–132, 239, 254, 255
    Allport, Susan, A Natural History of Parenting, 132
    elephants, 132, 239
    Glenn, quoted, 130–132
    penguins, emperor, 239–240
Anxiety, as messenger of intuition, 26

Apprehension, 6, 8
  as messenger of intuition, 26
Armed conflicts, 278
Arneson, Mary, 242, 311–321
Artificial intuition systems, 307–308
Asperger, Hans, 316
Asperger's syndrome (see Autism)
Assertiveness, 168
Autism, 242, 253, 311–321
Autism Society of America, 296, 321
Away from home, 128–147
  day care (see Day care)
  sleepovers, 133–136

Baby and Child Care (Spock), 7
Baby-sitters, 20, 103–127
  agencies, 108–109, 120
  age of, 117–118
  background investigations of,
    115–116
  child abuse and, 121–127
  emergency situations and, 112–113,
    118
  hidden camera systems and,
    121–122
  male vs. female, 119–120, 124–125
  preemployment questions for,
    111–114
  references and recommendations of,
    103, 106, 109, 111, 116–117
  sexual orientation of, 16, 120
  vignettes, 104–107, 120–127
Basketball Diaries, The (film), 244
"Battered Child Syndrome, The"
    (Kempe), 256
Beauty Bites Beast (Snortland), 214
Behavioral predictions, 30
Belknap, Raymond, 232–234, 236, 238
Berendzen, Richard, 277
Bergman, Ingmar, quoted, 24
Big Brothers/Big Sisters of America,
    139, 293
Blankenhorn, David, 239
Body parts, naming, 166–167
Bok, Sisela, 237

Born to Rebel (Sulloway), 247
Boryczewski, Rachel, 223
Bosnia, 278
Boyd, David, 153–154
Boyd, Rita, 153–154
Boys Clubs, 279
Boy Scouts of America, 139
Brazelton, T. Berry, quoted, 128
Brothers, Leslie, 67
Bryant, David Morris, 284
Buddha, quoted, 60
Bullying, 218–222, 241–242

Calling home, 96
Camera systems:
  baby-sitters and, 121–122
  in day-care facilities, 141
Campus crime statistics, 180
Cancer deaths, decrease in, 100
Can't Fool Me training program, 167
CAP (Child Access Prevention) laws,
    227, 305–306
Carneal, Michael, 244, 245
Cassidy, Anne, 18, 32, 270
Caster, Elliott, 218–222
Certainty, search for, 8–10, 20
Charm, 65, 67–68, 210, 212
Cheerios, 137
Child abuse. (see also Sexual abuse)
  baby-sitters and, 121–127
  in day care, 128–130, 137, 140
  in de Becker's family, 21–23,
    247–250, 266–267
  evolutionary issues, 254–256
  infants, 251–253
  leaving alone, 271–274
  protective custody, 256–257
  social policies, 256–257
  stepfathers and, 152, 257–259
Child Access Prevention (CAP) laws,
    227, 305–306
Child Care Aware, 137
Child-care facilities (see Day care)
Child Development Act of 1971, 142
Child Lures Ltd., 167–168, 292

*Child Lures* (Wooden), 80
Child-welfare agencies, 275–276
Child-welfare workers, 271–275
CIVITAS Initiative, 293
Clinton, Bill, 257
Clinton, Hillary, quoted, 53
Conscience, 267
Consent, withdrawing, 165
Consumer Product Safety Commission, 224
Context, of details, 68–69
Corpus callosum, 227
Country Walk Daycare Center, Florida, 128–130, 137
Curiosity, as messenger of intuition, 26

Dark humor, as messenger of intuition, 26
Date rape, 202, 203, 213–214
Davis, Noy S., 139
Day care:
  background investigations of, 115–116
  camera systems in, 141
  child abuse in, 128–130, 137, 140
  employer-sponsored, 143–144
  policy book, 140
  screening and evaluation of, 137–140
  vignettes, 128–130, 144–147
  visiting, 141, 142
Death.
  maternal fear of, 50–51
  schedule and method of, 46
de Becker, Gavin, 309
  childhood of, 21–23, 247–250, 266–267
DeBernardo, Caren, 243–245
Defensive gun uses (DGUs), 303–305
*Demonic Males* (Wrangham and Peterson), 254
Denial, 14, 126, 251, 265
  of intuitive signals, 27–29
  of sexual abuse, 15–17
  signals of, 28–29
Dental records, 50

Diary keeping, 31
Dietz, Park, 309
Discipline, questioning baby-sitters about, 111, 112
Discounting the word No, 65, 71–75, 210, 212
Divorce, 125, 152
DNA samples, 50
Dogs, intuition of, 38–39
Domestic violence, 247–268. (*see also* Child abuse)
  pre-incident indicators of, 259–261
Domestic Violence Council, 295
Domination, safety and, 21, 280–284
Don't tell/tell! (role-playing game), 94
Don't Wander Off in Public Rule, 89–90
Don't yell/yell! (role-playing game), 93
Doubt, 6
  as messenger of intuition, 26, 71
*Drama of the Gifted Child, The* (Miller), 276
Drug screening, 109, 114
Drug use, 236, 244, 245
  questioning baby-sitters about, 113
  by schoolchildren (PRIDE study), 184
Drunk driving, 215

Eckman, Paul, 84
Edison, Thomas, 319
Emergency situations, questioning baby-sitters about, 112–113
*Emotional Intelligence* (Goleman), 245
Employer-sponsored day care, 143–144
Excuse-making, as signal of denial, 28, 29

Facial expressions, 84
Faith, role of, 9–10
Family, changes in modern, 132–133
*Fatherless America* (Blankenhorn), 239
Fathers, 239–240
Fear, 2–6, 46, 50–51
  as messenger of intuition, 26

Federal Bureau of Investigation (FBI), 48
Feminism, 119
Fight or flight concept, 95
Fiji, 110
Fingerprint-based background information, 138
Firearms (*see* Guns)
Forced teaming, 65, 66–67, 210, 212
*Fortune* magazine, 143
Fromm, Erich, 54
Fuster, Frank, 128–130
Fuster, Ileana, 128–130

Gang violence, 233
Gavin de Becker, Incorporated, 19, 307–308
Gender, of baby-sitters, 119–120, 124–125
*Gift of Fear, The* (de Becker), 32, 262
Girl Scouts USA, 139
Golden, Drew, 240, 245
Goleman, Daniel, 245
Gordon, Robert, 124
Gordon, Scott, quoted, 269, 276
Guidelines for the Screening of Persons Working with Children (Justice Department), 139, 145, 185
Guilt, parental, 131, 133
Guns, 100, 218–231. (*see also* School shootings)
  access to, 223, 226–227, 231, 244
  CAP (Child Access Prevention) laws, 227, 305–306
  defensive use of, 230, 303–305
  male fascination with, 227–229, 236, 244
  manufacturers, 224, 226, 301–302
  parental policies concerning, 229–230
  safety features, 223–226, 229
Gurian, Michael, 131, 133, 228, 238
Gut feelings, as messenger of intuition, 26, 31

Harvard School of Public Health, 184
Health and Human Services, U.S. Department of, 230
*Heart of Man, The* (Fromm), 54
Help-giving resources, 291–296
Herley, Peter, 227
Heroin, 214
Hesitations, 6, 7, 9, 10
  as messenger of intuition, 26, 27
Hidden camera systems, 121–122, 141
Hillside Strangler, 87
Hinkleman, Mary, 264–265
Hoffman, Dustin, 313
Hoffmann-La Roche, 214
Homosexual men, 16, 120
Hotlines, 48, 294
Hubler, Shawn, 45
Hudson, Larry, 263
Hudson, L.D., 262–263
Hudson, Marlow, 263
Hunches, as messenger of intuition, 26
Hunting, 228

Identification kits, 48, 50
If You Are Ever Lost, Go to a Policeman Rule, 86–88
If You Are Ever Lost, Go to a Woman Rule, 87
IMPACT FOR KIDS, 94, 168, 214, 291–292
IMPACT Personal Safety, 94, 291
Infants, 8, 11–12
  abductions of, 49–50
  abuse of, 251–253
  mortality rate, 278
Internet, the, 322
Intuition, 6, 9, 24–40
  of dogs, 38–39
  listening to, 14
  origin of word, 27
  prediction and, 24–26, 30–31
  signals of (*see* Intuitive signals)
  trusting, 55
  vignettes, 32–38

Intuitive signals:
  anxiety, 26
  apprehension, 26
  curiosity, 26
  dark humor, 26
  denial of, 27–29
  doubt, 26, 71
  fear, 26
  gut feelings, 26, 31
  hesitation, 26, 27
  hunches, 26
  nagging feelings, 26
  persistent thoughts, 26
  suspicion, 26
  worry, 55–56
Iraq, 278

Johnson, Mitch, 240, 245
Jonesboro, Arkansas, shooting, 186, 240
*Journal of the American Medical
    Association,* 226
Judas Priest, 232–233, 235, 237, 238
Justice, U.S. Department of, 139, 190,
    230, 303, 304
  Guidelines for the Screening of
    Persons Working with Children,
    139, 145, 185
Justification, as signal of denial, 28, 29

Kaye, Mitchell, 184
Keener, Patricia, 115
Kelland, Clarence, 262
Kempe, C. Henry, 256
Kent, Jamon, 186
Kidnapping, 34, 59, 60–78
  baby abductions from hospitals, 49–50
  by divorced parents, 48
  worry about, 47–50
KIDPOWER, 168, 214, 296
Kids 'R' Kids, Marietta, Georgia, 141
King, Stephen, 244
Kinkel, Bill, 188–190
Kinkel, Faith, 189, 190
Kinkel, Kip, 186, 188–190, 242–243,
    245

Kortum, Sarah, 31
Kregor, Betty Baird, 280–284

Landis, Vince, 128–129
Latchkey children, 226
Leaving children alone, 271–274
Lennon, John, 87
Leonard, China, 24–25
Leonard, Richard, 24–25
Lincoln, Abraham, quoted, 270
Little League Baseball, 279, 295
Loan-sharking, 65, 70, 210, 212
Locking systems for guns, 224, 225
Logic brain, 6–7
Lost children, 20
  Don't Wander Off in Public Rule,
    89–90
  Go to a Policeman Rule, 86–88
  Go to a Woman Rule, 87
  talking to strangers, 85–86
Louikaitais, Barry, 244
LSD, 214
Lynch, Thomas, 52, 54, 58

*Making an Issue of Child Abuse*
    (Nelson), 256–257
Male baby-sitters, 119–120
Male fascination with guns, 227–229,
    236, 244
Mandela, Nelson, quoted, 41
Mandell, Deborah, 28, 29
Manufacturers of guns, 224, 226, 236,
    244
Masters, Cara, 181–183
McDonnell, Anna, 13, 84–85, 96,
    122–123
McGee, James, 243–245
McGowan, Dorothy, 173–174
Media products, addiction to, 236–237,
    243, 244
Media provocation, 244, 245
Medical records, 158
Menninger, Karl, 58
Miller, Alice, 276
Mindblindness, 313–314

Minimization, as signal of denial, 28, 29
Missing children, 48
Mones, Paul, 265, 266
Mother's Brigade, Long Beach,
    California, 101–102
Music albums, 232–235, 238

Nagging feelings, as messenger of
    intuition, 26
Naming body parts, 166–167
Nannies (see Baby-sitters)
Nanny-cam, 121, 122
National Center for Health Statistics,
    230
National Center for Missing and
    Exploited Children, 48, 294–295
National Center for Victims of Crime,
    166, 230, 294
National Child Protection Act of 1993
    (Oprah Winfrey Act), 139
National Children's Advocacy Center,
    275, 293
National Conference of State
    Legislatures, 143
National Crime Prevention Council,
    230
National Domestic Violence Hotline,
    294
National Institute of Mental Health,
    152
National Rifle Association, 229
National Survey on Private Ownership
    and Use of Firearms, 303–305
National Victims Center, 310
Natural Born Killers (film), 244
Natural History of Parenting, A
    (Allport), 132
Negotiation, word No and, 71–72
Nelson, Barbara, 256–257
Neuville Industries, North Carolina,
    143
Never Talk to Strangers Rule, 79–86
Niceness, 65, 67–68, 210
Nixon, Richard, 142

NO, 201
No Place Is Safe warning, 88–89
Northridge Hospital, California,
    143–144
Northrup, Christiane, 31

Obsession, 237
    with safety, 18–19
Office of Juvenile Justice and
    Delinquency programs, 139
Oprah Winfrey Show, 32, 80
Organizations, 48, 291–296
Orr, Gregory, 309
Owner-recognition technology for guns,
    224, 226

Parenting Packs Web site, 122–123,
    294
Parent Patrol, Chicago, Illinois, 102
Parents Who Think Too Much (Cassidy),
    18, 32
Parker, Kathy, 124
Parker, Michael, 124
Patriarchy, 14
PAX, 306
PC (Privacy and Control), 207–210
Pearl, Mississippi, shooting, 243
Pediatricians, choosing, 153–159
Peer influence, 232–240
Pennington, Gary, 243–244
Persistent thoughts, as messenger of
    intuition, 26
Persuasion-predators, 64–65, 77, 208
Pickup lines, 205–206
Pixley, Latrena, 257
Police Foundation, 303, 304
Police officers, 275
Politeness, 13
Pollack, William, 243, 246
Pop Warner Football, 279
Posner-Weber, Gregory, 160–161, 165
Powerlessness, 54
Power-predators, 64, 208
Predatory types, 64–65

Preemployment questions for baby-
    sitters, 111–114
Pre-incident indicators (PINS), 6, 64,
    235–238. (see also Survival signals)
    of domestic violence, 259–261
    of violence by schoolboys, 244–246
PRIDE study, 184
Primate behavior, 254, 255
Principals, school, 176–180, 182
Promises, unsolicited, 65, 70–71, 210
Protection process, 153–168
Protective custody, 256–257
Protest masculinity, 239
Public, children alone in (see Alone in
    public)

Rage (King), 244
Rage disorder, 317–318, 320
Rain Man (film), 313
Ramsey, Evan, 243
Rape (see also Sexual abuse)
    by children, 177–180
    of children, 152
Rapport-building, 66–68
Rationalization, as signal of denial, 28, 29
Real Boys: Rescuing Our Sons from the
    Myths of Boyhood (Pollack), 243
Reality, acceptance of, 16–17, 28, 265
Reassurance, requests for, 29
References:
    of baby-sitters, 103, 106, 109, 111,
        116–117
    of volunteer day-care workers, 138
Refusal, as signal of denial, 28, 29
Remarriages, 152
Resignation, from responsibility, 16
Responsibility:
    for child's own safety, 91
    resignation from, 16
Reward insurance, 48
Right to bear arms, 224
Risk:
    actual vs. imagined, 53
    as human experience, 18

teaching, without excessive fear,
    98–99
worry and, 14–15
Ritzert, Theresa, 258–259
Rogers, Betsy, 182–184
Rohypnol, 213–214
Rudeness, 66, 72–73, 75
Rules, for baby-sitters, 107
Runaways, 48

Safe Corridors, Downey, California,
    102
Safe Sitter program, 114–115
Safety. (see also School safety)
    domination and, 21
    maxims, 21
    obsession with, 18–19
    for parents, 13
Safety features of guns, 223–226, 229
Safe Walk Home, Escondido,
    California, 102
Saturday Evening Post, The, 256
Saying No, 201–206
School safety, 20, 175–190. (see also
    School shootings)
    guns in school, 184, 186, 188–190
    letter to principal, 185–186
    policy book, 179–180
    questions on, 181, 186, 297–299
    teachers and, 181–184
    threats, 186–188
    vignettes, 173, 175–177, 179–180
School shootings, 243–245
    Jonesboro, Arkansas, 186, 240
    Pearl, Mississippi, 243
    Springfield, Oregon, 186, 188–189,
        242
    West Paducah, Kentucky, 244
Second opinions, pediatricians and,
    158, 159
Secrecy, 162
Security guards, 86–87, 178–179
Self-defense training, 214
Sensationalism, 99–100

Sex offenders, registered, 138
Sexual abuse, 20
  as act of violence, 15
  behavioral signs of, 151
  by children, 177–180
  denial of, 15–17
  detecting evidence that has occurred,
    153–160
  detecting evidence that is likely to
    occur, 160–162
  by family members, 15
  incidence of, 15, 152
  physical signs of, 151
  protection process, 153–168
  questioning baby-sitters about,
    109–111
  questioning pediatricians about,
    155–157
  of teenage girls, 193–198
  vignettes, 148–149, 169–172
  what children should know,
    165–168
  withdrawing consent, 165
Sexual orientation, of baby-sitters, 16,
  120
Sexual predators, 65, 148–174. (see also
  Sexual abuse)
Shurlock, Arthur, 259
Siegler, Ava L., 99
Signals of denial, 28–29
Sleepovers, 133–136
Smiles, Samuel, quoted, 189
Smiling, 84
Snortland, Ellen, 214
Society for the Prevention of Cruelty to
  Animals, 256
Society for the Prevention of Cruelty to
  Children, 256
Solar plexus, 31
Son of Sam killer, 87
Soto, Omar, 222
Southall, David, 251–252
Spanking, 111
Spock, Benjamin, 7
Spousal abuse, 259–261

Springfield, Oregon, shooting, 186,
  188–189, 242
Stained Class (Judas Priest), 233
Stalking, 202, 203
Status and worth, seeking through
  violence, 237, 243
Stepfathers, 152, 257–259
Stone, Elizabeth, 45
STOP position, 72
Strangers:
  kidnapping by (see Kidnapping)
  Never Talk to Strangers Rule, 79–86
  talking to, 85–86
Strong, Sanford, 93, 94
Strong on Defense (Strong), 93
Suicide, teenage, 215–216, 230,
  232–234
Sullen, Angry, Depressed (SAD), 244,
  245
Sulloway, Frank, quoted, 247
Survival signals, 65–76
  charm and niceness, 65, 67–68, 210,
    212
  discounting the word No, 65, 71–75,
    210, 212
  forced teaming, 65, 66–67, 210, 212
  loan-sharking, 65, 70, 210, 212
  too many details, 65, 68–69, 210, 212
  typecasting, 65, 69, 210, 212
  unsolicited promise, 65, 70–71, 210
Suspicion, 6
  as messenger of intuition, 26

Tamper-proof containers, 225
Teachers, 181–184
Teenage boys, 218–231
  fathers, 218–220, 222
  and guns, 218–223, 226–227,
    229–231
  violence, 218–222, 243
  violent friends, 218–222, 243–244
Teenage girls, 191–217
  date rape, 202, 203, 213–214
  drunk driving, 215
  PC (Privacy and Control), 207–210

saying No, 201–206
sexual abuse of, 193–198
suicide, 216
Teenage suicide, 215–216, 230,
    232–234
Test of Twelve, 92–94, 101, 165, 168
Testosterone, 219, 229, 239
Threats, in schools, 186–188
*Time* magazine, 236–237
Todd, Joseph "Colt," 245
Too many details, 65, 68–69, 210
Tourette syndrome, 314
Trust, 27, 55, 76, 161, 162
    misplaced, 65
TV news reports, 49, 50, 56, 99–101,
    236
Twain, Mark, 222–223
21st Century (21C) Schools, 142
Tylenol case, 225
Typecasting, 65, 69, 210

*Understanding & Preventing Workplace
    Violence* (videotapes), 309–310
*Undertaking, The: Life Studies from the
    Dismal Trade* (Lynch), 52
Universality of violence, 12–13
University of Chicago, 168
Unsolicited promise, 65, 70–71, 210
*Untouched Key, The* (Miller), 276

Vance, James, 232–238
Vehicle fatalities, decrease in, 100
Verbrugge, Joseph, Jr., 24–25
Victory Over Violence, 295–296
Video games, 237, 240
Vignettes:
    abuse by baby-sitters, 104–107,
        120–127
    Betty and her children, 280–284
    Blair and the college roommates,
        32–35
    bullying, 218–222, 241–242
    day care, 128–130, 144–147
    Dinner with Andre, 85–86
    Donovan and violent nanny, 120–121

Elias left alone, 271–274
Elliot Caster and bullying, 218–222
Eve's feeling of power, 51
Gail and Vince, baby-sitter who let
    boyfriend into garage, 104–107
Ginger the dog, 38–39
Holly and daughter at the movies,
    1–6, 26, 64
Holly and daughter with the string,
    41–42
Holly and worry, 43–45
Jason, molested by man he meets at
    ball park, 169–172
Jess's kidnapping, 60–64
Kim, Rocky, and Karl, 193–199
Leonard, China, and operation,
    24–25
Marta, nanny working for Ally and
    Bill, 125–127
Melanie and her son, Brian, 35–38
rape by children, 177–180
school safety, 175, 177–183
sexual abuse, 148–149, 169–172,
    193–198
sleepovers, 133–136
suspicion, 26
undertaker's worries, 52
Violence, universality of, 12–13
Volunteers for Children Act, 138–139

Walking to school, 20, 96–97,
    101–102
West Paducah, Kentucky, shooting, 244
*What Should I Tell the Kids?* (Siegler),
    99
*When a Child Kills* (Mones), 265
Wild brain, 6–8, 10, 40
Wilson, Mary Ellen, 256
Winfrey, Oprah, 139
*Women's Bodies, Women's Wisdom*
    (Northrup), 31
*Wonder of Boys, The* (Gurian), 131,
    228
Wooden, Ken, 80, 168
Woodham, Luke, 243

Workplace, shooting in, 244, 309
Worry, 41–59
    action as antidote to, 58
    actual vs. imagined risk, 53
    excessive, 53–54
    exercises to help, 56–57
    inability to shake, 57
    as intuitive signal, 55–56
    of kidnapping, 47–50
    meaning of word, 54
    as risk enhancement, 14–15

    true vs. unwarranted, 54–55
    vignettes, 41–45, 51, 58
Wrangham, Richard, 254, 255, 258
Wurst, Andrew, 245

Yelling for help, 92, 93
Yello Dyno, 292
YMCA/YWCA, 139, 279, 295
Yugoslavia, 278

Zimbalist, Efrem, Jr., 309